THE CONCERT OF CI

# Rethinking Political and International Theory

Series Editors:
Keith Breen, Dan Bulley and Susan McManus,
all at Queens University Belfast, UK

Committed to show you in what ways traditional approaches in political and international theory may be applied to twenty-first century politics, this series will present inventive and pioneering theoretical work designed to build a common framework for the latest scholarly research on political theory and international relations.

Intended to be international and interdisciplinary in scope, the series will contain works which advance our understanding of the relevance of seminal thinkers to our current socio-political context(s) as well as problematise and offer new insights into key political concepts and phenomena within the arena of politics and international relations.

*Also in the series*

Virtue and Economy
Essays on Morality and Markets
*Andrius Bielskis and Kelvin Knight*
ISBN 978 1 4724 1256 0

Revolutionary Subjectivity in Post-Marxist Thought
Laclau, Negri, Badiou
*Oliver Harrison*
ISBN 978 1 4724 2133 3

Human Rights, Human Dignity, and Cosmopolitan Ideals
Essays on Critical Theory and Human Rights
*Edited by Matthias Lutz-Bachmann and Amos Nascimento*
ISBN 978 1 4094 4295 0

Knowing al-Qaeda
The Epistemology of Terrorism
*Edited by Christina Hellmich and Andreas Behnke*
ISBN 978 1 4094 2366 9

# The Concert of Civilizations

## The Common Roots of Western and Islamic Constitutionalism

JEREMY KLEIDOSTY
*University of Jyväskylä, Finland*

LONDON AND NEW YORK

First published 2015 by Ashgate Publishing

Published 2016 by Routledge
2 Park Square, Milton Park, Abingdon, Oxon OX14 4RN
711 Third Avenue, New York, NY 10017, USA

First issued in paperback 2017

*Routledge is an imprint of the Taylor & Francis Group, an informa business*



**British Library Cataloguing in Publication Data**
A catalogue record for this book is available from the British Library

**The Library of Congress has been applied for**

ISBN 13: 978-1-138-30700-1 (pbk)
ISBN 13: 978-1-4724-1480-9 (hbk)

# Contents

# Acknowledgements


> "The world will little note nor long remember what we say here," but I will never forget the overwhelming support of so many people during the course of writing this book.[1]

Much credit for the actual completion of this book is due to colleagues at the University of St Andrews, particularly Professor Anthony Lang. He read through countless drafts and offered a number of key methodological suggestions that allowed me to grapple with a very unwieldy topic. Likewise, Professor Nicholas Rengger was instrumental in helping me to find a niche within political theory early on in my scholarly career. His suggestions on readings and conceptual frameworks were extremely formative and helpful.

I also wish to give my sincere thanks to those who made it financially possible for me to pursue this work. Countless friends and family members donated money for our initial move to Scotland. The support from the Binks Trust and teaching and conference grants from the School of International Relations are likewise appreciated.

Thank you to my parents, extended family, and amazingly supportive circle of friends for believing in me and my work. I continue to strive to deserve your confidence and to make you proud. Finally, I wish to give my love and thanks to my wife Elizabeth, whose willingness to let me put in the hours needed to see this through and constant encouragement saw me through many difficult times. You and our children give my work meaning and purpose that cannot be overstated.


1 See Lincoln, Abraham. "Gettysburg Address."

# Preface

In the spirit of comparative political theory, this book analyzes the ideas that have shaped Western and Islamic constitutional discourse and assesses the extent to which they intersect at key historical and philosophical points. This goal is placed within a larger debate of whether Islam and constitutionalism are mutually exclusive.

The book begins by positioning itself against Elie Kedourie, who argues that Islam is inherently incompatible with constitutional governance. It then addresses the idea of constitutionalism as described by Western thinkers on three constitutional concepts: the rule of law, reflection of national character, and placing boundaries on government power. These are examined through the lens of a particular canonical text or thinker, Cicero, Montesquieu, and *The Federalist Papers*, respectively. This is followed by a comparison of the *Magna Carta* and Muhammad's *The Constitution of Medina*. Islamic corollaries to the constitutional ideas discussed earlier are then examined. Al-Farabi's *On the Perfect State*, ibn Khaldun's *asabiyya* (group feeling) in the *Muqaddimah*, and the redefinition of the state in the 19th century Ottoman *Tanzimat* reforms are discussed. Following this, the book looks at a moment in history where these two traditions intersected in 19th century Tunisia in the work of Khayr al-Din al-Tunisi, undertaking a detailed analysis of the introductory section of his book *The Surest Path to Knowledge Concerning the Conditions of Countries*.

The abstract philosophical questions that motivated this inquiry suddenly have unquestioned practical implications. In recognition of this, the conclusion of the book looks at how theorists are addressing the pressing concerns of various states and peoples.

## Introduction

# The Challenge of Comparative Constitutional Analysis, Questions and Methods

A word said but not heard does not make language. Therefore, realization is made through dialogue ... The general commonalities that languages share, both in terms of wisdom and numerous similar functions stem from the common humanistic nature of humans. Their differences, however, stem from their historical, geographical and civilizational differences as well as due to their different social and cultural experiences. And since we grow inside cultural and lingual surroundings, rather than outside them, recognition of this point, that the cultural and lingual surroundings of fellow nations originally differ from our history, culture and language is extremely difficult. Nonetheless we may accept these differences, interpreting them in the context of cultural and religious pluralism.

(Mohammad Khatami, "The Theoretical Foundations of the Dialogue of Civilizations")[1]

The West's universalist pretensions increasingly bring it into conflict with other civilizations, most seriously with Islam and China ... The survival of the West depends upon Americans reaffirming their Western identity and Westerners accepting their civilization as unique not universal and uniting to renew and preserve it against challenges from non-Western societies. Avoidance of a global war of civilization depends on world leaders accepting and cooperating to maintain the multicivilizational character of global politics.

(Samuel Huntington, *The Clash of Civilizations and the Remaking of World Order*)[2]

... dialogue means exposure to an otherness which lies far beyond the self ... it signals an alternative both to imperialist absorption or domination and to pliant self-annihilation ... it requires a willingness to 'risk oneself,' that is, to plunge headlong into a transformative learning process in which the status of self and other are continuously renegotiated.

(Fred Dallmayr, *Beyond Orientalism*)[3]

---

1 University of St Andrews International Lecture, speech delivered 31 October, 2006.

2 Huntington, Samuel P. *The Clash of Civilizations and the Remaking of World Order*. New York: Simon & Schuster, 1996, pp. 20–1.

3 Dallmayr, Fred R. *Beyond Orientalism: Essays on Cross-Cultural Encounter*. Albany, NY: State University of New York Press, 1996, p. xviii.

As the above words of former Iranian President Khatami's illustrate, a great deal of debate and controversy has been generated by the idea of a "clash of civilizations" between the Western and Islamic worlds. The outcome of this debate, in real terms, is one which has taken on a particular urgency as it appears that a significant number of Muslim citizens may soon have the opportunity to form truly representative forms of government, which may or may not be amenable to Western aims and norms depending upon whom one believes. A casual reading of Samuel Huntington and Fred Dallmayr's work could easily lead one to conclude that they approach the question of civilizational conflict from diametrically opposed positions. As the above quotes reveal however, even thinkers from opposing camps in the "clash of civilizations" debate may have important commonalities. In this case, it quickly becomes clear that both writers are advocating the continuation of disparate traditions rather than the triumph of any one mode of civilization. Huntington's prescription of relying upon "world leaders accepting and cooperating to maintain the multicivilizational character of global politics," is not altogether different from Dallmayr's contention that dialogue is "an alternative both to imperialist absorption or domination and to pliant self-annihilation." In other words, the clash of intellectuals can be easily overstated and used to purposes opposite of those intended by their authors.

It is fair though, to note that the crucial difference between these two points of view is as, or perhaps even more, important than their shared advocacy of civilizational pluralism. Huntington approaches these entities as unique, opposite, potentially conflictual, and in discrete categories of "I" and "other." His concern is couched in warlike, existential terms like "survival of the West" and "global war of civilization." This could be considered scholarship via hyperbole. It also poorly reflects the fact that Islam is very much a part of Western civilization. Aside from millions of Muslims living in Western states, the influence of Muslim scholars upon Western philosophy and political thought has been substantial since at least the time of Thomas Aquinas (who borrowed liberally from al-Farabi), even when this influence has not been readily acknowledged. Thus the primary problem with Huntington's thesis is that it is based on false premises of discrete civilizations and concludes with a false choice between civilizational war and civilizational détente achieved through Western assertions of its distinct and irreconcilably different civilizational character.

On the other hand, Dallmayr's approach is one in which the bounds of the civilizations themselves are not taken for granted as having any real and clear definition, but rather they are evolving entities which, much like individuals in relationships, "risk themselves" in the process of interacting openly in the "transformative learning process in which the status of self and other are constantly renegotiated." This is far more reflective of the overlapping and evolving relationship between the categories of Christendom, or the West, and the "Muslim world," since they collided so violently in the Crusades. If any historical time period would validate Huntington's thesis it would be this particularly bloody era with its cycle of religiously-inspired conquest and bloodshed, yet the Crusades concluded with a wholesale infusion of ideas, products, and cultural influences from the Middle East into Europe. Far from losing its civilization, Western culture thrived under this new infusion of ideas and the dynamism they helped to unleash laid the groundwork for what would come to be considered Europe's Renaissance. This is exactly the type of process Dallmayr describes in his theories of comparative politics. Indeed, it is fair to ask if this is the result of the Crusades, which occurred in an age of far less communication technology and cultural mobility, how much more likely is it that the present challenges posed by conflicting philosophies (the West and Islam cannot be assumed to be in conflict when they are sometimes united in individual people and ideas) will result in an even greater level of accommodation and understanding, and possibly even genuine and popularly accepted cultural pluralism.

It goes without saying that the subject of this book cuts across a variety of disciplinary boundaries and engages with an equally great variety of theoretical concerns. Its original contribution to the field lies primarily in its use of comparative political theory methods to redefine constitutionalism for use in a globalized and pluralist context. By freeing constitutionalism from its liberal teleology it then becomes possible to examine Western and Muslim thinkers in a mutually constructive fashion, advancing the stated aim of civilizational dialogue.

It is this effort to examine pre-defined boundaries, reassess them, and to create a discursive space between and beyond these boundaries which this book seeks to undertake. Since so much of the discussion about the relationship between the West and Islam operates in an atmosphere of assumptions about the respective values, goals and governmental models they embody, the subject of the following examination can be broadly defined as constitutionalism, and more narrowly as the narratives of constitutional ideas and values as they have developed across various times and places in both Western and Islamic contexts.[4] This is done with a view to demonstrate both the commonalities and distinctive elements that these philosophies of government have with the further aim of being able to elucidate potential avenues for how they may evolve, overlap, coexist and blend in the future. No claims are made that the accounts of constitutionalism given are exhaustive or representative of the whole breadth of their respective traditions. Indeed, each of the traditions could easily form the subjects of multiple books, so the account here is one which is intentionally simplified into these core constitutional concepts in order to provide a starting point for a comparative analysis based upon an exegesis of key texts.

In order to advance its argument, the book will first examine what constitutionalism is and why it matters, highlighting its most basic and fundamental components. Due to the comparative element of this work, it will interrogate whether the aims and characteristics of constitutionalism are essentially different in different cultural contexts, or if there are relatively universal aspirations and qualities that it lays claim to. Specifically, it will develop a narrative of Western

4 Western and Islamic are terms used primarily for simplicity and readability. They are not meant to signify exclusive or essentialist typologies.

and Islamic notions of the state and constitutionalism in parallel to allow them to be more easily compared. Drawing from various political thinkers in each canon, along with actual constitutional texts it will contribute to a larger understanding of the constitutional concepts of rule of law, government that is reflective of those it governs, and limited government. The ultimate goal of this book is to allow a reasoned, though perhaps not conclusive answer to whether, based on both historical and philosophical grounds, Western and Islamic political and constitutional values bound for a civilizational clash. If not, have the boundaries of these two discourses been previously misunderstood? Did such boundaries ever truly exist? How can these traditions and their mutual understandings of one another be renegotiated fruitfully in light of the demands of international law and universal humanitarian demands?

> Generally speaking, the project of comparative political theory introduces non-Western perspectives into familiar debates about the problems of living together, thus ensuring that "political theory" is about human and not merely Western dilemmas.7 This presumes an understanding of political theory as defined by certain questions rather than particular answers. As Salkever and Nylan (1991, 1994) argue, emphasizing shared dilemmas and questions rather than universal answers enables the project of comparative political philosophy to avoid the conclusion that cultures are morally and cognitively incommensurable without imposing supposedly universal categories and moral rules. Additionally, I want to suggest that recognizing the possibility of and conditions for conversations between and among thinkers across cultures is transformative, opening theoretical discourse to admit of parallels and comparisons that narrower conceptions of political theory occlude.[5]

The methodology used in the various textual analyses in this work is largely inspired by the hermeneutical approach to comparative political theory used by thinkers like Roxanne Euben, who is quoted above, and other contemporaries like Andrew March, Jürgen Gebhardt, and Kimberly Hutchings. Euben's claim that comparative theory is "about human and not merely Western dilemmas," is one which was decisive in focusing on constitutionalism as a discourse of social goods and values rather than as various institutional arrangements for governing a people.

It seems likely that focusing on institutional differences can obscure as much as it illuminates the underlying visions of social good and the role of government that actually animate a given state. Britain and the United States, for instance, have radically different styles in political campaigning (party-driven vs. personality-driven), equally divergent methods for the creation and execution of law (parliamentary vs. presidential), and even quite different methods for restraining

5 Euben, Roxanne L. "Comparative Political Theory: An Islamic Fundamentalist Critique of Rationalism." *The Journal of Politics*, 59:1 (1997): 32.

law-making powers (there is no real equivalent of Marbury vs. Madison in British jurisprudence). However, these real and important institutional differences do not alter the fact that both systems rest on a political and legal tradition that is inherently rationalist, liberal, and constitutional. The illustrative power of the different evolutionary arcs of British and American constitutional arrangements actually lies in its vivid demonstration of how groups with strikingly similar values and even origins (after all the United States was once part of the British Empire and its laws reflect a great deal of reliance and respect for British jurisprudence) can nonetheless pursue a wide variety of institutional arrangements in pursuing the societal values they most wish to prioritize. If this is true for the United Kingdom and the United States, there is no reason to assume the same may not be true of majority-Muslim states. Whilst most of them may claim a constitutional basis in Islam and the *sharīʿa*, their interpretations of what this means in both theory and practice vary widely depending upon cultural, historical, social, economic and other factors traditionally considered in political study.

"Constantly changing and in the throes of novelty, such a dynamic universe may never be completely transparent or fully grasped by traditional conceptual categories."[6] This statement from Dallmayr's *Integral Pluralism* could easily be applied to the ever-evolving concepts of constitutionalism. Its preoccupation with society and its organization into political units means that the avenues for its expression are potentially as numerous as the human race. Contrary to the assertions of Elie Kedourie or Steven Emerson, the application of Islam in the political process is not bound to any particular fate and there is perhaps less separating the fundamental assumptions of Western and Islamic constitutional narratives than is usually suggested. Rather, as Mark Tessler contends, "The influence of the religion thus depends to a very considerable extent on how and by whom it is interpreted. There is no single or accepted interpretation on many issues, nor even a consensus on who speaks for Islam."[7]

The methodology Dallmayr proposes is one which this work aspires to emulate, recognizing that its call to avoid representing people in monolithic categories and to maintain a type of Kantian notion of people as ends unto themselves is far more difficult to achieve than it may at first appear. Although a great deal can be written about his framework for comparative political theorizing, his conclusion in his book *Border Crossings: Toward a Comparative Political Theory* encapsulates this approach. In it he writes the following:

> In the context of postmodernity, globalization (or the globalization of truth) acquires and distills a radically new meaning: it is wary of "ethnocentric chauvinism" on

---

6 Dallmayr, Fred R. *Integral Pluralism: Beyond Culture Wars*. Lexington, KY: University Press of Kentucky, 2010, p. 3.

7 Tessler, Mark. "Islam and Democracy in the Middle East: The Impact of Religious Orientations on Attitudes toward Democracy in Four Arab Countries." *Comparative Politics*, 34:3 (2002): 340.

> the one hand and "faceless universalism" on the other … It cannot be mistaken for and confused with ethnocentric identification or essentializing totalization. Rather, it subverts and transgresses the Eurocentric *enframing* (Heidegger's *Gestell*) of truth … it is the result of a cross-cultural intertwinement or chiasm in which one culture can no longer be the "negative mirror" of another … (Harmonization) itself—like making music together—is not inimical to difference; it *is* rather the play of difference(s), of heterogeneity, not of homogeneity. It accentuates the *eccentricity of difference*. Cosmopolitanism is not the question of merely discovering a Plato, an Aristotle, a Machiavelli, a Descartes, a Kant, or a Hegel in the non-Western world but also of finding a Confucius, a Mencius, a Nishida, a Watsuji, a Hu, a Tagore, or a Radhakrishnan in the West.[8]

A few elements of this paragraph are worth highlighting. Firstly, this book is addressing concerns about the compatibility of ideas in a cross-cultural globalized context that have been presented in an alarmist and problematized fashion by thinkers like Kedourie, Huntington, Emerson and others. As such, Dallmayr's use of globalization as a positive force that mediates between ethnocentrism and universalism is one which is highly attractive for its recognition that not all consequences of globalization are necessarily negative. Additionally, since there is no sign of globalization reversing or even slowing, it behooves political thinkers and people generally to find ways to cope with its various socio-cultural effects. Specifically, the rejection of framing and categorizing that has characterized Western thought since at least the Enlightenment, and brought to its culmination in scientific schemes of evolutionary trees and classification of individuals into genus, species, etc., is one which can allow analyses to go beyond their pre-defined disciplinary boxes and potentially to more accurately and effectively deal with the interdependent, multi-polar and global political and cultural context that characterizes the present. By recognizing similarity and difference simultaneously, and by acknowledging their contingency, it is possible to have difference without conflict. It is his admonition to find the Western cognates of non-Western thinkers in addition to finding resonances of Western thought in Islamic contexts, which this work seeks to follow by analyzing key texts not only in civilizational/cultural/religious terms, but also simply on their own merits as representations of constitutional themes which seem to persist across eras and civilizations.

It is hoped the reader will appreciate al-Farabi, not only as a Muslim neo-Platonist, but as an original and formidable philosopher in his own right. Likewise, though both Montesquieu and Ibn Khaldun write about the nature of societies, Ibn Khaldun is not being presented as the Muslim Montesquieu, but rather as a thinker who can be considered the global "Father of Sociology" and whose novel approach and vast scope of study on the rise and fall of society is without precedent. Finally, it may be noted that both Dallmayr and I have still been forced to resort to terms

8 Dallmayr, Fred R. *Border Crossings: Toward a Comparative Political Theory*, Global Encounters. Lanham, MD: Lexington Books, 1999, p. 288.

like "Western" and "non-Western" or "Islamic." In some senses it is unfortunate that these labels are so pervasive. On the other hand, if one recognizes that these too are subject to change and negotiation, and even combination, then they can be used to make one's case more readily understood while avoiding the most pernicious types of essentializing and stereotyping.

In some respects, this monograph is also an attempt to engage in the type of comparative political theory articulated in Andrew March's "What is Comparative Political Theory?" In this critique he notes that beyond the simple goal of expanding the scope of the canon of theorists beyond the West, the "justifications are often more ambitious and tend to coalesce around the following five themes: the epistemic, global-democratic, critical-transformative, explanatory-interpretative, and the rehabilitative."[9] Each of these goals is potentially admirable, but as March notes, there is the question of whether they are properly part of the scholarly enterprise. One cannot be engaged in scholarship if there is a presumption of validity or inherent worth in a given work simply by virtue of the fact it is derived from a non-Western or third world source.[10] He argues that the "strongest warrant for a comparative political theory is that there are normative contestations of proposals for terms of social cooperation affecting adherents of the doctrines and traditions that constitute those contestations."[11] Elsewhere he states that these should be semi-autonomous traditions and that in particular, "religious thought helps us set boundaries (however porous) between traditions of thought, (and) it does so without leading to the problem (discussed above) of patronizing non-Western thinkers by treating them as important or interesting merely because of their cultural identity or because of the fact that they were once colonized by Europeans."[12] This is not a perfect delineation by any means. As Kimberly Hutchings comments, comparative theory and insights for International Relations will not stem "from a dialogue between the 'West' and the 'non-West' constructed on either Socratic or Habermasian terms, but from conversations between multiple, fractured self-identities, which acknowledge the imperfect and provisional nature of the insights that they generate."[13]

In an effort to avoid some of the essentializing that can occur when analyzing a culture other than one's own, this book will bring together an analysis of both Western and Islamic traditions in a way that illustrates common roots and applications of their respective political theories in addition to pointing out their distinctive characteristics. It also attempts to assess the application of these ideas

9 March, Andrew F. "What is Comparative Political Theory?" *The Review of Politics*, 71:4 (2009): 538.

10 Ibid., pp. 564–5.

11 Ibid., p. 565.

12 Ibid., p. 552.

13 Hutchings, Kimberly. "Dialogue between Whom? The Role of the West/Non-West Distinction in Promoting Global Dialogue in IR" *Millennium—Journal of International Studies*, 39:3 (2011): 647.

in terms derived from native thought. Thus, the discussion of the role of national character in Islam for example, will be conducted using ibn Khaldun's concept of *asabiyya*, or group feeling, rather than Montesquieu's "spirit of the law." Likewise, each text will be approached with an assumption of validity, even if it did not necessarily make much practical impact at the time of its writing.[14] This simply recognizes that fact that political actors draw inspiration for their political movements and reforms from all manner of religious, philosophical, and historical repositories and that any of them can become relevant when made so by another thinker who uses them.

## Working Definition of Constitutionalism and Limitations of this Enquiry

For the purposes of this analysis, constitutionalism will be defined as a mode of governance which is defined by adherence to a written or generally agreed body of law, equally applied to all adult members of society. Furthermore, it reflects the cultural values and civilizational goals of its citizens, establishing both the boundaries of the state's role in society as well as the scope of action of the various institutional organs of the state. This view of constitutionalism is one which is located within the classical tradition of viewing the constitution as an organic political/institutional representation of a society and with the more modern approach which looks at constitutions as legal documents which codify the architecture and operation of the state.[15]

The subject of constitutionalism can be broken down into a wide variety of approaches. Due to its focus on limiting and directing government power, discussions of constitutionalism are often tightly focused on the language or rights and duties, with an emphasis on rights, in accordance with certain pre-established liberal guarantees of personal rights. Institutional examinations tend to examine constitutional regimes in terms of the three established branches of government: executive, legislative, and judicial (or monarchy, oligarchy, and democracy in classical terms). Case-based approaches look at the extent to which constitutional

14 This specifically applies in the case of al-Farabi. Given his historical context, it is likely he was very careful in his choice of words and may have self-censored. As such, Leo Strauss' approach of looking for hidden meaning in the text may lead to a fuller understanding of the text.

15 This definition is developed further throughout the thesis and is directly influenced by the work of C.H. McIlwain and Adbullahi An-Na'im. It is also informed by Nathan Brown's contention that whereas constitutions, as simple "legal frameworks for governing" can be non-liberal and not provide guarantees of personal rights, constitutionalism is necessarily concerned with the ideological and institutional "arrangements that promote the limitation and definition of means of exercising state authority." See Brown, Nathan J. *Constitutions in a Nonconstitutional World: Arab Basic Laws and the Prospects for Accountable Government*, SUNY Series in Middle Eastern Studies. Albany, NY: State University of New York Press, 2002, p. 8.

regimes adhere to various liberal values and how relevant constitutions are, or are not, to the day to day political process and state function. In Middle Eastern and Islamic cases, there is widespread agreement that a state's written constitution is often little more than a formality and is not applicable to an analysis of the actual structures or power in the state.[16]

In order to compare constitutional narratives between Western and Islamic thinkers and historical contexts, it is necessary to focus on the ideas that inform the institutional arrangements of the state rather than on the organs of the states themselves, as these are often highly conditioned by custom and historical practice. As the following chapters will demonstrate, there are concerns and issues which seem to transcend historical and civilizational divides and which would be generally seen as central to constitutionalism and/or governance by both traditions. Although there are more topics which could be found in common, this book will examine in particular how Western and Islamic thinkers have conceived and applied the principals of the rule of law, the reflection of national[17] character in the state, and the limitation and definition of state power. This is what might be termed a "thin" definition of constitutionalism, which is necessary for the purposes of balancing the universal and local elements that are always part of a comparative endeavor.

The overall plan of the work then, proceeds in the following manner:

The remainder of the Introduction identifies the central hypotheses of the book and then provides an overview of some of the literature in the relevant sub-fields of Comparative Politics, Constitutionalism, and Islamic Constitutionalism.

Chapter 1 further defines what is meant by constitutionalism for the purposes of this work. This is done by examining the debates between Western scholars about both the derivation of the term constitution and the way it has come to be used in Western parlance. C.H. McIlwain, as one of the most respected theorists of constitutionalism, and Hans Kelsen, as the standard bearer of legal positivism and crucial role in drafting the Austrian constitution, are also consulted for their invaluable contributions to the practical implications of constitutionalism as a mode of government and legality. Finally, it looks at the context of constitutional dialogue concerning Western and Islamic norms. Specifically, it outlines and refutes the contentions of Orientalists like Elie Kedourie, whose work denies the possibility of a genuinely Islamic constitutionalism. As an alternative, it

16 See, for example, Owen, Roger. *State, Power, and Politics in the Making of the Modern Middle East*. 2nd ed. London and New York: Routledge, 2000, pp. 27–8. Owen discusses "a huge expansion in the power and pervasiveness of the state" in the "post-independence Middle East," but his explanation of this expansion never mentions either constitutions or constitutionalism. Rather, the discussion is couched in terms of power, security, and pan-Arab nationalism.

17 This term is used for the purposes of simplification. More accurately, it could be said to represent the characteristics of the people living within a state's territorial boundaries or otherwise under its sovereignty.

then discusses Noah Feldman's *The Fall and Rise of the Islamic State*, which is particularly interesting as a text which seeks to learn from the mistakes of the US-led regime change project in Iraq, and Abdullahi Ahmed An-Na'im's *African Constitutionalism and the Role of Islam* and his *Islam and the Secular State,* which represent the work of a liberal Muslim scholar who has practical experience living under different regime types, and their implications for future constitutional discourse in majority-Muslim contexts.

Chapter 2, "Western Constitutionalism," begins by further defining what is meant by constitutionalism for the purposes of this work. This is done by examining the debates between Western scholars about both the derivation of the term constitution and the way it has come to be used in Western parlance. C.H. McIlwain and Hans Kelsen are again consulted for their invaluable contributions to the practical implications of constitutionalism as a mode of government and legality. From this perspective it is then possible to look at the more specific constitutional concepts of the rule of law, national character, and limiting government power. This is done through exegesis of Cicero's *Republic*, Montesquieu's *The Spirit of the Laws*, and *The Federalist Papers*, respectively. Other relevant secondary literature is consulted throughout to illustrate how these works can further understanding of the core constitutional values, rather than particular state structures, that lay the foundation of Western constitutionalism.

One may legitimately question why these particular thinkers have been chosen instead of others. In part, they were chosen because their ideas seemed to have a greater resonance with key thinkers from the Muslim canon. Additionally, each of these texts is nearly always included in the discussion of how Western constitutionalism evolved, and furthermore they distill the conceptual constitutional categories considered by this text in a way that is readily understandable and comparable. Cicero's *Republic*, for example, is far less contentious than Aristotle's *Politics* when it comes to discussing the primacy of law and the *telos* of the state. His particular conception of the rule of law is appealing because it is the theory of an actual politician who has led a major state and who has a reputation as a wordsmith, politician, and philosopher. Likewise, Montesquieu, despite some problematic sections that appear to smack of the worst kind of Orientalism and cultural determinism, articulates one of the clearest formulas for how the state as an institution should relation to its populace as a people with its own unique history and characteristics, requiring a tailored constitutionalism, rather than a one-size-fits-all solution. Finally, *The Federalist Papers* are the public argument made in favor of adopting the world's first modern constitution and the oldest one still in force. The role of the United States as a global hegemon and the only superpower with a reputation for constitutionalism makes it an exemplar for other states. Moreover, the ideological commitment to constitutionalism, particularly democratic constitutionalism, is so strong within the USA, that it is willing to support this commitment with considerable financial and military resources, meaning that its core constitutional story is absolutely essential to understanding the international context of constitutional debates and developments in the present.

The third chapter creates a philosophical bridge between the two constitutional traditions by taking a closer look at a key (perhaps *the* key) foundational moment in each of them. By looking at the *Constitution of Medina* promulgated by Muhammad and the *Magna Carta* signed by King John, it is possible to compare the political realities that compelled these rulers to establish covenants with those they were ruling, and to compare the means by which they established legitimacy, a distinctive sense of political identity, and codified the rights and duties assigned to the respective rulers and subjects. These texts in particular were chosen because of Muhammad's role not just as religious prophet, but as exemplary ruler, and because the story of constitutionalism in the West nearly always traces its origins to the capitulation of King John to his nobles at Runnymede.

Chapter 4 is in many ways a mirror of Chapter 2, and intentionally so. It looks at Islamic versions of the rule of law, national character, and restrictions on power through the lens of al-Farabi's *On the Perfect State*, ibn Khaldun's *Muqaddimah*, and the 19th century Ottoman reforms collectively called the *Tanzimat.* It must be emphasized that these works are not presented as approximations or corollaries to Western versions of these values, but are treated as much as possible as concepts worthy of study in their own contexts and in their own right. Farabi is a problematic thinker for theorists working in Islamic political thought because his orthodoxy has often been suspect and his work has primarily been of interest to philosophers and thinkers rather than politicians. However, he has been chosen for examination in this book not only because his notions of the rule of law are intricately developed within the framework of an Islamic view of civilization, but also because his influence outside the context of the Muslim-ruled world provides one of the finest examples of how political and constitutional theory transcend and blend the civilizational boundaries so often imposed upon them. Without Farabi, there is no Aquinas as we know him. His interpretations of the ancient Greek texts are some of the first and most foundational interpretations to launch the reincorporation of these texts into the Western tradition when it became clear that Christianity was not sufficiently political to comprise the entire constitutional framework of the state.

In a similar manner, Ibn Khaldun is included because his reputation as a progenitor of the sociological approach to politics exceeds civilizational boundaries and has made his *Muqaddimah* a central text for theorists from any tradition seeking to understand the cyclical (rather than linear) approach to constitutional development. The fact that he is writing in a Muslim context as someone affected by the *Reconquista* of Spain makes his theory especially relevant to a time in which Islam and West are being posed as essential and conflictual others. His concept of *asabiyya* foreshadows what present scholars have come to see as the paradox of constitutionalism, as it demonstrates how the cohesion of a group can be responsible both for creating and empowering a state, but also for its ultimate decay and destruction.

Like the *Federalist Papers*, the Ottoman *Tanzimat* reforms represent an actual approach to governance and to the establishment of constitutional norms in the context of major social and political upheaval. Where the US Constitution substituted subjects for citizens, these reforms renegotiated the relationship between Empire and province, changed the political unit from semi-autonomous religious communities with distinct rights and responsibilities, and created equal political communities with an aspirational national identity that was not specific to any religion. Although not nearly as radical as the reforms to come under Ataturk, these mark the beginnings of constitutional reform in the modern Muslim world, one which was struggling to fight the twin forces of internal independence movements and European encroachment and colonialism. These reforms also comprise the backbone of Khayr al-Din al-Tunisi's argument for a constitutional Tunisian state, and so also serve the vital function of ideological context for later sections of the book.

The fifth chapter looks at one instance in which the dialogue of these two traditions did in fact overlap in significant ways and led to new interpretations and fusions of both Western and Islamic concepts in the work of Tunisia's Khayr al-Din al-Tunisi. After detailing the contemporary historical and political scene, along with his personal biography, it undertakes a sustained exegetical analysis of his book *The Surest Path to Knowledge Concerning the Conditions of Countries*. This book, written by the man who helped to write and enact the Arab world's, indeed one of the entire world's first written constitutions, the Tunisian Constitution of 1861, describes a brief but comprehensive and coherent political philosophy that seeks to negotiate a path between Western and Islamic traditions, subverting some and creating new combinations of others, in order to both assert autonomy and to participate more fully in the globalizing industrial age in which it was written.

The concluding chapter, in addition to reexamining the topics discussed thus far, looks at how Dallmayr's type of comparative civilizational analysis can work in practice from a constitutional perspective. In particular, it engaged with the Arab Spring, not to draw conclusions or to speculate about the longevity of new constitutional movements, but rather to highlight the challenges and questions these events pose to constitutionalism as a discipline and as a normative idea.

# Chapter 1
# Constitutional Conversations—Alternative Models for the Challenge of Civilizational Conflict

## Contextualizing the Argument

In the case of the present work there is very little literature that fits within the discourse of Comparative Constitutionalism from Western and Islamic Political Theoretical Perspectives. A recent undertaking can be found in Antony Black's *The West and Islam* (2008). The stated argument of this particular work is that

> up to c.1050 Christian Europe, Islam, and the Byzantine world had more in common than is usually thought; and, secondly, that what decisively differentiated them was the papal revolution of the late eleventh century followed by Europe's twelfth-century renaissance … it goes without saying that in 1450 western political theory as we know it today had barely got off the ground. Since then, western political thought has become more and more different from anything that had gone before, either in its own past or in other cultures. Islamic political thought remained almost completely fixed. The West and Islam simply became more and more different, and that is about all there is to say by way of comparison after the fifteenth century.[1]

This discussion however, addresses fundamentally different concerns and comes to equally different conclusions, although perhaps with a degree of similar motivation in seeking to understand "in which respects ideas put forward in one culture differed from, or were similar to, those put forward in another."[2] Any comparative work likely has such an aim. Rather than focusing on political thought generally however, and rather than primarily assessing that thought during a fixed period of time that ends with a proposed fundamental divergence, this book looks specifically at foundational constitutional values as they are and have been enumerated in Western and Islamic contexts. Furthermore, it ultimately interrogates the very categories of "Western" and "Islamic" and questions their continued usefulness in light of the relentless growth of globalization and

1 Black, Antony. *The West and Islam: Religion and Political Thought in World History*. New York: Oxford University Press, 2008, pp. 1–4.

2 Ibid., p. 5.

particularly in light of the ubiquity of the modern state and adherence, at least in the sense of being treaty signatories, to various human rights and international legal conventions.[3] It may even be, that upon closer examination, the constant intercourse of European (and later North American) ideas and people with those of the majority Muslim regimes stretching from North Africa to Southeast Asia will be so sustained, substantial, and significant that the categories of Western and Islamic will be shown to be contrivances meant to reinforce a sense of otherness that may not be entirely justified by philosophical and historical analysis.

Having addressed the aforementioned comparative study of Western and Islamic political thought, this overview of relevant literature will address the key components of the book. The first of these is comparative political theory. The second is constitutionalism as an object of study separate from discourses on political theory and particularly as distinct from democratization. Finally, the third area of relevant literature looks at some of the work being done on the specific subject of Islamic political thought.

## On Comparative Political Theory, Constitutionalism, and Islamic Political Thought

As discussed above, the relatively new field of comparative political theory is one which is still struggling to differentiate itself from other subfields of comparative politics, area studies, and political though. Excellent examples of the quest to properly define this field include Andrew March's "What is Comparative Political Theory?"[4] and Roxanne Euben's more specific articles on comparing Western and Islamic political theory.[5] Equally important is Kimberley Hutchings admonition that comparativists recall that their work contains insights from people whose identities cannot simply be amalgamated under simplistic labels and which are highly contingent and fractured. Thus, the insights gleaned from comparative work must be treated with a healthy dose of humility and appreciated for their contingency.[6] Jürgen Gebhardt's "Political Thought in an Intercivilizational

3 In the sense in which it is being used here, globalization, or the process by which ideas, people and goods are exchanged between and amongst cultures in a way that gradually and mutually changes these cultures has been ongoing since the earliest days of human navigation. Indeed, it is difficult to find a single historical period in which there were not some forms of significant contact between Christendom and the House of Islam.

4 March, Andrew F. "What is Comparative Political Theory?" *The Review of Politics*, 71:4 (2009): 531–65.

5 See Euben, Roxanne L. "Comparative Political Theory: An Islamic Fundamentalist Critique of Rationalism." *The Journal of Politics*, 59:1 (1997): 28–55 and Euben, Roxanne L. "Contingent Borders, Syncretic Perspectives: Globalization, Political Theory, and Islamizing Knowledge." *International Studies Review*, 4:1 (2002): 23–48.

6 Hutchings, Kimberly. "Dialogue between Whom? The Role of the West/Non-West Distinction in Promoting Global Dialogue in Ir." *Millennium—Journal of International*

Perspective," is also highly instructive in its proposition that comparative political theorizing is properly and meaningfully located in "the common ground of the intercivilizational modality of human existence in history and society" because it "intends to bring to our attention the essence of the political in all of its historical modalities."[7] There are several more comparative thinkers treated throughout this work, and many more like Charles Taylor who are incredibly significant to this sub-field, but these and Fred Dallmayr are by far the most influential on this text.

In terms of literature on constitutionalism as a broad subject of enquiry, the array of writers and various related subjects is truly vast. The primary limitation of most of this literature, at least until recently, is that despite many of its universal claims, it is predominantly and overwhelmingly Western in orientation. In terms of this traditional approach to constitutionalism, Charles McIlwain's *Constitutionalism, Ancient and Modern* is absolutely essential reading and will be discussed in much greater detail later in this work. It established many of the methodologies and discourses surrounding constitutionalism and also helped to solidify the Western political canon while simultaneously developing a canon of literature specific to constitutional thought. Furthermore, it presents a cogent defense of the constitution as a natural growth of a given society, and as such, provides an implicit defense of the natural law school of constitutional thought. This is in stark contrast to the work of Hans Kelsen, as seen in his *General Theory of Law and the* State, which is perhaps far more influential in terms of its application by policy makers and presents a thoroughly positivist vision of constitutionalism. A much more recent and self-aware book on constitutionalism is Loughlin and Walker's (2007) *The Paradox of Constitutionalism*. This edited volume contains chapters from several present scholars, the most relevant of which for this work are those in its final section on "Extension and Diversification of Constituent Power." It may be noted that this title emphasizes the element of identity and individuals in the idea of a constitution as being a representative social arrangement, rather than simply an amalgamation of various legal norms and institutions. As such, Stephen Tierney's chapter on "Plurinational States" and James Tully's argument about the "Imperialism of Modern Constitutional Democracy" make incredibly cogent points on the challenge of claiming representativeness in states with mixed populations and the problematic conflation of constitutionalism with democratization.[8] Larry Alexander's *Constitutionalism: Philosophical Foundations*, and Alan Brudner's *Constitutional Goods* are excellent volumes to read alongside this discourse as

*Studies*, 39:3 (2011): 639–47.

7 Gebhardt, Jürgen. "Political Thought in an Intercivilizational Perspective: A Critical Reflection." *The Review of Politics*, 70:1 (2008): 5.

8 Loughlin, Martin, and Neil Walker. *The Paradox of Constitutionalism: Constituent Power and Constitutional Form*. Oxford and New York: Oxford University Press, 2007. See particularly Tierney, Stephen, "'We the Peoples': Constituent Power and Constitutionalism in Plurinational States": 229–46, and Tully, James, "The Imperialism of Modern Constitutional Democracy": 315–38.

they highlight the questions posed by constitutionalism from a philosophical perspective, in contrast to the history of political thought method of McIlwain.

Of course, constitutionalism is often broken down into institutional works that discuss the functions of various organs of state. These works are essential, but not directly relevant to this discussion. However, as this work is primarily concerned with constitutional values, the other main sub-category of constitutionalism that focuses on particular ideas like justice, the rule of law, etc. is crucial. These works are extremely diverse in their normative orientation and philosophical underpinnings, but they generally advocate stronger adherence to a particular core constitutional norm. These would include *Justice* by Sandel, Richard Tuck's *Rights of War and Peace*, Tom Bingham and Brian Tamanaha, both on *The Rule of Law*, Kymlicka's work on nationalism and identity,[9] and Larry May's *Global Justice and Due Process*. Additional considerations on issues such as the tension between positivist and natural law justifications for constitutionalism will be considered later in this text.

The Western constitutional canon itself does not require repeating in depth here, but it bears mentioning that it generally traces the evolution of Western thought from Socrates onward, with a great deal of emphasis on the Enlightenment ideals of rationality and individuality. Therein lays one of its key weaknesses from a comparative perspective. The canon, as such, is designed with an often unacknowledged teleology that is meant for the reader to arrive philosophically convinced of the inevitability and suitability of the modern liberal state as the definitive political model, representative of the pinnacle of social achievement, and worthy of universal imitation and perhaps even imposition. Thus, when one searches for resources on constitutionalism, references to democracy and liberalization are absolutely rife. Mohammed Khatami identified this very danger in the speech quoted at the start of this book. He cautions that "We cannot simplistically speak of an end to history, as liberalism cannot be introduced as the sole image of wickedness or the sole symbol for perfection of social thought."[10] Whether from institutional approaches like those of Donald Lutz[11] or theoretically-based works like those of Bellamy,[12] Elster and Slagsted's (1998) *Constitutionalism and Democracy*, and Cass Sunstein's (2001) *Designing Democracy: What*

9 Key works include: *Justice in Political Philosophy*. 2 vols, An Elgar Reference Collection. Aldershot and Brookfield, VT: E. Elgar, 1992. *Politics in the Vernacular: Nationalism, Multiculturalism, and Citizenship*. Oxford and New York: Oxford University Press, 2001. *Multicultural Odysseys: Navigating the New International Politics of Diversity*. Oxford and New York: Oxford University Press, 2009. *Liberalism, Community, and Culture*. New York: Clarendon Press, 1989.

10 Khatami (2006), p. 6.

11 See "Thinking About Constitutionalism at the Start of the Twenty-First Century." *Publius*, 30:4 (2000): 115–35. Also, *Principles of Constitutional Design*. Cambridge and New York: Cambridge University Press, 2006.

12 Bellamy, Richard. *Political Constitutionalism: A Republican Defence of the Constitutionality of Democracy*. Cambridge: Cambridge University Press, 2007.

*Constitutions Do*, the conflation of these closely-related, yet nonetheless distinct, concerns is pervasive and generally goes unquestioned.

This leads to a great deal of spillover once one ventures into the rather newer field of Islamic political theory, which can be broken into two further groupings of writings which proceed on a history of thought or history of philosophy model, and others which seek to use Islamic thinkers to advance a particular normative political agenda. The first category includes works by Patricia Crone, who provides a sophisticated and extremely thorough historical and philosophical context for understanding medieval Muslim thought in books such as *God's Rule: Government and Islam*.[13] One could also include Antony Black's *History of Islamic Political Thought* in this group, which is more or less a literary introduction to various Muslim thinkers arranged in a chronological fashion.[14] John Esposito largely subscribes to this approach, but with a more explicitly conciliatory aim in works including *Islam: the Straight Path* and *Islam and the West: Muslim Voices of Dialogue*.[15] In contrast, Nathan Brown deals with concrete observation of majority Muslim states and their constitutional norms, and his primary normative argument seems to be quite simply for a constitutional, though not necessarily liberal, mode of governance. In light of recent events, his *The Rule of Law in the Arab World: Courts in Egypt and the Gulf* is highly relevant and may offer some explanation for why revolution has broken out in some states and not others. From a more general perspective, his insistence on decoupling constitutionalism and democratization, seen in *Constitutions in a Nonconstitutional world*, is crucial to this project.[16]

Providing a bridge between these works and those advocating a particular political vision are the writings of Tariq Ramadan. Key amongst his writings for the present enquiry are *Islam, the West, and the Challenges of Modernity*, *Globalisation: Muslim Resistances*, and *The Quest for Meaning: Developing a Philosophy of Pluralism*.[17] Working with an explicitly pluralist and liberal perspective, Abdullahi an-Naim's *African Constitutionalism and the Role of Islam* and his more recent *Islam and the Secular State* lay out a role for Islam as

---

13 Crone, Patricia. *God's Rule: Government and Islam*. New York: Columbia University Press, 2004.

14 Black, Antony. *The History of Islamic Political Thought: From the Prophet to the Present*. Edinburgh: Edinburgh University Press, 2001.

15 Esposito, John L. *Islam: The Straight Path*. 3rd ed. New York and Oxford: Oxford University Press, 1998. See also Esposito, John L., and John O. Voll. "Islam and the West: Muslim Voices of Dialogue." *Millennium—Journal of International Studies*, 29:3 (2000): 613–39.

16 Brown, Nathan J. *The Rule of Law in the Arab World: Courts in Egypt and the Gulf*, Cambridge Middle East Studies 6. Cambridge and New York: Cambridge University Press, 1997. See also, Brown, Nathan J. *Constitutions in a Nonconstitutional World: Arab Basic Laws and the Prospects for Accountable Government*, SUNY Series in Middle Eastern Studies. Albany, NY: State University of New York Press, 2002.

17 For an applied version of his thought, see his most recent *The Arab Awakening: Islam and the New Middle East*. London: Allen Lane, 2012.

guarantor of social and political rights and advocates pluralist government to be the only form of political organization that can satisfy the demands of *sharīʿa.*[18] These works will be discussed in greater detail later in the book. Likewise, Noah Feldman seeks to create a role for the *'ulama* within a liberalized context in his *The Fall and Rise of the Islamic State*. As someone who participated in the Iraq reconstruction effort following the 2003 Iraq invasion, his intellectual arc has undergone a substantial transformation from advocating a more or less Western state with Iraqi vernacular, seen in his book *After Jihad*, to advancing a far less concrete vision of a constitutional regime in which the institutions reflect local practice and are open to negotiation.[19]

## Constituting Vocabulary—The Derivation of "Constitution," Sartori vs. Maddox

Lest one be tempted to think that the study of constitutionalism is the study of a settled field with well-defined and agreed upon boundaries, it is helpful to first examine how contestable the very concepts of what a constitution *is* and *means* are. An illuminating example of the very fundamental disagreements on these issues can be found in an interesting debate on the very nature of the word *constitution*, which occurred between the 1960s and 1980s as seen in two articles by Giovanni Sartori and Graham Maddox, both of which appeared in *The American Political Science Review*. The earlier of these arguments, Sartori's, takes particular care to show that what most scholars think of as constitutions from the 19th Century onwards does not derive, as is suggested by some scholars and even standard dictionaries,[20] from the Latin *constitutio*, because for him it simply meant "an enactment," and later in its plural form "came to mean a collection of laws enacted by the Sovereign."[21] This is problematic especially because, for Sartori, the mother country of constitutionalism is Britain, which seems to "delight" in confounding outsiders by claiming for itself a constitution that is present but largely unwritten, or according to some, even entirely unwritten but strongly underpinned by a variety of "particularly solemn written documents: the Magna Charta (*sic*), the

18 Na'im, Abdullahi Ahmad. *African Constitutionalism and the Role of Islam*. Philadelphia, PA: University of Pennsylvania Press, 2006. Also, *Islam and the Secular State: Negotiating the Future of Sharīʿa*. Cambridge, MA: Harvard University Press, 2008.

19 See his *After Jihad: America and the Struggle for Islamic Democracy*. 1st paperback ed. New York: Farrar, Straus and Giroux, 2004. Also, *The Fall and Rise of the Islamic State*. Princeton, NJ: Princeton University Press, 2008.

20 See for example the Oxford Dictionary of English entry on "constitution," which states its origin is Middle English (denoting a law, or a body of laws or customs): from Latin *constitutio(n-)*, from *constituere* "establish, appoint."

21 Sartori, Giovanni. "Constitutionalism: A Preliminary Discussion." *The American Political Science Review*, 56:4 (1962): 853.

Confirmation Acts, the 1610–1628 Petition of Rights, the Habeas Corpus Act of 1679 … etc."[22] This is ultimately of only secondary importance however, as his primary concern is with the *telos* of the constitution, which written or not, in examples from England, the Continent, and America is concerned with a common goal, what the Italians and French call *garantisme*. "In other terms, all over the Western area people requested, or cherished, 'the constitution,' because this term meant to them a fundamental law, or a fundamental set of principles, *and* (emphasis mine) a correlative institutional arrangement, which would restrict arbitrary power and ensure a 'limited government'." However, post-World War I this "situation of over-all basic agreement has come to an end rapidly and radically."[23]

What is the basis for Sartori's claim for a "radical" shift in the way constitutions themselves are understood? It is here that his argument would seem especially open to scrutiny, as he himself says that the problem is that "legal terminology … shares the same destiny as political terminology in general: that is, it tends to be abused and corrupted."[24] In essence, the political atmosphere of the mid-20th Century led politicians to abuse the term constitution to whip up nationalistic impulses to suit their own purposes and Continental scholars to seek out universals when defining constitutionalism, which brought about the parsing of the term into two components: a constitution which was a formalized set of rules for governing, and *being constitutional*, which required enumeration of individual liberties/rights and the means of protecting them.[25] This leads, in the end, to an ability to say any order is a constitution, rendering the word both dangerous to the masses for its positive emotive content, and useless for the scholar for its lack of a normative element that would reattach the word to its role in protecting rights as well as delineating rules and duties.[26] Sartori concludes this discussion by proposing a starting point for his own definition of constitution that is able to account for the word's normative and descriptive properties whilst still allowing for significant variation in the norms it promotes and the institutions it develops to enact and protect them. Oddly though, this is boiled down to what he calls a "role theory" approach which appears to be a blend of function and process that looks at a constitution "*vis-à-vis* the role-taking of the power holders … does it help to enforce, and if so to what extent, a desired 'role performance' upon the persons in office."[27]

This seems entirely unsatisfactory based on his own arguments for political terms to be assessed in light of historical experience rather than political expedience, and given that this approach seems unlikely to address the totality of a constitution as not only a set of laws, institutions and rights, but also as an embodiment of the national sovereign will and character that the term has carried

22 Ibid., p. 855.
23 Ibid.
24 Ibid.
25 Ibid., pp. 856–7.
26 Ibid., pp. 855–9.
27 Ibid., p. 864.

since at least the time of Aristotle, who even Sartori notes spoke of the *politeia* as conveying "the idea of the way in which a polity is patterned."[28] It is based on similar and additional critiques of Sartori that Graham Maddox seeks to enlarge, or at least enlarge the discursive space, for the word *constitution* in his 1982 article "A Note on the Meaning of 'Constitution'." He systematically analyses Sartori in light of other key constitutional scholars and demonstrates the need for a broader definition of the word if it is to be useful for comparative and analytical purposes.

One of Maddox's first qualms with Sartori's work is that he finds it disingenuous to separate the Latin term *constitutio* from constitution simply because the meaning of the term changed through time. He points out that the term itself derives from the root *constituere*, which means 'to set up, establish, erect, construct, arrange, to settle or determine,' and that even in imperial Rome the emperor's decrees were called *constitutiones* "because they collectively defined the limits of state action."[29] This seems perfectly in line with Sartori's idea of the constitution being centrally concerned with limiting government. Maddox then goes on to show how several writers including Cicero, Tacitus, St. Augustine and Boethius all used the term in fairly consistent fashion, satisfying the historical criterion laid down by Sartori himself and contradicting his dismissal of Cicero's usage as imprecise (a charge that is especially serious as Cicero is known as much for rhetoric and his care with words as he is for his philosophical and political thought).[30]

Interestingly, this feeds into a later concern of Sartori's that scholars of political thought not project present issues into the past.[31] Maddox makes the basic observation that various scholars of constitutionalism (including Loewenstein, Ostwald, and McIlwain) have thoroughly shown the classical lineage of constitutionalism and that even in antiquity the "idea of constitution as the total establishment of a state system rested alongside more restricting notions of the limitations on government power by the 'power of the people'."[32] Further to this, the entire idea of limits on government power being the true and universally agreed *telos* of the constitution is highly questionable. Is it not possible, Maddox asks, for there to be more than one end to which constitutions aim? If it is indeed not the case that all earlier scholars of Greek were wrong in translating the Greek *politeia* and Latin *constitution* as "constitution," then to what extent can the term be widened without losing its specificity and usefulness? Here, he very effectively refers to one of the foremost 20th Century scholars of constitutionalism, CH McIlwain, to note that over the centuries, including recent ones that saw the development of the American constitution amongst others, there was an equally urgent need to have a "strong *gubernaculums*, government power, to control inordinate private

28 Ibid., p. 860.

29 Maddox, Graham. "A Note on the Meaning of 'Constitution'." *The American Political Science Review*, 76:4 (1982): 805–6.

30 Ibid., p. 807.

31 This idea finds quite full expression in the work of Quentin Skinner.

32 Ibid., p. 808.

interests to the benefit of a peaceful civil order, along with the essential *jurisdictio* which implied a civil control on government power."[33] If one accounts for the divergent aims of constitutions, Maddox contends, then "the balance between strong government and the firm control of government may then remain a more open question."[34]

## Putting the "Norm" in Normative—Constitutionalism as an Instrument in the Work of C.H. McIlwain

Exploring the open question of what constitutions do and should aim to accomplish is the overarching concern of most of the work of CH McIlwain, whose works include influential titles like *The Growth of Political Thought in the West* (1932) and *Constitutionalism: Ancient and Modern* (1947). A sustained examination of his contribution to the development of constitutionalism as an academic discipline is warranted not only by his substantial list of books and articles, but also by the influence he exercised on other scholars in his role as professor at Harvard University in the first half of the 20th Century. As Douglas Sturm suggests he was "both historian and political theorist. In his case this was a fruitful combination."[35] Over the course of his career he developed a historically-based theory of constitutionalism that eschewed the type of limited definition advocated by Sartori and instead viewed it as a history and developmental process in its own right. Sturm compares this view of constitutionalism to that of the lawyer of the common law tradition who prefers it to "black letter law" because it is fluid rather than fixed, and "definitions are *pro tempore* and not *in aeturnum*."[36] It would seem that this view would lend itself most strongly to a view of the constitution as an accretion of laws, customs, and institutions rather than as a written code, but McIlwain in fact spent a great deal of energy examining the written manifestations of constitutional order, particularly as it related to the US Constitution. The general motivation and normative element of his works is best summed up in his own words in his book *Constitutionalism: Ancient and Modern* in which he states the following:

> The earlier history of the growth of our constitutionalism can, of course, furnish no definite or conclusive answer to many of these questions, because the conditions under which they exist now are in so many ways different from those which surrounded their growth in past ages. Nevertheless, I do believe that

33 Ibid., p. 809.

34 Ibid.

35 Sturm, Douglas. "Constitutionalism: A Critical Appreciation and an Extension of the Political Theory of C.H. McIlwain." *Minnesota Law Review*, 54 (1969): 217.

36 Ibid., pp. 217–18.

> careful unbiased study of this past growth is not without its practical value in helping us to analyze our own pressing problems, if not to answer them.[37]

This is coupled with the dual-natured view of government that Maddox mentioned that takes an inherently conservative line that seeks a steady, rather than reactionary, dialectic between strengthening and limiting government in order to create a regime that is strong enough to rule and a population that is strong enough to hold its rulers accountable.[38] This struggle is one that McIlwain sees present through the historical record beginning at least as early as the Ancient Greek polis and continuing through the Roman era, the Medieval Period, the Early Modern/ Enlightenment age, and finally into the Modern present.[39]

Now that the nature and method of his work have been summed up, it is helpful to look at the actual definition he gives to constitution. He sees present constitutions as first and foremost self-conscious creations made by "direct and express constituent action."[40] This differs from earlier versions of constitutionalism in which law was identified with custom as much as with legislation and it was seen as binding in a legal sense. It also excludes arguments in which consent of the governed is taken to be implicitly present simply by their continued presence within the territorial sphere of a given regime.[41] Despite these differences, what makes constitutionalism something that can be studied as a tradition and as a recognizable quantity is that it "has one essential quality: it is a legal limitation on government; it is the antithesis of arbitrary rule; its opposite is despotic government, the government of will instead of law … the most ancient, the most persistent, and the most lasting of the essentials of true constitutionalism still remains … the limitation of government by law."[42]

37 McIlwain, Charles Howard. *Constitutionalism: Ancient and Modern*. Rev. ed. Indianapolis, IN: Amagi/Liberty Fund, 2007, p. 139.

38 See Ibid., p. 45, which says: "If reaction is truly to be avoided, we must preserve our legal guarantees. We must keep them intact, but we dare not stop there. There is corruption which feebleness in government makes possible, and this can only be ended by making government, within its legal limits, actually stronger than it is. This strength, however, is itself a danger if it is not completely responsible to the people, and to all the people, at all times."

39 Ibid., p. ix. Doubtless he would have continued this into the post-modern era had he lived to see it, despite its rejection of -isms and identities previously taken for granted.

40 Ibid., p. 21.

41 This would seem to take into account criticisms, such as those of David Hume in "Of the Original Contract," that contract theorists of the state took the ability of a subject to leave a domain for granted and did not acknowledge the overwhelming difficulties the common person would confront in attempting to leave an unsatisfactory regime. Indeed, even in recent times, and in what is called "the West," examples like the former East Berlin reveal how a state can make leaving nearly impossible.

42 Ibid., p. 22.

In using this approach of definition by examining both advocacy and opposition, McIlwain brings the discussion of constitutionalism and its meaning full-circle. Like Sartori and others he does not hide his enthusiasm for constitutionalism as an instrument (as well as a tradition that can be studied for insight into present questions and difficulties). He also agrees with the view that the primary role of the constitution is to limit state power by codifying and defining it. This in turn gives the state the legitimacy and strength that it needs to enforce the law and to remain stable when the people enforce their will upon the state through some sort of consensual mechanism. However, what is for Sartori a *telos*, is ultimately for McIlwain the means to achieving an altogether larger *telos* that derives from the ancient conception of government existing to promote the good/virtuous/ just life. As McIlwain says in his 1936 "Government by Law," "The problem of constitutionalism, then, is everybody's problem, whatever economic or social system he may prefer. It is law alone that gives protection to rights of any kind in any individual, personal as well as proprietary, whatever form the state..."[43]

## Positively Constitutional—Hans Kelsen and the Constitution as Legal Foundation

Law, of course, is the singular obsession of legal positivist Hans Kelsen. His strain of constitutional thought is important because in addition to spending the majority of his career in academia, he also personally drafted the Austrian constitution of 1920, which continues to form the basis of Austrian constitutional law and constitutional review, which in turn has influenced constitutional theory in various parts of Europe.[44] As Nicoletta Ladavac points out, this legacy is further extended due to political events in Europe that forced him, as someone of Jewish heritage, to emigrate, first to Switzerland and then to the United States.[45] In the United States he quickly established himself as an authority on law and wrote a detailed critique on the then new United Nations charter and assessed its various components for their effectiveness and adherence to a consistent vision of law. Any new regime seeking statehood finds itself needing to demonstrate conformity with these UN ideals, and therefore finds itself too under the significant weight of Kelsen's positivist vision. His influence can be seen not only through his writings, but also

43 McIlwain, CH. "Government by Law." *Foreign Affairs*, 14:2 (Jan. 1936): 185. Note also the use of the word "proprietary," which seems especially apt in a time when state's are judged by their ability to foster economic growth and to protect the intellectual wealth, along with more material products, that they produce. It seems that there is an ongoing and increasing appreciation for the relationship between the political economy and the stability of the state and its constitution.

44 Ladavac, Nicoletta. "Hans Kelsen (1881–1973) Biographical Note and Bibliography." *European Journal of International Law*, 9 (1998): 391.

45 Ibid., pp. 392–3.

through his teaching, as his students included eminent scholars and theorists like Adolf Merkl, Alfred Verdross, Felix Kaufmann, Eric Voegelin, and Franz Weyr.[46]

In order to fully appreciate the scope of his work, it would require an examination far too involved for the confines of this dissertation. However, a reasonably nuanced understanding of his contribution to constitutional and legal theory can be gained through examining his seminal work *General Theory of Law and State* in consultation with some of his shorter articles and lectures. His work is at once both philosophical and legal, and as such proceeds carefully from definition of an issue or case, to definition of terms, to use of evidence, and then to drawing conclusions. Using his own organization, we will first look at his definition of law, particularly from a positivist perspective (in contrast with natural law), then examine how he thinks it is used to define the ends for which a State exists, what the State itself is, the role of the constitution in the State, the separation of powers of constitutional organs, and finally the question of which order of law is supreme between national and international law.

> Law is an order of human behavior. An 'order' is a system of rules. Law is not, as it is sometimes said, a rule … It is impossible to grasp the nature of law if we limit our attention to the single isolated rule. The relations which link together the particular rules of a legal order are also essential to the nature of law.[47]

Much has been written about the virtues and dangers of Kelsen's view of law and its basis.[48] His definition of law itself, seen above, is however equally notable and important. The first thing that strikes the reader is that law is supposedly not grounded in nature, but is "an order of human behavior." On what basis can Kelsen argue that this behavior itself is not derived from nature or natural instinct? This seems to require an assumption that human agency is something that exists apart from the natural order and is an order unto itself. If there is a physical order made of Newtonian objects with their own relationships and rules of motion, then Kelsen argues here that there is also a legal order, made of legal objects (laws) with relationship to legal subjects (citizens, corporations, governments, etc.) and that the relationships of these laws to one another and to their subjects are important in their own right. Indeed, they are "essential to the nature of law." In rejecting natural law, Kelsen nonetheless creates something that would appear very akin to an organism, composed of different parts which must be properly ordered for mutual benefit, and which has its own identity that is greater than

46 Ibid., p. 392.

47 Kelsen, Hans, Anders Wedberg, and Wolfgang Herbert Kraus. *General Theory of Law and State, 20th Century Legal Philosophy Series: Vol. I.* Cambridge, MA: Harvard University Press, 1945, p. 3.

48 See for instance, TC Hopton's "Grundnorm and Constitution: The Legitimacy of Politics," in *MacGill Law Journal* (1978) and its discussion of the errant use of Kelsen's theory in judicial rulings within the British Commonwealth.

the sum of its parts. This conception of the law seeks to maintain "purity" that is devoid of relations to appeals to supernatural codes, morals, or natural law in order to recognize as equally valid (at least potentially) any legal system regardless of the ends to which the order may aspire. As he goes on to say,

> (Law) designates a specific technique of social organization. The problem of law, as a scientific problem, is the problem of social technique, not a problem of morals ... There are legal orders which are, from a certain point of view, unjust. Law and justice are two different concepts. Law as distinguished from justice is positive law.[49]

Here can be seen Kelsen's effort to achieve a definition of law that can be universally valid, but in so doing does he create a definition that is essentially meaningless? One of his more vociferous opponents and contemporaries, Carl Schmitt, mocked his conception of law as one in which a norm is "'valid if it is valid and because it is valid,' but not because it refers to a more fundamental moral ideal. Consistent normative thereby evolves into a mode of 'bourgeois relativism'."[50]

This critique seems justified in light of Kelsen's further point that the very existence of so many ideas of justice in the world makes the discussion of the term as an absolute entity which can be discovered via deduction from the natural order, divine inspiration, or any other means, in the end, absurd.[51] What Schmitt and others with similar critiques do not account for, however, is that although Kelsen is divorcing law from morality and natural law in his pure theory in order to create a definition that is functional in any context, he is not arguing that the law must remain devoid of this normative element in individual contexts. Indeed, in his article on the Preamble of the UN Charter, he argues the following:

> The content of a statute or treaty is legally relevant, that is to say, has binding force only if it has a normative character. It has binding force if its meaning is to establish by itself or in connection with other contents of the statute or treaty an obligation. A statement whose meaning is to establish an obligation is a norm.[52]

---

49 Kelsen (1945), p. 5.

50 As cited in Scheuerman, William E. "Carl Schmitt's Critique of Liberal Constitutionalism." *The Review of Politics*, 58:2 (1996): 303.

51 See Kelsen (1945), p. 8 where he states, "Since humanity is divided into many nations, classes, religions, professions and so on, often at variance with one another, there are a great many very different ideas of justice; too many for one to be able to speak simply of 'justice'."

52 Kelsen, Hans. "The Preamble of the Charter—A Critical Analysis." *The Journal of Politics*, 8 (1946): 142.

This means that law should contain an element of what people should or should not do. Without this element it is meaningless because it cannot be enforced.[53] What this means then is that whilst the morals may differ between systems and be "relative," they must nonetheless be present in some manner in order to give the law social impetus. This *should* element is what Kelsen calls an "obligation." What results then, is a system of statements that create obligations (either for the citizen to do or not do something, or for the state to assign penalties for disobedience), these norms provide the normative character to law, which socially justifies the contents of the laws and the charters that underpin their validity. What Kelsen offers is a flexible account of constitutions that can accommodate all types of human social organization and mores, past, present, and future. The constitution can be reconstituted in a variety of forms for a variety of reasons but it remains a constitution so long as it is a self-sustaining system of law that is socially valid.

Kelsen seems keenly aware that the long tradition of natural law theory will provide ample grounds for criticism of his ideas by those who hold to its general assumptions. He acknowledges that "Faced by the existence of a just ordering of society, intelligible in nature, reason, or divine will, the activity of positive law makers would be tantamount to a foolish effort at artificial illumination in bright sunshine."[54] This does not trouble him greatly though as he is convinced that,

> The usual assertion, however, that there is indeed a natural, absolutely good order, but transcendental and hence not intelligible, that there is indeed such a thing as justice, but that it cannot be clearly defined, is in itself, a contradiction. It is, in fact, nothing but a euphemistic paraphrase of the painful fact that justice is an ideal inaccessible to human cognition.[55]

This hostility to natural law theory forces Kelsen to seek out an alternative to justice as a basis upon which a legal order can be founded. Here, he creates the idea of *Grundnorm*. TC Hopton sums up this term as one whose "validity cannot be objectively tested; it must be presupposed or assumed."[56] Here one is drawn inexorably back to the criticism of Schmitt and must ask why this assumption of validity is a strong enough reason to justify its perpetuation. Perhaps Kelsen could reply that natural law theorists argue that justice can be discovered through observation of nature, so why can he not argue that the social base from which law springs likewise can be discovered, even if its existence is purely socially constituted and ephemeral rather than something eternal and transcendent. It may

53 This same reasoning can be seen in Hobbes' contention in *Leviathan* that the state cannot outlaw what goes on in one's mind because it has no jurisdiction or enforcement in the internal realm of thought.

54 Kelsen (1945), p. 13.

55 Ibid., p. 13.

56 Hopton, T.C. "Grundnorm and Constitution: The Legitimacy of Politics." *McGill Law Journal*, 24 (1978): 82.

have horrified people of an earlier age to conceive of our entire planet floating through the void of space, held in check by non-material bonds of gravitational attraction, but this non-material force of attraction is nevertheless strong enough to keep our material existence secure for the time being. To argue that law is based upon anything greater than this is, for Kelsen, intellectually dishonest.

This concern for utmost, brutal honesty is what leads him to definitely rule out the existence of law outside of positive law.[57] Consequently, he must also reject any considerations of *telos* that so heavily figure in the works of other constitutional scholars, including the aforementioned Sartori and McIlwain. To his mind the very idea that the State serves "some sort of ultimate end" is problematic as it follows that "some sort of definite regulation of human behavior, proceeds from 'nature,' that is, from the nature of things or the nature of man, from human reason or the will of God. In such an assumption lies the doctrine of so-called natural law."[58]

If natural law is rejected, along with the notion of finding and delivering justice, what then is the identity and the role of the State? Where other thinkers see the state as an entity with its own character, lifespan and will, for Kelsen there is "no sociological concept of the State different from the concept of the legal order; and that means, that we can describe the social reality without using the term 'State'."[59] The State then, is simply shorthand for the amalgamation of norms and laws which a given society follows and creates. This has enormous implications for the idea of the State as a continuous and coherent actor with prerogatives in both the domestic and international spheres. If there is no inherent national identity being expressed through the state, no consolidation of wills, or no conception of the state as an entity beyond its statutes and ordinances, then what justifies its position as an agent with the power of life and death over its subjects or citizens? Does every change in the law change the very identity of the state?

To these questions Kelsen makes a couple observations. The first is that the State is not simply a territorial unit existing in space. It also exists "in time ... Just as the State is spatially not infinite, it is temporally not eternal ... The point of time when a State begins to exist, that is, the moment when a national legal order begins to be valid, is determined by positive international law according to the principle of effectiveness. It is the same principle according to which the territorial sphere of validity of the national legal order is determined."[60] That is, the State exists as an actor because other actors of a similar nature recognize it as

57 See Kelsen (1945), p. 114, where he states: Law is always positive law, and its positivity lies in the fact that it is created and annulled by acts of human beings, thus being independent of morality or similar norm systems.

58 Ibid., p. 8. This is not to say that his theory is not normative. For an interesting discussion of the parallels between Kelsen and Kant, see Stanley Paulson, "The Neo-Kantian Dimension of Kelsen's Pure Theory of Law." *Oxford Journal of Legal Studies*, 12:3 (1992): 311–32.

59 Kelsen (1945), p. 192.

60 Ibid., p. 219.

an entity existing within certain territorial and temporal boundaries. The agency that the State appears to possess and exercise is, in fact, merely due to the fact that it is recognized by international law, which confers upon the State both rights and duties. Since the State does not exist apart from the social context however, "International law obligates and authorizes the state to behave in a certain way by obligating and authorizing human beings in their capacity as organs of the state to behave in this way."[61]

Of course, though this conception of sovereignty is one that is to some extent observable and based upon the actual exercise of international law, it is not wholly satisfactory as it still leaves open the question of the basis upon which international law is valid. Professor Kelsen admits that ultimately, the determination of where sovereignty properly lies, at the national or international level, is a chicken and egg argument to which one's answer is greatly influenced by one's identity being, or not being, fundamentally shaped as part of a given nation or state. Taken from the point of view of law as science, it "remains totally indifferent towards both" points of view and merely "frees the way to political development of either without postulating or justifying the one or the other."[62] In fact, Kelsen may go beyond this question to an almost post-structural view that there is neither chicken nor egg in the Platonic sense of something material approximating an ideal, but rather simply two collections of molecules with certain characteristics that society recognizes as chickens and eggs.[63]

This leads finally, to his conception of the foundational law of the state, or its constitution. Here again, Kelsen is frustratingly circular in his description of what a constitution is, what it does, and on what basis it exists. He defines the constitution of a state as "its 'fundamental law,' (it) is the basis of the national legal order … as used in political theory, the concept is made to embrace also those norms which regulate the creation and competence of the highest executive and judicial organs."[64] In a way then, the constitution is a sort of *Grundnorm* for the legal system of a state, and in particular for the organs through which the state will enact and enforce its laws. The importance of this role of constitutions is that

61 Kelsen, Hans. "Sovereignty and International Law." *The Georgetown Law Journal*, 48:4 (1960): 628.

62 Ibid., p. 640.

63 Further discussion of this concept can be seen in Kelsen (1945), p. 388 where he states: "A person whose political attitude is one of nationalism and imperialism will naturally be inclined to accept the hypothesis of the primacy of national law. A person whose sympathies are for internationalism and pacifism will be inclined to accept the primacy of international law. From the point of view of the science of law, it is irrelevant which hypothesis one chooses. But from the point of view of political ideology, the choice is important since tied up with the idea of sovereignty … Science can make the jurist aware of the reasons for his choice and the nature of the hypothesis he has chosen, and so prevent him from drawing conclusions which positive law, as given in experience, does not warrant." Kelsen himself uses the chicken and egg analogy in his "What is a Legal Act?" which first appeared in English in 1984 in *The American Journal of Jurisprudence*, 29: 209.

64 Kelsen (1945), pp. 258–9.

it more firmly grounds national law within its own local context on the basis that it "receives its validity from the constitution, since it has been established by the competent organ in the way the constitution prescribes."[65] This means that law is valid not only when socially recognized but it must also be enacted in a lawful manner by the appropriate state body or bodies as specified in the constitution. This clearly lays the groundwork for a justification of judicial review of the constitutionality of individual statutes and for the separation of powers within a government. Strangely however, Kelsen rejects most of the assumptions of the doctrine of Separation of Powers. He contends that

> The concept of 'separation of powers' designates a principle of political organization. It presupposes that the three so-called powers can be determined as three distinct coordinated functions of the State, and that it is possible to define boundary lines separating each of these three functions from the others. But this presupposition is not borne out by the facts. As we have seen, there are not three but two basic functions of the State: creation and application (execution) of the law ... Further, it is not possible to define boundary lines separating these functions from each other, since the distinction between creation and application of law—underlying the dualism of legislative and judicial power (in the broadest sense)—has only a relative character, most acts of State being at the same time law-creating and law-applying acts.[66]

Granted that significant overlap does in fact exist between the branches of governments and their spheres of authority, it is difficult to understand why Kelsen so thoroughly rejects the idea of the Separation of Powers. It could perhaps be that it contradicts his quest for purity because it assumes that a true legal (constitutional) order *must* have this division in order to be valid, which contradicts his goal of looking at constitutions as a framework devoid of content. He explicitly says that in his Pure Theory of Law the "contents of the norms of a positive legal order are determined exclusively by acts of will of human beings ... constituted by acts of human beings and instituted by the constitution as a law-creating fact."[67]

If constitutions are simply the framework for the apparatus of the State, then what is the source of their validity?[68] Kelsen answers that, "If we ask why the constitution is valid ... ultimately we reach some constitution that is the first historically and that was laid down by some individual usurper or assembly. The validity of this first constitution is that last presupposition, the final postulate, upon

65 Ibid., p. 115.

66 Ibid., p. 269.

67 Kelsen, Hans. "On the Basic Norm." *California Law Review*, 47 (1959): 109–10.

68 This contention is evidenced in Kelsen (1945), p. 260, where he argues "'Constitution' in this sense ... means nothing but a specific procedure of legislation; a certain legal form which may be filled with any legal content."

which the validity of all the norms of our legal order depends."[69] Once again, there is no ultimately satisfactory answer as to where the validity of the constitutional order comes from in any sense beyond the fact that it is recognized as valid by those participating in it. This opens the possibility that the constitutional order itself can change. Though this idea is anathema to many political actors, particularly in the United States, it is clearly seen in history. France, for instance, is on its 5th constitution since the creation of the Republic in 1789. Although the 5th Republic is not bound to the constitutions of its predecessors, there is nonetheless a large degree of continuity in its very basic assumptions and values. This seems to demonstrate that the constitution cannot be "the final postulate," but that the true *Grundnorm* must lie in some deeper source, even if that source is simply social custom. That is why he argues that despite the efforts of framers to create a document that is unchanging through time, "There is no legal possibility of preventing a constitution from being modified by way of custom, even if the constitution has the character of statutory law, if it is a so-called 'written' constitution."[70] This is because ultimately even the most fundamental or basic norm is "hypothetical."[71]

Though it would seem logical to conclude that any positivist constitutional order would necessarily be one with a written constitution, this is not necessarily the case. He notes that for one thing, "Very often the constitution is composed of norms which have partly the character of statutory and partly the character of customary law," and that furthermore "The distinction made by traditional theory between 'written' and 'unwritten' constitutions" is simply "the difference of constitutions the norms of which are created by legislative acts and constitutions whose norms are created by custom."[72] In other words, the distinction does not matter except that customary bases for law would appear to be stronger in many instances than statutory bases. The value of the constitution is somewhat dubious in this conception. As Michel Troper points out in "Marshall, Kelsen, Barak and the constitutionalist fallacy," Kelsen would argue that "the constitution is superior to the law because it governs the drafting of laws. It is supreme simply because there is no other positive rule of law in which it could find the basis for its own validity."[73]

For a legal positivist then, the ultimate justification for the creation and maintenance of a constitutional order is to provide a framework in which law can be created and enforced to act towards some socially agreed order. This order can take on an endless variety of forms and moral injunctions. There is no means of using this theory to describe a just order or one which is morally correct, but its value lies in its ability to make obvious the contingency of law, the necessity of

69 Kelsen (1945), p. 115.

70 Ibid., p. 260.

71 Kelsen (1984), p. 209.

72 Ibid., p. 260.

73 Troper, Michel. "Marshall, Kelsen, Barak and the constitutionalist fallacy." *I-CON*, 3:1 (2005): 30.

maintaining some sort of social agreement that allows the law to be seen as valid and enforced. Avoiding chaos and stasis were the primary objectives of Greek constitutionalism, and in the end, despite his rejection of a *telos* for the state, Kelsen can be seen to implicitly demonstrate the value of having order over none, even if it cannot be cosmically justified. It is this very quality of creating order seemingly out of nothing more than agreement to do so, that makes law appear almost magical and which ultimately sustains it as a system.[74] As he concludes in his 1952 article "What is a Legal Act?" it is the "principal of efficacy, which as the content [*Inhalt*] of the basic norm" and which is of "specifically legal cognition," which "offers an adequate guarantee that legal theory cannot ever lose sight of the connection between legal norms and what we call 'social reality'."[75] It is the assumptions that lay behind Elie Kedourie's historical critique of the "social reality" of constitutionalism in Muslim contexts, found in the introduction of his work *Politics in the Middle East* which this book next examines. Much as Kelsen's *Grundnorm* creates the foundation for all subsequent law, this set of pre-determined beliefs about the nature of Muslim societies colors the subsequent examinations of historical cases to the extent that, contrary to common perceptions, it is the assumptions themselves which most deserve analysis.[76]

## Kedourie's Critique—A Conservative Orientalist Perspective on Islam and Governance

The beliefs, norms, and attitudes of Islam, the experiences, triumphs, and vicissitudes that Muslims have encountered over the centuries have combined to bring about a society of a highly distinctive character ... Even today, when the Western world is the source of industrial techniques and military weapons, and is seen as providing intellectual and political norms, Islam as a religion is far from being defeated or silenced. And its influence as a culture, whether acknowledged or not, obstinately persists in permeating and shaping institutions, attitudes, and modes of discourse. This is nowhere more true than in government and politics, and in the mutual responses of the rulers and the ruled.[77]

74 See Dhananjai Shivakumar's "The Pure Theory as Ideal Type: Defending Kelsen on the Basis of Weberian Methodology." *The Yale Law Journal*, 105:5 (1996): 1389. He points out that in addition to law evolving in its own orbit, Kelsen's account importantly combines the American concern with judge-made law and the Continental concern with the historical roots of codified law.

75 Kelsen (1984), p. 212.

76 Of course, many writers could arguably be better targets for this criticism, but Kedourie's claims of historical objectivity and case-based analysis, claims common to most arguments against the compatibility of Islam and constitutionalism, make his work especially important to criticize.

77 Kedourie, Elie. *Politics in the Middle East*. Oxford and New York: Oxford University Press, 1992, p. 1.

Constitutionalism was thus the Western political tradition which was adopted earliest in the Middle East. It had a long, albeit very checkered career. It proved, as has been seen, to be a failure everywhere…[78]

It would be easy to mistake the above sentiments as having derived from the text of a 19th century European treatise on the nature of colonial possessions in the Middle East. The tone of the language and the way in which Islamic civilization is clearly painted as an "other," makes equally clear the author's opinion of the prospect of Islamic societies finding a way to remain true to themselves and to pursue a constitutional form of governance. This quote however, does not come from the 1890s but from the 1990s, or 1992 to be specific, and it comes from Elie Kedourie's succinctly titled *Politics in the Middle East*. The date is important because it illustrates that in some quarters it remains acceptable to accuse by implication when it comes to Muslims and Islam. It is also important because it marks a major turning point in recent history, when the Cold War had just come to a resounding end in favor of Western liberal democracy. Perhaps the downfall of one long-lasting enemy, the Soviet communists, partly explains the rise, or at least the perception of a rise, of a new threat, Islamic fundamentalism and violence. The pedigree of this type of writing extends back to thinkers like Bernard Lewis, Montesquieu, and even Dante. It continues in more strident tones in the work of writers like David Horowitz, Steven Emerson and Robert Spencer.[79]

This is not to say however, that the contentions of these thinkers should not be examined seriously. Precisely because Kedourie's arguments are couched in academic language and conducted along historical lines, it is possible to engage with them in order to understand the particular historical events and political concerns that comprise his wide-ranging critique. Mark Tessler, for example, refers to his work by acknowledging that he was "a prominent student of Arab and Islamic society" who "gave forceful expression to" the point of view that Islam is inimical to a restrained political system.[80] As mentioned before, the period of history in which Kedourie wrote this book ranged from the immediate aftermath of the Iranian Islamic Revolution to before the beginning of Gorbachev's *glasnost* and *perestroika* to after the fall of the Berlin Wall and the USSR.[81] The end of the Cold War saw Middle Eastern states able to act more independently than ever before as they had mostly been consolidated into relatively stable (or what appeared to be stable) states, had resoundingly cast off official colonial administration, and no longer were divided into client states or spheres of influence between the

78 Ibid., p. 268.

79 Their recent book titles, *Unholy Alliance: Radical Islam and the American Left*, *American Jihad: The Terrorists Living Among Us*, and *Stealth Jihad: How Radical Islam is Subverting America without Guns or Bombs*, respectively, are all alarmist to say the least.

80 Tessler, Mark. "Islam and Democracy in the Middle East: The Impact of Religious Orientations on Attitudes toward Democracy in Four Arab Countries." *Comparative Politics*, 34:3 (2002): 340.

81 See Kedourie (1992), Acknowledgements.

Americans and Soviets. This was a time in which there was space for an Islamic identity to fundamentally reassert itself. It is also a setting in which the rise of fundamentalism in the Middle East was in stark contrast to the wave of liberal democratization cresting in Eastern Europe and some parts of Central Asia.

Kedourie himself did not address his immediate historical setting in any sustained manner, but rather laid out a historical case of the Islamic polity from its founding under Muhammad, continuing to the days of the Ottomans, and finally to post-Ottoman nationalized states. Beginning with Muhammad's rule, he states that Islam, as instituted by its founder, "was not only a religion, but also a government, and a fast-rising international power."[82] As will be seen later in this book, this statement is accurate. The nature of the Islamic movement has been both religious and political from its inception. His next contention however is more problematic. Kedourie claims that what "Western Christianity from very early times distinguished as temporal and spiritual were *ab initio* inextricably intermixed in Islam. Islam made all Muslims one community where all concerns, spiritual and temporal, were attended to and codified in the Divine Law."[83] Although the earliest Christians seem to have abstained from making many religiously-based political claims, from at least the time of Constantine until the Reformation, in real terms, Christianity experienced centuries of a very similar mixing of religious and political power with often only the thinnest of veneers masking the Church's maneuvering within the state. One must therefore question Kedourie's application of Muhammad's legacy as one which necessarily remains definitive within Muslim societies, despite the overwhelming variety of governmental institutions and mores found within Islamic society.

In terms of the constitutional concepts that form the basis of this book, his critique of Islam's relationship with the rule of law can be briefly summarized as one that is beset by endemic corruption,[84] frequent opportunistic amendments to the law itself, the legitimization of power relations that are inherently illiberal and despotic,[85] outbreaks of political violence, and sham elections that make a farce of the idea of accountability and representation.[86]

In a similar fashion, *Politics in the Middle East* also tackles the subject of what could be termed the cultural and political character of Islam and Islamic states. Kedourie argues that the first slate of 19th Century reforms imitated Europe with little regard for local custom.[87] Even worse, according to Kedourie, is that some constitutions were written to gain recognition by Europeans with little effect in the

82 Ibid., p. 1.

83 Ibid., p. 2.

84 Ibid., p. 16.

85 Ibid., p. 14.

86 These contentions are laid out in detail in two chapters Kedourie titled, "Constitutionalism and Its Failure: 1," and "Constitutionalism and Its Failure: 2," on pp. 49–91 and 155–267.

87 Ibid., pp. 36–46.

actual governance of the state.[88] In other cases, European powers mistakenly allowed themselves to be bullied and misled into allowing groups like the Wafd in Egypt to take over the political life of a country in the name of respecting representation of the majority, whilst in reality they may have had little public support to begin with.[89]

In terms of restricting the power of government, Kedourie's argument is even more forceful and remains firmly tied to the historical record of certain Islamic states. He claims that government power is unfettered and citizens are lacking in rights and expect virtually nothing of their governments. For instance, al-Ghazali's theological injunction of the religious requirement and practical benefit of political obedience, which is quoted at length, is oddly characterized as one in which readers will see "a clear-eyed, skeptical pessimism, or even desperation, about what the ruled can at best expect from the rulers."[90] The only problem with this is that the entire passage simply talks about the chaos of a world without a strong leader, in a manner very similar to that of Hobbes. It never discusses expectations of the ruler or ruled at all; aside from the reason religion requires obedience.[91]

Kedourie's only nod to any conception of limited power in the Islamic state is confined to a recognition that the scope of government action traditionally did not touch upon private or family law, which was dealt with by shari'a courts. This is given only the most limited treatment, and by way of criticism. He begins this admission by saying that "Traditional Middle Eastern rulers simply took no interest in a vast range of issues in which modern governments of all colors assume it their right and duty to intervene." They didn't bother to educate their subjects or to ensure that the most basic elements of sustenance were provided for. Instead,

> just as non-Muslims were left a large measure of freedom in their communal affairs, so the ruler took it for granted that certain affairs relating to the *umma* were the subject of divine prescription with which no one could tamper and were to be regulated by the *qadis*, or religious judges, according to the *shari'a*. All these, then, were built-in limitations on the activities of government under oriental despotism.[92]

He sums up the various efforts of Muslim thinkers and political actors to contain the government with this gloomy assessment.

88 See for example Kedourie's discussion of the Egyptian constitution of 1923, pp. 174–7. His discussion of the development of the regime of the Iranian Shah in the mid-20th century is also instructive, pp. 249–67.

89 Ibid., pp. 177–80.

90 Ibid., pp. 6–7.

91 Ibid., p. 9, where he quotes a Moroccan saying that "To him who holds power obedience is due."

92 Ibid., p. 20.

> The establishment of the Islamic Republic of Iran, the military *coups d'état* in Egypt, Syria, and Iraq, and the regimes issuing from them, the destruction of the Lebanese Republic, and the mixed fortunes of the constitutional and representative government in the Turkish Republic are the outcome, thus far, of one hundred and fifty years of tormented endeavor to discard the old ways, which have ceased to satisfy and to replace them with something modern, eye-catching, and attractive. The torment does not seem likely to end soon.[93]

One cannot help but ask how Kedourie can so easily lump Islam's experience with government into such generalized descriptions and how he can even dismiss the very secular example of a place like Turkey, which is not only predominantly Muslim, but is at the heart of the last great Islamic empire. Indeed, the very contentious nature of its present debates on the role of Islam in society and the state show that politics is alive and well in that state and that Turkish society itself is trying to find its own understanding and method of interpreting Islam's role through popular and democratic means.[94]

Throughout the book, much of Kedourie's argument is focused either directly or indirectly upon the Ottomans and their successors, the Turks. After detailing the various reforms carried out in the 19th century which ostensibly provided a variety of liberal guarantees of personal protection and freedom, he then goes on to show how they were ultimately meaningless because they simply transferred absolute power from the sultan to the bureaucracy.[95] If the same standards were applied to the early iterations of liberalizing Western reforms they could also be roundly dismissed as historically insignificant and therefore mere aberrations. The Constitution of the United States, for example, was meant to institutionalize the convictions laid out in the Declaration of Independence that "all men are created equal," yet it permitted the institution of slavery and included the infamous "Three-fifths Compromise," which gave slave states three-fifths of a person in apportioning representation in the Congress and the Electoral College. Likewise, the much earlier and often cited *Magna Carta* protected very narrow segments of society from arbitrary rule and was a far cry from present-day standards of equality. Kedourie actually directly compares the 1808 Ottoman *sened-i ittifak* or "deed of agreement" between the Sultan and the Janissaries to the *Magna Carta*. He mentions that Sultan Mahmud was forced to sign a legal contract which, in return for obedience and acknowledgment of his authority, he would recognize the property and inheritance rights of the nobles. Although comparing "this document to *Magna Carta* is natural," he argues that it is a false comparison because the

---

93 Ibid., p. 346.

94 The Turkish debate on allowing the wearing of headscarves in public institutions, for example, generated considerable domestic controversy. In many ways it could even be compared with the similar secular impulses present in a Western state like France, which also places a variety of controls upon public expressions of religion.

95 Kedourie (1992), pp. 49–91.

*sened* did not accurately reflect Ottoman power relations and was "speedily proved to be a dead letter." Nowhere does he mention that King John, who signed the *Magna Carta*, also quickly rescinded it by giving the Pope lordship of England.[96] Should these documents then be dismissed as mere political conveniences that did little during their time to enshrine or enlarge liberty?

What emerges then from this examination of Kedourie's portrayal of Islamic governance? Firstly, there is an inherent temptation to analyze foreign traditions in a way that makes them more distinct and "othered" than is necessarily justified by their histories. Secondly, the nuances found in localized versions of these traditions can easily be glossed over in the pursuit of finding generalized concepts that can be said to apply to an entire civilization. Finally, there is a glaring double standard in the way Islamic history and reform movements are treated when compared with the way in which the Western tradition is discussed.

In order to further assess the validity of the critiques of Kedourie, Huntington, and others, and to gain an understanding of what the long-term prospects for constitutionalism in an Islamic context might be, it is helpful to look at two very distinct alternative paths outlined by two equally distinct scholars, Noah Feldman and Abdullahi Ahmed An-Na'im.

## The Fall and Rise of Islamic Constitutionalism—A Brief Analysis of Noah Feldman and Abdullahi Ahmed An-Na'im

> The new Islamic state, if it is to succeed, must do for itself the difficult and slow work of establishing new institutions with their own ways of operating that will gradually achieve legitimacy ... Borrowing, with all of its limitations, still seems easier than invention. Nevertheless, with all its risks and dangers, the aspiration to re-create a system of government that draws upon the best of the old while coming to terms with the new is as bold and noble a goal as can be imagined.[97]

As seen above, scholars like Noah Feldman take the future existence of Islamic states as a virtual given. Written in 2008, his book *The Fall and Rise of the Islamic State* came well before protestors took on the regimes of Ben-Ali and Mubarak and won the right to work out a new solution to the problem of how to govern justly, legitimately, and accountably. Considering the unprecedented pace of change surging through North Africa and the Middle East, this section will bring together the threads of narrative between Western and Islamic scholars by examining two fairly recent works on Islamic government. By comparing how a former U.S Supreme Court law clerk and constitutional adviser to the interim

96 Ibid., pp. 24–5.

97 Feldman, Noah. *The Fall and Rise of the Islamic State*. Princeton, NJ: Princeton University Press, 2008, p. 151.

Iraqi government envisions the future of Islamic government, with the way it is portrayed by a former political refugee and practicing Muslim law professor from the Sudan, it may be possible to ascertain whether a consensus is emerging on the viability and applicability of Islamic constitutionalism and what that consensus may be.

Noah Feldman's view of historical Islamic government is simple and elegant. He argues that:

> A common constitutional theory, developing and changing over the course of centuries, (was) obtained in all (Islamic states). A Muslim ruler governed according to God's law, expressed through principles and rules of the *sharīʿa* that were expounded by the scholars. The ruler's fulfillment of the duty to command what the law required and ban what it prohibited made his authority lawful and legitimate.[98]

This view shares a universalizing element with earlier Western accounts of Islamic government. Thus far there is little to distinguish it from those of the Orientalists. What immediately sets his work apart, however, is this statement:

> When empires fall, they tend to stay dead … There are, however, two prominent examples of governing systems reemerging after they had apparently ceased to exist. One is democracy, a form of government that had some limited success in a small Greek city-state for a couple of hundred years, disappeared, and then was resurrected some two thousand years later. It re-creators were non-Greeks, living under radically different conditions, for whom democracy was a word handed down in the philosophy books, to be embraced only fitfully and after some serious reinterpretation. The other is the Islamic state.[99]

From the very beginning then, his argument consistently makes reference to Western historical and political precedents that in some way mirror those of the Islamic world. The way Feldman creates a comparison between democracy and the Islamic state as political systems is unexpected to say the least. Though there are certainly reasons to question the validity of this comparison (it is difficult to see what Greek democracy and traditional Islamic government share in common beyond their philosophical preoccupations), it serves to notify the reader that the Islamic tradition will be treated as an equally valid alternative to that of the West.

Not only is the Islamic state potentially experiencing a reformulation and rebirth, but it is doing so in a way that is necessarily breaking new ground in order to find a voice that is authentically Muslim but still able to participate in global discussions of politics and commerce.

---

98 Ibid., pp. 1–2.

99 Ibid., p. 1.

> The movement toward the Islamic state is riding a wave of nostalgia, but it is also looking forward. The designers and advocates of the new Islamic state want to recapture the core of what made the traditional Islamic state great. They declare their allegiance to the *sharīʿa*, while simultaneously announcing an affinity for democracy. This means the new Islamic state will be different from the old one. There is no turning back the clock of history, no matter what anyone says.[100]

This recognition of Feldman's also puts him well outside the traditional Orientalist camp. Rather than emphasizing the backwardness and "obstinacy" of Islamists, he makes a point of describing the movement as one that is forward-looking regardless of the claims made on its behalf by groups that claim to be "returning" to the rule of *sharīʿa*. Instead of being a reactionary conservative retrenchment, "The call for an Islamic state is therefore first and foremost a call for law—for a legal state that would be justified by law and govern through it."[101] The preoccupation with law and with an exemplary past is something that is intrinsic to both Western and Islamic constitutional discourse.[102] The contours of the law may be different, but the desire for a supreme rule of law is of paramount importance to the entire project of constitutionalism in both traditions. Thus it is not an absence of the rule of law that threatens the future of the Islamic state, but the "greatest challenge facing the new Islamic constitution derives from the uncertainty about identifying who is in charge of specifying the meaning of the *sharīʿa* and by what authority."[103] This is the type of fundamental question that Western philosophy has wrestled with for decades. Liberal democracy is one answer to this dilemma because it provides a mechanism for citizens to have a representative and regulated voice in the creation of new laws and in the institutions that will implement them. The general lack of democracy in Muslim states is often cited as one reason that they are either despotic or unstable. It is argued that they need a strong figure to dictate the source of state authority and impose a unified vision of the state's purpose.[104] To such critics, Feldman offers the following reply:

---

100 Ibid., p. 3.

101 Ibid., p. 9.

102 Feldman notes on p. 5 that "There is nothing unique to Muslims about this active and continuing engagement with the constitutional past. Madison, Jefferson, and Hamilton continue to shape the American constitutional tradition from beyond the grave. It is impossible to understand the American Constitution today without taking these founding fathers into account, and no one would maintain that this makes constitutional debate in the United States premodern. Yet much analysis of the Muslim world insists on an artificial distinction between the historical past, the preserve of a professional guild of historians, and forward-looking political analysis, itself divided between university political scientists and think tank or government analysis."

103 Ibid., p. 13.

104 See Feldman's statement on pp. 21–2, where he says that "To Westerners, and even to those Muslims educated under Western-influenced conditions, it may sound extremely strange to describe the classical Islamic state of the Ottoman Empire and the

> From the perspective of the *sharīʿa* as a totalizing legal methodology, it can be claimed that the written constitutions of the state is legitimate only to the extent that it makes the *sharīʿa* paramount. This viewpoint would assimilate the new Islamic state into the logical structure of the old. But from the standpoint of the written constitution, matters are much less clear, because the meaning of the *sharīʿa* is explicitly being made the province of the legislature and courts of the state. This confusion—does the *sharīʿa* come before the state or the state before the *sharīʿa*?—is in fact a version of a familiar problem in the constitutions of liberal states. Americans have never fully resolved the question of whether the inalienable rights of life, liberty, and property preexist the U.S. Constitution or derive from it. It is more than possible to run the constitutional system of a legal state without resolving this thorny and ever-controversial difficulty.[105]

By refusing to be sidetracked by tangential philosophical concerns, Feldman is illustrating a way to move the conversation about Islamic government and the role of *sharīʿa* forward. Plenty of Americans would argue that the principles upon which their constitution is based are derived from Christian ethics and scripture. The fact that this lends extra legitimacy to the state actually helps consolidate the constitutional rule of law despite the fact that it raises the problem mentioned above of determining whether rights or the codification of rights are prior in existence.

The argument that Feldman ultimately makes is that the one sure way to introduce more control over the Islamic state is to create, or more accurately reinstate, a stronger role for the religious scholars. He contends that historically they acted as an important check on the power of the sultan because they "accepted the yoke of the law as interpreted by the scholars—a position of subservience to the law otherwise unheard of in the annals of great empires. Justinian's great *Digest* stated that "[t]he prince is not bound by law." No less powerful or extensive in their reach, the sultans earned the caliphate at the price of accepting that God and his law were above them."[106] In this manner, the scholarly class could serve as a check on any executive or legislative power because they would ensure that any new regulations or laws conformed to their understanding of the *sharīʿa*.

Feldman's prognosis for the viability and stability of the Islamic state is one which is ultimately very uncertain. This lack of confidence is reassuring in its humility even if it lacks the compelling force of alternative arguments. He sums up the present situation of the Muslim world as follows:

---

many dynasties that preceded it as fundamentally legal. Western writers have for centuries gone to great lengths to describe the Muslim world as the home of Oriental despots who did what they would, free from the constraints supposedly imposed on Western rulers. In fact, many of the most enlightened, law-loving Western thinkers—Montesquieu is one famous example—used the image of the Islamic East as a literary device for projecting their vision of the worst possible non-legal regime."

105 Ibid., p. 13.

106 Ibid., p. 54.

> … mainstream Islamism has in principle accepted the compatibility of the *sharīʿa* and democracy … the most prominent proposed solution is for the constitution of the state to acknowledge divine sovereignty rather than establish popular sovereignty and then use it to enact Islamic law. On this theoretical model, the people function somewhat as the ruler did in the classic constitutional order: they accept the responsibility for implementing what God has commanded…
>
> Yet for all its creativity as a solution to the challenges of modernity and egalitarianism, the democratized *sharīʿa* faces a deep question: to what does it owe its authority? If the *sharīʿa* is to be the ultimate source of law in the state, then it must also be the source of law for the constitution. Yet the constitution is enacted by actually existing citizens, and legislation is enacted by actually existing legislators. The classical *sharīʿa* dealt with this problem by claiming that the task of the scholars was solely to interpret, not to legislate, and that this task of interpretation was authorized by the *sharīʿa* itself. For the democratized *sharīʿa*, the same answer cannot be given because laws are actually being passed and because the classical *sharīʿa* nowhere envisions an elected legislature.[107]

Ultimately, the dilemma Feldman sees may or may not be as important as he makes it out to be. Present events would seem to indicate that the desires to have jobs with decent wages, the prospect of a good future, and basic political freedoms may very well be more important to Muslim citizens than more abstract questions of the basis of legal authority.

A similar, but distinct vision for Islam's role in the state can be found in Abdullahi Ahmed An-Naʿim's books *African Constitutionalism and the Role of Islam* and *Islam and the Secular State: Negotiating the Future of Sharīʿa.* Coming from the Sudan and with an admitted normative goal of seeing constitutionalism take a stronger hold of African and majority Muslim states, he shows less propensity to resort to cultural or religious defenses of practices that offend Western constitutional norms. Being well aware of the potential for laws to be worth little more than the paper they are written on, he emphasizes that "such rights as freedom of expression and association are not useful without the institutional means for exercising the sort of judgment and continuous accountability of government officials envisaged by the principle of constitutionalism."[108] One such mechanism of accountability that he discusses is the Islamic concept of *shura*, or consultation. Although the "meaning of the Arabic term shura … at most indicated a requirement to seek advice, without necessarily being bound by it," he makes the point that this meaning does not need to be considered sacrosanct and timeless. There is no reason it "cannot be used today as a basis for

107 Ibid., pp. 119–20.

108 An-Naʿim (2006), p. 6. See also An-Na'im, Abdullahi Ahmad. *Islam and the Secular State: Negotiating the Future of Sharīʿa*. Cambridge, MA: Harvard University Press, 2008, pp. 106–8 for a discussion of *shura* as practiced by Muhammad and its potential for reinterpretation as binding consultation.

institutionalized constitutional principles of democratic government that are legally and politically accountable to the population at large."[109]

A distinct, but related, notion of accountability and representation can be found in the *bay'a*, which was a "traditional oath of allegiance" which An-Na'im argues "should now by seen as an authoritative basis for a mutual contract between the government and the population at large, whereby the former assumes responsibility for the protection of the rights and general well-being of the latter in exchange for their acceptance of the authority of the state and compliance with its laws and public policy."[110] This is yet another idea that is thoroughly rooted in Western social contract theory. The fact that it is being advocated by a devout Muslim would seem to challenge those who describe Islamic opposition to Western ideas in monolithic terms and who would proscribe the possibility of people freely adopting and adapting those ideas which they find suitable for their present needs and goals, regardless of their origins. This is highly reminiscent of Khayr al-Din's argument that the *'ulama* should not reject a technology or idea out of hand simply because it came from a non-Muslim. To put it simply, if something is good, then its goodness is not altered by its origin but will be confirmed by its demonstrable effectiveness.

An-Na'im's perspective on constitutional concepts and their cross-cultural application is nicely summarized as follows:

> I hold that the universal validity and applicability of concepts like constitutionalism is a pragmatic necessity in view of the universalization of the European model of the nation-state through colonialism and postcolonial relations. This model is likely to continue as the dominant form of organization in national politics and international relations for the foreseeable future ... In other words, the commonality of tensions in state-society and state-individual relations recommends giving notions like constitutionalism and democracy broader applicability by expanding their meaning to include the experiences of other societies now seeking to adapt the same notion to their own respective contexts.[111]

His concern is thus imminently practical but also highly normative. The state as defined on the European model seems to be here to stay, so Muslim states need to find a way to exist and hopefully thrive within this system. It does not mean, however, that they must subvert their identities to the Western other. The basic universal concerns with reconciling the rights and duties of the social contract and creating mechanisms by which it can be successfully maintained are enough to provide a common discursive and legally compatible space for the international aspect of constitutional government to work.

There are many practical and potentially beneficial lessons to be drawn from the arguments of An-Na'im and others who approach the constitutional question

109 Ibid., p. 12.
110 An-Na'im (2008), p. 110.
111 An-Na'im (2006), p. 17.

from the perspective of non-Western, often post-colonial states. If comparative constitutional dialogue is indeed conducted openly and with as few preconceptions as possible, then it is possible that not only will non-Western powers move toward governments that are law-governed in a way that is acceptable to Western norms, but that those Western states themselves will have the benefit of drawing upon new sources of political ideas and organization that may be revolutionary in addressing hitherto insurmountable political crises in regards to communitarian concerns for medical care, the elderly, and the environment. As he says, "Each society is constructing its own constitutional development on its own terms, and that includes its own retrieval and adaptation projects, as well as internally generated responses to current challenges and concerns."[112]

It is clear that the literature on constitutionalism is becoming increasingly vast, as are the disagreements about its meaning, viability, and applicability to non-Western contexts. It bears repeating that this concern with universal application primarily stems from a fundamental mistake that occurs when constitutionalism is conflated with democratization, thus inheriting all the normative and cultural baggage that comes with it. By divorcing these two compatible, yet very distinct concepts, this work allows for constitutional thinkers to be analyzed outside the dialogue of where they fall on the democracy spectrum, and furthermore avoids the assumption that liberal democracy is the only true goal of constitutional regimes. Recalling the basic English use of the constitution as a word which refers to the body, not just the body politic, also recalls its history as an organic conception of the state which naturally develops from a given populace, rather than an institutional artifice imposed upon it.

Prior to analyzing the viability of these new applications of constitutionalism and Islamic political thought, particularly in light of the Arab Spring and subsequent political events in the Middle East and North Africa, it is first necessary to look at some of the key values underpinning constitutionalism from a Western perspective. It is this perspective that dominates constitutional discourse and sets the terms of the debate on issues like freedom and human rights. The universalist aspirations of the Western constitutional tradition must therefore be interrogated in order to understand the degree to which certain ideas and values may indeed be universally valued by humanity and shared between Western and Muslim thinkers who have pondered them.

112 Ibid., p. 35.

# Chapter 2
# Western Constitutionalism—Universal Norms or Contingent Cultural Concepts

In order to assess these questions and to address the critics of constitutionalism generally and of constitutionalism in Islamic contexts specifically, it is vital to first take a comprehensive view of Western constitutional development as it is the dominant point of reference and voice in constitutional discourse. Briefly, this chapter will examine constitutionalism in terms of three fundamental constitutional values that directly respond to the critiques of Elie Kedourie and others by examining the relationship between constitutionalism and 1) The Rule of Law, 2) National Character and 3) Limits on Political Power. Again, this is by no means an exhaustive list of constitutional ideas, values, or institutions. Rather, it is an intentionally circumscribed inquiry designed to allow for comparison of a thin model of constitutionalism which can be examined in various cultural and historical settings. Each of these values will be examined primarily in light of the work of one key Western thinker or text: Cicero, Montesquieu and the *Federalist Papers*, respectively. The arguments of these texts and the surrounding literature will be explored in order to arrive at a more developed and holistic understanding of each term.[1]

It is the use of the rule of law to create a potentially eternal social reality, i.e. The Roman State, which will first be examined in the work of Cicero.

## The Eternal and Universal Constitution—Cicero's Dream of a Law-Governed World

> Cato used to say that our constitution was superior to others, because in their case there had usually been one individual who had equipped his state with laws and institutions, for example, Minos of Crete, Lycurgus of Sparta ... Our own constitution, on the other hand, had been established not by one man's ability

---

1 The selection of texts is not meant to be exhaustive or exclusive. The scope of Western constitutional thought is vast and extends at least from the work of Plato and Aristotle onwards. There is no shortage of discussion of these Greek classics, but as the American constitutional paradigm is the one that presently dominates and since it explicitly draws heavily upon Roman thought in particular, it seems important to give the work of Cicero the centrality it is otherwise denied in more general accounts of constitutionalism from a purely theoretical sense.

> but by that of many, not in the course of one man's life but over several ages and generations. He used to say that no genius of such magnitude had ever existed that he could be sure of overlooking nothing; and that no collection of able people at a single point of time could have sufficient foresight to take account of everything; there has to be practical experience over a long period of history.[2]

In the introductory section of Book 2 of his *Republic*, Cicero discusses the founding of Rome and its distinctiveness. He is keen to show that Rome is an exemplar not just of the ideal society, but primarily of the ideal state, which alone can deliver the opportunity at the good life that all people long for.[3] From the passage above it is crystal clear that he sees constitutions as derived from collective experience and the accretion of ancestral mores and customs over a long period of time.[4] In turn, this allows for the gradual acceptance and consolidation of law such that it becomes largely self-enforcing.[5] As Scipio continues in Cicero's dialogue:

> ... states in which the best men strive for praise and honour, shunning disgrace and dishonour. They are not deterred so much by fear of the penalty prescribed by law as by a sense of shame—that dread, as it were, of justified rebuke which nature has imparted to man. The statesman develops this sense by making use of public opinion, and completes it with the aid of education and social training. So in the end citizens are deterred from crime by moral scruples as much as by fear.[6]

This manner of looking at the constitution seems perfectly in line with the scope and definition given constitutionalism by McIlwain with its emphasis on historical development. It is also interesting to note the almost explicit advocacy of a pluralist, consensus-based approach to establishing a ruling order and the way in which Cicero combines a conservative concern with observance of the ancestral ways with a modernizing twist that accepts the need for constant, gradual change in actual legislation. In effect, Cicero is arguing that the consolidation of a legal order over the generations ultimately should make enforcing that order relatively easy because the succession of steward-statesmen who help to enact law do so in consultation with "public opinion." This same majority of the public will be those who provide the education and social training Cicero says are needed to foster the best kind of citizens, again doing much of the hard work of the state by accepted custom and free will, minimizing the need for force and naked expressions of

---

2 Cicero (1998), *The Republic*, Book 2.2, p. 35.

3 Ibid., p. 83.

4 EM Atkins gives further weight to this idea, noting the especially important role that aristocrats played in Roman society and that they "represented their ideal as inherited; they made frequent appeal to an amalgam of moral and constitutional precedents they described as *mos maiorum*, 'the customs of the ancestors.' History and tradition mattered."

5 See Cicero, *The Republic*, Book 5.6.

6 Cicero (1998), p. 83.

power. As President Reagan's Attorney General Edwin Meese III cites in his "Law of Constitution" speech,[7] "We are heirs to a long Western tradition of the rule of law. Some 2,000 years ago, for example, the great statesman of the Roman Republic, Cicero, observed, 'We are in bondage to the law in order that we may be free'."[8]

In effect, this idea of being bound to the law, even if one does not agree with a particular law or set of laws, is the very essence of the much used, and much less often defined term, the Rule of Law. Tom Bingham undertakes a historical and detailed look at the term's development and contemporary meaning in his aptly named book, *The Rule of Law.* "The core of the existing principle," he argues, "is … that all persons and all authorities within the state, whether public or private, should be bound by and entitled to the benefit of laws publicly made, taking effect (generally) in the future and publicly administered by the courts."[9] Bingham evocatively demonstrates that this condition of equality before the law is not one to be taken for granted or to be assumed universal, reminding the reader that the manifestations of a regime that does not embrace this concept are present in a nasty variety of horrors:

> the midnight knock on the door, the sudden disappearance, the show trial, the subjection of prisoners to genetic experiment, the confession extracted by torture, the gulag and the concentration camp, the gas chamber, the practice of genocide or ethnic cleansing, the waging of aggressive war. The list is endless.[10]

Interestingly, Bingham's formulation of the Rule of Law and its antibook is one that does not mention democracy or representation. He clearly favors government that is democratically elected and accountable, but for the purposes of his topic it is not essential. The same goes for constitutional discourse more generally. An order can be governed by law and constitutional without also being representative, republican, or otherwise democratic. In fact, the abuses of state power he catalogues may very well be sanctioned by popular majorities. Placing the rule of law at the forefront of assessing the constitutionality of a regime removes the temptation to conflate constitutionalism and democratization, and emphasizes the role that constitutionalism plays in placing sovereignty outside the hands of any would-be tyrant or tyrants so that equal protection and equal "benefit of laws publicly made" are available to all citizens. This also allows the conceptual tools of constitutionalism and the rule of law to be applied to various historical

7 This speech was given on the important occasion of the investiture of Supreme Court Chief Justice Rehnquist and Associate Justice Scalia in 1986.

8 Cicero, *Pro Cluentio*, 146, as cited in Meese, Edwin. "Law of Constitution." *Tulsa Law Review*, 61 (1986): 989.

9 Bingham, T.H. *The Rule of Law*. London and New York: Allen Lane (2010), p. 8.

10 Ibid., p. 9.

and political contexts, even allowing one to define which parts of a given state's institutions are or are not run constitutionally.

It is well known that the Roman Republic was not a democracy in the mode of the New England town hall, nor were all people within its jurisdiction equally protected by the law. All *citizens*, however, were indeed equally protected by the laws and entitled to various rights according to their position. Thus, it is the historical role of Roman aristocracy that is essential to understanding Cicero's conception of the idea of being bound to a sovereign law. Although certainly not a democrat according to modern understandings, he is well aware that power in the Republic is very fluid and quickly changes hands. Although there were societal ceilings on certain groups, lesser noble families could potentially achieve fame, honor, and wealth in a relatively short span of time should they do well politically. As E.M. Atkins point out, the reason that ancestral custom was so important to the ruling class was three-fold. "First, these men learnt their ethics from their predecessors, especially from exemplary stories of heroism. Secondly, the pre-eminent position of the elite had *remarkably little protection in law; it relied upon a powerful respect for precedent* (emphasis mine). Thirdly, the family rather than the individual was the primary location of reputation and of pride."[11]

This suggests that legitimacy, as much as power, is key to the establishment of the Rule of Law. The imperial experience of Rome likewise shows that sovereignty, rather than being an intrinsic part of a state's national character, is in fact a characteristic that is anthropomorphized onto the state via the recognition of its legitimacy and its beneficence by its subjects. This implies, and Cicero explicitly states, that the statesman must be persuasive as well as just because it is vital that society be convinced of the wisdom of his rule, otherwise he will be unable to be elected to a further term of office.[12] Furthermore, the laws passed by the legislative body must meet certain standards if they are to attain what Cicero calls "law in the proper sense," which is "right reason in harmony with nature."[13] The danger for the state is that if it does not pass laws in accordance with this higher law, the state itself could die, which is "never natural … when a state is destroyed, eliminated, and blotted out, it is rather as if (to compare small with great) this whole world were to collapse and pass away."[14] To briefly recapitulate, Cicero traces a linear thread of legitimacy that uses natural law as its basis, which in turn is recognized by human reason and codified into laws, and these laws are given legitimacy because the community accepts their accordance with reason and the overriding value that reason places upon the law to create a society in which the good of society and the maintenance of the state that upholds it are paramount.

11 Atkins, E.M. "Cicero." *Cambridge Histories Online*. Cambridge: Cambridge University Press, 2008.

12 Atkins (2008), p. 492.

13 Cicero, *The Republic*. Book 3.33, pp. 68–9.

14 Cicero (1998), p. 69.

One may be tempted to suggest that Cicero's view of law is inherently imperialistic and self-serving for a Roman aristocrat however when he claims for the virtuous law of nature that it "cannot be countermanded, nor can it be in any way amended, nor can it be totally rescinded. We cannot be exempted from this law by decree of the Senate or the people ... There will not be one law at Rome and another in Athens ... but all peoples in all times will be embraced by a single and eternal and unchangeable law."[15] It is important to note that although he prescribes to natural law doctrine along with its inherent difficulties in assuming reason as a given, and more troublingly the conclusions of reason as also foregone conclusions, Cicero never suggests that the particular edicts of any regime are eternal or universal, nor does he argue that institutions and state organs are themselves likewise eternal and/or universal. The very structure of his work in *The Republic* recognizes the development of different types of regimes and that they are derived from local experience as well as universal values.

This lesson has particular relevance to various development projects that emphasize what Frank Upham calls the "Rule-of-Law Orthodoxy." This concept, according to Upham is a concerted effort by development agencies to encourage/compel developing states to follow a formalist version of the Rule of Law in which there is "strict adherence to established legal rules and freedom from the corrupting influences of politics ... promoters contend that such reforms are essential to establishing stability and norms that encourage investment and sustainable economic growth."[16] It has gained currency amongst powerful state actors and NGOs as a way of creating accountability in the use of development aid funds and in providing a means to create opportunities for economic investment (some may say exploitation) that should allow these states to eventually sustain themselves. Aside from Upham's criticisms that the language used by development agencies on the Rule of Law tends to be either composed of platitudes, exclusive, and evangelical, he highlights a danger that these development regimes pose that could have implications beyond simply offending cultural sensibilities. Rather, the very drive to create stability can in fact weaken existing, and therefore likely internally legitimized, societal structures. This potentially places at great risk "the existing informal means of social order, without which no legal system can succeed ... Legal anarchy can result in a society that has a new, formal legal system but lacks the social capital, institutions, and discipline to make use of it."[17]

In addition to being concerned with development, Rule of Law discourse is often conflated with security discourse, and although Cicero seems to think that providing for security is certainly essential, his main concern is that the government itself functions in a way that provides for the longevity and overall

15 Cicero (1998), p. 69.

16 Upham, Frank. "Mythmaking in the Rule-of-Law Orthodoxy." *Promoting the Rule of Law Abroad*. Thomas Carothers, (ed.). Carnegie Endowment for International Peace: Washington DC (2006), p. 75.

17 Upham (2006), p. 100.

benefit of the state itself. This, he believes, provides the best chance at the good life for its citizens. Here it is useful to look at his *On Duties*, in which Cicero imparts various pieces of wisdom to his son. Regarding warfare and security he takes a moderate approach quoting the maxim: "Let arms yield to the toga, and laurels to laudation."[18] Discussing the pinnacle of his own career in averting civil war he goes on to say, rather immodestly,

> Through my vigilance and my counsel the very arms swiftly slipped and fell from the hands of the most audacious citizens. Was any achievement of war ever so great? What military triumph can stand comparison? I am allowed to boast to you, Marcus my son. For yours it is both to inherit my glory and to imitate my deeds ... Therefore the courageous deeds of civilians are not inferior to those of soldiers. Indeed the former should be given even more effort and devotion that the latter ... In this field the civilians who are in charge of public affairs provide no less a benefit than those who wage war. And so it is by their counsel that a war may be avoided and terminated, and sometimes declared ... We must therefore value the reason which makes decisions above the courage which makes battle; yet we must be careful to do that because we have reasoned about what is beneficial, and not merely for the sake of avoiding war. Moreover, war should always be undertaken in such a way that one is seen to be aiming only at peace.[19]

Providing security and leadership for the state requires both wisdom and practical experience. Upon examining this text one sees traditional security terms like vigilance, triumph, and declaration of war. On the other hand, the emphasis is clearly on political resolution of conflicts within proper channels and this endeavor will only be successful if vigilance is accompanied by "counsel" and the "courageous deeds of civilians." This is why reason is to be valued above courage because it is only reason that can provide the wisdom needed to decide whether to undertake battle in the first place and to do so only when aiming at peace and the benefit of the state rather than personal glory. As if to ensure this message hits its mark, Cicero warns that "The dangers attending great undertakings fall sometimes upon their authors and sometimes upon the nation. Again, some are called to put their lives at risk, others their glory and the goodwill of their fellow-citizens. We must, therefore, be more eager to risk our own than the common welfare."[20]

Thus unlike his hero Plato, Cicero's ideal ruler is the Wise Politician rather than a Philosopher King. Both may have similar knowledge and regard for philosophy, but the former has the benefit of applying philosophy in an earthly context and understands the value of accommodation and compromise in keeping the various parts of government and society in synch. That is why the ideal ruler is not an

---

18 Cicero quoting his own poem "On His Own Times," in *On Duties*. Book 1.77, p. 31.

19 Cicero (1991) *On Duties*, pp. 31–2.

20 Ibid., p. 33.

unattainable mystic but someone who can actually "offer himself as a mirror to his fellow-citizens."[21]

This balancing of sectors within society and government should create a symphonic harmony of interests that restrains any one group from dominating the others, whether in society or government.

> Just as with string instruments or pipes or in singers' voices a certain harmony of different sounds must be maintained ... and as that harmony, though arising from management of very different notes, produces a pleasing and agreeable sound, so a state by adjusting the proportions of the highest, lowest, and intermediate classes, as if they were musical notes, achieves harmony. What, in the case of singing, musicians call harmony is, in the state, concord; it constitutes *the tightest and most effective bond of security* (emphasis mine).[22]

Note that this metaphor says that society's classes should be adjusted in proportion "as if they were musical notes." This implies that the means for creating stability and the "tightest and most effective bond of security" is the subtle raising and lowering of groups, or very gradual and incremental adjustments so as not to create a jarring discord, in order to create a society that is cohesive, a recognizable entity in its own right as much as the instruments by which its politics and relationships are played out. These instruments then must be the mechanisms by which the state is organized and creates and enforces legislation, in short, its constitution.

Ultimately, this is why the mixed constitution is the only one which potentially satisfies Cicero's desire for longevity, stability, and justice that can allow the accepted rule of law to embed itself firmly within a society and avoid stasis. Although fragmentary, he explicitly states this preference in Book 2 of *The Republic* saying "the best possible political constitution represents a judicious blend of these three types: monarchy, aristocracy, and democracy."[23] Brian Tamanaha describes the essence of Cicero's constitutional contribution to the Western tradition as one in which this mixed constitution allocated more power to rule to the best citizens, who are the most educated and wise, as they "have the capacity to discern the requirements of natural law that should govern society."[24]

---

21 Cicero (1998) *The Republic*, p. 58.

22 Ibid.

23 Cicero (1998) *The Republic*, Book 2. Fragment 1, p. 58.

24 Tamanaha, Brian. *On the Rule of Law: History, Politics, Theory*. Cambridge: Cambridge University Press (2004), p. 11.

## Monte-skewed, Constitution as Character or Caricature?—Montesquieu's Vision of National Spirit and National Law

A casual reading of Montesquieu's *The Spirit of the Laws* could easily lead one to conclude that this work is typical of its time (1748) in its treatment of the issue of culture and governance, particularly in its deterministic statements on non-Western peoples and the effects of climate, religion, and culture upon the types of constitutional regimes that exist and can possibly exist. Although many critiques of this work by an 18th Century French aristocrat are undoubtedly deserved, it is nonetheless vital to understand the impact his writings have had upon the development and understanding of constitutionalism in the West and the Western understanding of its potential elsewhere. Melvin Richter contends that contrary to what some of his critics say,

> in both his *Considerations* and the *Spirit of the Laws*, Montesquieu moved toward a qualified determinism that made room for positive intervention and correction of abuses, injustices, or practical defects by legislators and statesmen. Increasingly, his argument took the form of pointing out that the causes of all human practices may be understood by analysis both of physical nature and by the study of history, government, law, and society.[25]

Richter himself is forced to admit, however, that although there "are a number of national character sketches scattered throughout Montesquieu's work. On the whole, they are difficult to reconcile with the project of arriving at a science based on a few laws applicable to all societies."[26] Despite this, Donald S. Lutz argues, "The culture-power-justice nexus that characterizes modern constitutionalism was first dissected by Montesquieu, and an examination of his approach to constitutionalism provides a useful window into why we developed the political technology of constitutional democracy and why the future of this technology is not a foregone conclusion."[27]

Furthermore, Montesquieu is credited (along with Gravina) of another key innovation, which is to separate civil society and the State. This is in direct contrast with Aristotelian[28] and Ciceronian thought, indeed with ancient and medieval thought generally, which saw the economic, political, and social as all part of the

---

25 Richter, M. "An Introduction to Montesquieu's 'An Essay on the Causes That May Affect Men's Minds and Characters'." *Political Theory*, 4:2 (1976): 134.

26 Richter, M. "Comparative Political Analysis in Montesquieu and Tocqueville." *Comparative Politics*, 1:2 (1969): 140.

27 Lutz, Donald. "Thinking About Constitutionalism at the Start of the Twenty-First Century," *Publius: The Journal of Federalism*, 30:4 (2000): 115.

28 See, for instance, the explicit conflation of state and society and lack of advocacy for any particular type of government in Aristotle's *Politics*, Book 8:1: "For each government has a peculiar character which originally formed and which continues to preserve it. The

same *polis* or *societas civilis*.[29] It is this separation that allows for the specifically cultural to be analyzed for its effects on the governmental or political. As long as they were conflated into one concept this was impossible. Foreshadowing and laying the groundwork for later thinkers like Hans Kelsen,

> in strict contradiction to the law-of-nature school, which assumes a uniform, everlasting law to be inferred once for all from a supposed contract which is essentially identical throughout the whole world, Montesquieu teaches that law depends on multifarious conditions and varies at once with these conditions. This idea of the correspondence of law with outward circumstances perhaps marks the greatest progress effected by a single man in legal science.[30]

The main concern then, of Montesquieu's work is to demonstrate the way in which the national spirit creates and animates the legal framework and its operation. Briefly, he notes that, "Many things govern men: climate, religion, laws, the maxims of the government, examples of past things, mores, and manners; a general spirit is formed as a result."[31] This general spirit then informs not only the mechanisms of the state, but its *telos* as well. In Book 11, Chapter 5 he gives some examples of the specific purposes of certain historical states as follows:

> Although all states have the same purpose in general, which is to maintain themselves, yet each state has a purpose that is peculiar to it. Expansion was the purpose of Rome; war, that of Lacedaemonia; religion, that of the Jewish laws; commerce, that of Marseilles; public tranquillity, that of the laws of China; navigation, that of the laws of the Rhodians; natural liberty was the purpose of the police of the savages...[32]

Even a cursory examination of this excerpt reveals two essential qualities about Montesquieu's vision of constitutionalism. The first is that he is attempting to address the concept of governance on a global and timeless level, as noted by his reference to "all states" and his inclusion of regimes from widely ranging historical eras and geographical regions. His wide reading is very useful in citing observable "facts" that can justify broad statements about the State generally and states specifically. The other tendency that evidences itself is an attempt to apply

---

character of a democracy creates democracy, and the character of an oligarchy creates oligarchy; and always the better the character, the better the government."

29 Richter, Melvin. "Montesquieu and the concept of civil society." *The European Legacy*, 3:6 (1998): 33.

30 Ehrlich, Eugene. "Montesquieu and Sociological Jurisprudence." *Harvard Law Review*, 29 (1916): 583.

31 Montesquieu, C. d. S., A. M. Cohler, et al. *The Spirit of the Laws*. Cambridge and New York: Cambridge University Press, 1989, Book 19, Ch. 4, p. 310.

32 Ibid., p. 156.

this same knowledge in a focused manner to distil the character of a given nation to its essence. Hence, he makes reference to the purpose of Rome being expansion; the Jewish laws, religion; etc.

Taking a cue from the scientific revolution, Montesquieu shows how he arrives at his characterizations of national character by analyzing observable factors that influence this character, and consequently the state that develops from it.[33] These factors include the manner of achieving subsistence or the occupation of the people, the primary religion practiced, the way in which equality and liberty are conceived and exercised, and the tolerance and type of tyranny that may be present. From these he is able to not only paint a portrait of a general national spirit, but also of the type of government or constitution best suited and most likely to emanate from that group.

One of the most easily observable aspects of a society is the way in which its members maintain subsistence and potentially achieve wealth. Closely related to this is the climate and terrain this group occupies. To this effect, Montesquieu states that "The goodness of a country's lands establishes dependence there naturally."[34] This statement is far from revolutionary. However, he continues by discussing a variety of climates and terrains and the types of societies and political arrangements that develop in them. He explains the connection as follows:

> The laws are very closely related to the way that various peoples procure their subsistence. There must be a more extensive code of laws for a people attached to commerce and the sea than for a people satisfied to cultivate their lands. There must be a greater one for the latter than for a people who live by their herds. There must be a greater one for these last than for a people who live by hunting.[35]

This arrangement is clearly hierarchical and may display a degree of prejudice toward commercial societies. The constitutional component of this passage though is notable in the emphasis on the economic function of society, which is seen in the whole context of the work to be itself a function of both the climate/terrain and the national mores. It is interesting that Montesquieu should spend so much time discussing the climates of Asia, America, and Europe and the effect of living on the plains (prone to attack and despotism) versus living in the mountains (independent and fiercely free), when he ultimately declares other causes to be more decisive in creating social arrangements and institutions.[36] Karl Kriesel, in his profession as a

33 See Suzanne Gearhart's discussion of Montesquieu's view of history as a science in "Reading De l'Esprit des Lois: Montesquieu and the Principles of History." *Yale French Studies*, 59 (1980): 175.

34 Montesquieu (1989), p. 285.

35 Ibid., p. 289.

36 For a very interesting discussion of the validity of the effects of hot vs. cold climates, which are found to have little impact on personality traits but very strong metaphorical power for people being "hot-blooded," or emotionally "cold," etc., see Robert

geographer, notes that the determinist label given to Montesquieu on account of the sections of *Spirit of the Laws* on climate is both misleading and unfair. He recounts Montesquieu's own defense of his work and himself when called to testify at the University of Paris on charges of being irreligious, that although he did indeed write that "There are climates where the impulses of nature have such a force that morality has almost none," that this in no way indicated that he dismissed the role of morality in the world. Rather, in the chapters on climate he discussed climate, and in the chapters on morality he discussed morality. Furthermore, he argued, when taken as a whole work, *The Spirit of the Laws* "presents a perpetual triumph of morality over climate, or rather over the physical causes in general."[37] This leads Kriesel to give him the label of "possibilist," rather than determinist.

Moving beyond the simplistic discussion of climate and terrain, the fruits of these seemingly odd chapters become more apparent. Because climate and terrain influence the way people engage with the land and what occupations they undertake, it also influences the way that they conceive of property. This, in turn, drastically impacts not only the type, but even the amount, of law that will be necessary to govern a given people.[38] Even societies that do not have a great deal of formal law are still governed by a sort of law. "One can call the institutions of these peoples' *mores* rather than *laws*."[39]

In discussing mores, it is natural to also examine their more formal incarnation in religion. The importance of religion in Montesquieu's thought is that it is extremely prejudicial in determining whether a regime is more or less likely to be despotic. He begins the section of *Spirit of the Laws* that deals with religion (Part 5) by noting the utility of religion. Interestingly, his emphasis is on its usefulness in reining in the ruler(s) rather than its effects on the morals of the citizenry as evidenced in his contention that "Even if it were useless for subjects to have a religion, it would not be useless for princes to have one and to whiten with foam the only bridle that can hold those who fear no human laws."[40] This of course assumes that the prince is not bound or restrained by human law as he ideally would be in a mixed constitutional system. It also implies that religion is particularly useful in regimes that tend toward despotism, as it is the only conceivable check upon the supreme power of the head of state.[41]

---

McCrae et al. "Climactic Warmth and National Wealth: Some Culture Level Determinants of National Character Stereotypes." *European Journal of Personality*. December 1; 21:8 (2007): 953–76. Also, see Kriesel, K.M. "Montesquieu: Possibilistic Political Geographer." *Annals of the Association of American Geographers*, 58:3 (1968): 557–74.

37 Cited in Kriesel (1968), p. 585.

38 See Montesquieu (1989), p. 291 where he writes: "It is the division of lands that principally swells the civil code. In nations that have not been divided there will be very few civil laws."

39 Ibid.

40 Ibid., p. 460.

41 A possible confirmation of the validity of this claim could be seen in the historical record of regimes, such as Stalinist Russia, that rejected and/or repressed religion and the

Conversely, religion can exercise its own sort of despotism and Montesquieu is clearly reticent of the conflation of religious and civil law. "Human laws made to speak to the spirit should give precepts and no counsels at all," he writes.[42] Likewise, "religion, made to speak to the heart, should give many counsels and few precepts."[43] In other words, the purpose of law is to tell people what they *must* do rather than what they *should* do, and the purpose of religion is primarily, though not entirely, to advise people on how they *should* live in order to live better. He gives as an example how the Christian counsel on the value of celibacy resulted in its being mandated for an entire class of people with the result that "the legislator tired himself, he tired the society, making men execute by precept what those who love perfection would have executed by counsel."[44] Clearly, the political state is not meant to be perfect, but simply good in the sense that it allows one to pursue the good life, "for perfection does not concern men or things universally."[45]

As regards political subjects, Montesquieu argues that the people themselves should seek a religion given by God, but where not able they should have a system of belief that conforms with the dictates of morality.[46] In its ideal form, that is, outside of a particular tradition or religious revelation, this can be seen in Stoic philosophy. The use of Stoicism brings together the principles of the Rule of Law as properly aspiring to emulate an eternal law and the formation of the character of a people worthy of wise rule as it seeks only to work for "men's happiness and (to exercise) the duties of society ... Born for society they believed their duty was to work for it ... it seemed that only the happiness of others could increase their own."[47] Here can be seen a preference for a society in which the individual good is subordinated to the greater social good. If a society were to be based on Stoicism this would have the benefit of being good for the individual as well, as they would count the happiness of others as important as their own, and thus increase their personal happiness.

In accordance with this ideal, religion and civil law should and do act in conjunction, whether in Protestant, Catholic, "Mohammedan," or other forms. The relationship between these two factors is inversely proportional for Montesquieu who says that: "As religion and civil laws should aim principally to make good citizens of men, one sees that when either of these departs from this end, the other should aim more toward it; the less repressive religion is, the more the civil laws should repress."[48] This sets up an interesting and ironic formula in which

corresponding impacts that repression had on various human rights and social freedoms.

42 Montesquieu (1989), p. 464.

43 Ibid.

44 Ibid.

45 Ibid.

46 Ibid., p. 465.

47 Ibid., pp. 465–6.

48 Montesquieu (1989), p. 468.

strict religious dogma could be argued to be a force for political liberalism.[49] As evidence of its validity, he cites the case of Japan, where there are "almost no dogmas" and a concept of "neither paradise nor hell," which requires law of "extraordinary severity" that is "executed with an extraordinary punctiliousness."[50] In the next breath however, Montesquieu seems to change his mind as to the causal nature of this relationship. Rather than seeing Islam, with its strict beliefs, as a religion which leads to greater political freedom, he notes that one of these beliefs is predestination (he conveniently omits significant Christian allegiances to this idea, most notably amongst Calvinists), and this belief stems from "laziness of the soul." On this dubious basis, he recommends that law be used to arouse these drowsy religious sluggards. He does not elaborate on what this would mean in practice however, leading one to argue that on the whole, Montesquieu provides theoretical support for arguments like Kedourie's that cite the "Arab mind" and other such deterministic factors in explaining the failure of constitutionalism. If however, one leaves out what Montesquieu specifically says about the values of one religion versus another, the actual theoretical framework of a successful constitution simply calls for a morality that is in line with the immutable values of Stoicism and the like, and where these values are religious they should encourage industry in business and restraint in manners. This would not seem to negatively prejudice non-Christian societies against very strong constitutional regimes. Indeed, Christianity and Islam both meet an important religious criterion for Montesquieu in that they have doctrines of both heaven and hell, or reward and punishment. Balancing these two ideas alleviates the danger of certain salvation which leads to "scorn for death." After all, "How can one constrain by the laws a man who believes himself sure that the greatest penalty the magistrates can inflict on him will end in a moment only to begin his happiness?"[51] Of course in reality, radicals of any religion seem to embrace this certainty nonetheless to often disastrous effect as evidenced by the ongoing appeal of martyrdom.

Religious ideals aside, Montesquieu is primarily concerned with happiness in the present life. This happiness varies as much as people vary, and as such is a function of both equality and liberty. Montesquieu's definition of equality is illustrative of this nuanced view. He states: "As far as the sky is from the earth, so far is the true spirit of equality from the spirit of extreme equality … It seeks not to have no master but to have only one's equals for masters."[52] This definition is notable in that it allows for a variety of political forms, assuming that the different classes of society have some degree of autonomy from one another. Indeed, he notes that "Men are equal in republican government; they are equal in despotic government; in the former, it is because they are everything; in the latter, it is

49 Indeed, this is echoed in early American thought regarding the necessity of a virtuous populous if liberty is to be preserved.

50 Montesquieu (1989), p. 468.

51 Ibid., p. 469.

52 Ibid., p. 114.

because they are nothing."[53] What Montesquieu calls "extreme equality" would seem to be something akin to Burke's "levelling" and amounts to a type of anarchy that he clearly believes will result in a Hobbesian State of Nature where all are equal by virtue of their equal ability to kill, and equal susceptibility to being killed. His definition of equality is thus tied into liberty such that people are considered free if they are only under the dominion of their peers. Given his apparent agnosticism on which form of government is best in a universal sense, this view could hold true in societies as simple and essentially egalitarian as hunter-gatherer tribes[54] or as stratified as a monarchy, so long as the powers of the various social classes are restrained and balanced by one another.

Where power within the State becomes imbalanced or unreflective of the national character, Montesquieu argues it gives rise to tyranny. Of tyranny, he states that there are "two sorts," "a real one, which consists in the violence of the government, and one of opinion, which is felt when those who govern establish things that run counter to a nation's way of thinking."[55] His argument nicely supports present-day "realists" who contend that Western nation-building exercises are counter-productive and often doomed to fail. Whereas today's commentators might cite ongoing instability in Iraq and Afghanistan, he appealed to the classics citing,

> The Parthians could not tolerate this king who, having been raised in Rome, made himself affable and accessible to everyone. Even liberty has appeared intolerable to peoples who were not accustomed to enjoying it. Thus is pure air sometimes harmful to those who have lived in swampy countries.[56]

Tyranny is thus not a condition only of actual oppression, but one in which a legal framework is imposed upon a social structure for which it is not fit for purpose. This could easily form the basis of an argument against imperialism of both political and cultural forms, and of the need for political change to change in response to social change, rather than attempting the reverse. The result of either form of tyranny will often be violence. Here again, he cites the example of Japan (an ironic example given its post World War II transformation into a parliamentary democracy by virtue of military *dictat*). In contrast to the extreme number and severity of laws and punishments under the Imperial government and feudal lords, he argues the following:

---

53 Montesquieu (1989), p. 75.

54 See ibid., p. 293. "What most secures the liberty of peoples who do not cultivate the land is that money is unknown to them … whereas, when one has signs for wealth, these signs can be amassed and distributed to whomever one wants … Among peoples without money, each man has few needs and satisfies them easily and equally. Equality, therefore, is forced; thus, their leaders are not despotic."

55 Ibid., p. 309.

56 Ibid.

> A wise legislator would have sought to lead men's spirits back by a just tempering of penalties and rewards; by maxims of philosophy, morality, and religion, matched to this character; by the just application of the rules of honor; by using shame as punishment, and by the enjoyment of a constant happiness and a sweet tranquillity.[57,58]

Upon examination of this passage, he reveals himself to be heeding his own advice, despite prescribing societal fixes from the outside. The means he recommends to establish peace and rule of law include concepts rooted in traditional Japanese culture like philosophy, morality, honor and shame. Likewise, one of the societal rewards he proposes is tranquility. This demonstrates that his view of the "spirit" of the law does not prohibit criticism and constructive dialogue from within or from without a society. It does indicate, though, that any change should be gradual, evolutionary, and should not upset the delicate balance achieved through the accretion of influences from climate, terrain, history, culture, religion, etc.

Ultimately then, *The Spirit of the Laws* can be seen as a sort of sociological account of a wide array of constitutions and corresponding nations/people groups. The development, maintenance, and alteration of these systems is clearly portrayed as an organic interaction of many disparate influences which can reinforce or counterbalance one another, but which nonetheless should be changed with the utmost care. Its inherent conservatism serves to actually restrain any type of ruler by virtue of its incredible breadth of national case studies which all reinforce Montesquieu's maxim that "The legislator is to follow the spirit of the nation when doing so is not contrary to the principles of government, for we do nothing better than what we do freely and by following our natural genius."[59] This idea of the natural genius, in counterpoint to those who would simply label Montesquieu a deterministic Eurocentrist, is one that opens the possibility of any group of people developing a rule of law that is uniquely tailored to their circumstances, customs, and concerns. Is this not, in essence, the very definition of what political freedom aims to accomplish? To the moralist, the bureaucrat, and the despot, Montesquieu makes this admonition:

> If there were in the world a nation which had a sociable humor, an openness of heart; a joy in life, a taste, an ease in communicating its thoughts; which was lively pleasant, playful, sometimes imprudent, often indiscreet; and which had

57 Ibid., p. 87.

58 In Montesquieu (1989), p. 85, this recommendation of shame as punishment seems to be a rare instance in which he subscribes to a natural law doctrine and unsurprisingly, a classical Greek idea of the ultimate societal sanction being ostracism, or social death. "Let us follow nature, which has given men shame for their scourge, and let the greatest part of the penalty be the infamy of suffering it."

59 Ibid., p. 310.

with all that, courage, generosity, frankness, and a certain point of honor, one should avoid disturbing its manners by laws, in order not to disturb its virtues.[60]

This endeavor of avoiding "disturbing the manners" of a state is one which is greatly aided by the next constitutional concept being discussed, the Separation of Powers doctrine.

## One Body, Many Members—The "Specialization" of Powers as a mechanism of restraint in the Federalist Papers

It may be useful to approach the doctrine of separation of powers by looking to the origin of that idea in the interaction of intellectual theory and practical problems during the American revolutionary era.[61]

The impulse to separate comes from *within* the departments: powered by the allegiance of individuals, each department pushes outward and expands to the limits of its power.

Imagine that the departments were parts of a machine-as the Framers were wont to do and that each part represented an expandable chamber sharing a wall with another part. In such a scheme, each chamber's *internal* expansion serves to limit the reach of the power of its coordinate branch. Interest fuels both this hydraulic pressure and its restraint by expanding the chamber to limits set by the expansion of neighbor chambers. In such a scheme, the interior structure of the departments has been "so contrived" that its "several constituent parts may, by their mutual relations, be the means of keeping each other in their proper places. (Quoting *Federalist 51*)[62]

In sharp relief to Montesquieu's concern that a society not be corrupted by law, is the recognition of later thinkers that society is almost never monolithic and nearly always contains majority and minority factions. In democracies then, it becomes an urgent matter for the government to ensure protection of minority rights whilst still respecting the will of the majority. This effort is usually given the neat doctrinal title of Separation of Powers. As the quote above suggests, the issue of the separation of powers is not simply one of assigning specific roles to the discrete branches of government, but rather is one of assigning power in such

60 Ibid.

61 Levi, Edward H. "Some Aspects of Separation of Powers." *Columbia Law Review*, 76:3 (1976): 372.

62 Nourse, Victoria. "Toward A "Due Foundation" For the Separation of Powers: *The Federalist Papers* as Political Narrative." *Texas Law Review*, 74:3 (1996): 481.

a way that no societal group can hold a preponderance of power over the others.[63] It is also meant to create specific proficiencies in the various departments so that they can specialize in the sphere assigned to them by the constitutional framework.

Just as a physical body is threatened when one group of cells multiply beyond their proper bounds resulting in cancer, so too is a government threatened when one specialized branch grows beyond its proper bounds. The question, however, is one of determining where those proper bounds lie, where they overlap, and to what extent government functions can or should be shared.

Of all the constitutional concepts discussed thus far, the idea that government power should be structured into separate departments that could check one another's power is arguably the latest to reach anything approaching its present form. Ancient theorists certainly philosophized about the government having different organs, but this was typically done in such a fashion as to ensure that the government would be efficient and just. Plato's Republic has its philosopher kings, but it is not assumed that they need to have their power limited. If the virtuous are ruling, then why limit that virtue?[64] Likewise, Thomas Hobbes' *Leviathan* features a frontispiece depicting a body politic rendered in actual corporeal form, with a king as its head and the assembled masses below him. The king is transcendent, and within the rest of the body there is no indication of any social groups or governmental divisions. To his mind, the paramount value delivered by the State is the protection of life and limb, which is achieved only through complete public submission to the will of the sovereign.[65]

The framers of the American Constitution were well aware of the historical development of government and the role they would potentially be playing in it. Alexander Hamilton himself boldly asserted this contention in *Federalist 9*, saying:

> The science of politics, however, like most other sciences has received great improvement … The regular distribution of power into distinct departments—the introduction of legislative balances and checks—the institution of courts composed of judges, holding their offices during good behaviour—the representation of the people in the legislature by deputies of their own election—these are either wholly new discoveries or have made their principal progress towards perfection in modern times. They are means, and powerful means,

63 In *Federalist 47*, p. 324, Madison states: "The accumulation of all powers legislative, executive and judiciary in the same hands … may justly be pronounced the very definition of tyranny."

64 Plato, G.R.F. Ferrari, and Tom Griffith. *The Republic*, Cambridge Texts in the History of Political Thought. Cambridge and New York: Cambridge University Press (2000), pp. 501–4.

65 Hobbes, Thomas, and Richard Tuck. *Leviathan*, Cambridge Texts in the History of Political Thought. Cambridge and New York: Cambridge University Press, 1991. Inside Cover.

> by which the excellencies of republican government may be retained and its imperfections lessened or avoided.[66]

It is clear from this excerpt that the principle of separation of powers was at the forefront in the process that yielded the particular institutions and powers enumerated in the Constitution. Clearly this division is one that aims, in a traditional sense, to achieve justice in minimizing harm and maximizing public good within government. That this principle should be so explicitly discussed in *The Federalist Papers* is somewhat surprising given that there is nothing actually written in the Constitution about this idea. It is implicit in the institutional arrangements, which themselves are worded in language designed to be vague enough to allow for flexibility. In his discussion of the term and its development, Supreme Court Justice Antonin Scalia says of the idea:

> The principle of the separation of powers was set forth in the Constitution of the Commonwealth of Massachusetts well before it found its way into the federal document ... with an economy of expression many would urge as a model for modern judicial opinions, the principle of separation of powers is found only in the structure of the document, which successively describes where the legislative, executive and judicial powers, respectively, reside. One should not think, however, that the principle was any less important to the federal framers. Madison said of it, in Federalist No. 47, that "no political truth is certainly of greater intrinsic value, or is stamped with the authority of more enlightened patrons of liberty."[67]

The adoption of the present US Constitution was an occasion of immense public debate and brought forth a whole series of arguments for and against the new institutional arrangements, with the primary concerns being to avoid repeating the mistakes of both authoritarian rule and mob rule. Equally important was to establish a more firmly federal union than that created by the Articles of Confederation, particularly one that would take into account the lessons gained from the functioning of the various state constitutions.

As the oldest written constitution still in use, the US Constitution was to have significant ramifications for all subsequent constitutional orders, particularly as the US came to a position of international dominance in the post-World War II era. This in turn, greatly affected constitutionalism in a general sense with the post-war era's corresponding proliferation of constitutionally conceived international institutions (the UN, the IMF, GATT, etc.) The most famous, and arguably influential, set of documents to emerge from the effort to enact the new constitution is *The Federalist*

---

66 Madison, James, Alexander Hamilton, and John Jay. *The Federalist Papers*, Classics of Conservatism. New Rochelle, NY: Arlington House (1966), p. 51.

67 Scalia, Antonin "The Doctrine of Standing as an Essential Element of the Separation of Powers." *Suffolk University Law Review*, 17 (1983): 881.

*Papers*, written by James Madison and Alexander Hamilton. In these essays, they marshal an array of theoretical support from classical and Enlightenment sources, in addition to existing constitutional documents, to answer specific objections that had been raised against establishing the stronger institutional framework that the new constitution embodied. In a sense then, the discussion of the Separation of Powers doctrine that is found in their words is one that is both the culmination and protector of the previously mentioned principles of constitutional orders being based upon the rule of law and in keeping with national character.

*Why Separate Power?—Maintaining Proper Organ Function in a Republican State*

Before the principle of separation of powers can be assessed in relation to the questions enumerated above, it is first necessary to examine what Madison and Hamilton saw as the key components of the state and their respective roles. According to Madison,

> Justice is the end of government. It is the end of civil society … In a society under the forms of which the stronger faction can readily unite and oppress the weaker, anarchy may truly be said to reign … even the stronger individuals are prompted by the uncertainty of their condition, to submit to a government which may protect the weak as well as themselves.[68]

This view is in stark contrast to the classical view that assumes virtuous rulers. The entire point, it seems, in creating countervailing forces in government is to ensure that the edifice of government itself creates and sustains a just order despite the self-seeking inclinations of human nature. The channeling of wills toward the public good occurs at two levels. On the one hand,

> among the great variety of interests, parties and sects which it (the United States) embraces, a coalition of the majority could seldom take place on any other principles than those of justice and the general good; and the being thus less danger to a minor from the will of the major party, there must be less pretext also, to provide for the security of the former, by introducing a will not dependent on the latter; or in other words, a will independent of the society itself.[69]

The first check on tyranny then is the very requirement of majority rule in passing legislation. Although one person's will may easily be corrupted and selfish, the Framers are more optimistic about the collective sensibilities of a community leading to just laws, particularly when aired in consideration of the facts afforded by a free press and the debate afforded by freedom of expression. The second

68 *Federalist 51*, p. 352.
69 Ibid., p. 353.

barrier to tyranny is cryptically referred to as "a will not dependent on the latter." What constitutes this "will independent of society itself?"

In answer to this question Madison continues, saying "It is no less certain than it is important ... that the larger the society, provided it lie within a practicable sphere, the more duly capable it will be of self government. And happily for the republican cause, the practicable sphere may be carried to a very great extent, be a judicious modification and mixture of the federal principle."[70] Again, it is clear that Madison thinks the very diversity of society will lend itself to self-government, but more than that, that this system can be further improved by "modification and mixture of the federal principle." The federal principle is entirely concerned with dividing powers between bodies with their own spheres of sovereignty, and his allusion to a mixture foreshadows both Madison's and Hamilton's later discussion of overlap between branches of government.

Having looked at the forces that restrict government as a whole, it is now possible to examine the way each branch of government is viewed both functionally and formally by the Framers. In his essay, "The Indeterminacy of the Separation of Powers and Federal Courts," William Gwyn discusses this doctrine's two competing camps as composed of "formalists" and "functionalists."

> The former are inclined to limit each branch of government to the exercise of a power assigned to it by the Constitution, unless that document has explicitly permitted an exception. The latter are inclined to take a flexible approach, emphasizing the need for a blending as well as a separation of powers, and insisting on a careful examination of each intrusion by one branch into the primary function of another in order to determine whether one has prevented the other from effectively exercising its function. The functionalists perceive the formalists as overly literal in their interpretation of the Constitution at the expense of governmental effectiveness. The formalists see the functionalists as substituting their personal judgments for the clearly stated requirements of the Constitution, placed there by the Framers to satisfy the prescriptions of the hallowed doctrine of the separation of powers. Although, as it will become evident, my own sympathies lie with the functionalists, one of the major conclusions of this essay is that any use of the separation of powers doctrine by American courts is bound to be unsatisfactory, no matter what approach is taken, because the doctrine is indeterminate.[71]

Gwyn's claim that the doctrine is indeterminate could be more strongly stated to the effect that this indeterminacy is intentional. This is because the simple division of government into Executive, Legislative and Judicial was not deemed sufficient to check power. Experience under The Articles of Confederation in various states

70 *Federalist 51*, p. 353.

71 Gwyn, William B. "The Indeterminacy of the Separation of Powers and the Federal Courts." *George Washington Law Review*, 57 (1988–1989): 474–5.

had shown how contrary to earlier concerns with abuses of executive power in the monarchical regime, in the new republican form of government it was the legislative branch that most required limitations. In *Federalist 48*, Madison asks

> Will it be sufficient to mark with precision the boundaries of these departments in the Constitution of the government, and to trust to these parchment barriers against the encroaching spirit of power? ... some more adequate defence is indispensably necessary ... The legislative department is every where extending the sphere of its activity, and drawing all power into its impetuous vortex.[72]

The terms used here paint a vivid image of the entire ship of state being sucked into a legislative Charybdis. Once a government cedes too much power to the legislature, it will be unable to steer itself away from disasters that occur due to legislative excesses imposed upon the society by the majority party on any given issue. There seems to be a belief that the Executive and Judicial powers are less susceptible to this same kind of gravitational pull for a multitude of reasons. First of all, the Executive is the most visible manifestation of state power. As such, the acts of this branch are bound to be more public and therefore there will be less temptation for it to usurp power improperly. Likewise, the Judiciary operates under very clear boundaries. It can only take cases brought to it by outside parties; it has only negative power in that it can only rule on the application and constitutionality of law; and finally, its members are under less public pressure to conform to majority will.[73] This is why Madison is at pains to explain that

> The legislative department derives a superiority in our governments from other circumstances. Its constitutional powers being at once more extensive and less susceptible of precise limits, it can with greater facility, mask ... the encroachments which it makes on the co-ordinate departments.[74]

Notice that he does not say that it can potentially encroach on the other departments, but instead that there are encroachments that "it makes." The more power a department has the more force it exerts on the entire state. Madison's observation that by its very nature the Legislative power cannot easily be limited to any precise sphere is especially significant because of its primary function being to exercise the positive power of creating new law and modifying existing law.

Historically-speaking, this fear of the legislative body, was founded by a situation in which

> Events in a great many of our jurisdictions must have brought clearly to the attention of leaders in the period from 1775 to 1790 the dangers of legislative

72 *Federalist 48*, p. 333.
73 See ibid., p. 334.
74 Ibid.

> supremacy in general, and "legislative justice" in particular. Popular rule on a large scale was a novel experiment in any case, and one can appreciate the a priori apprehension of those who carried it on. And experience strengthened the apprehension. Laws favoring debtors and dealing arbitrarily with criminals produced specific constitutional prohibitions. And exercises of "judicial power" by the legislatures, with similar effects, must have helped to impress many of the fathers with the importance of erecting an independent judiciary, with its own inviolable province. Such a judiciary would have, as well as the power to disregard unconstitutional statutes, the exclusive power to determine legal controversies.[75]

The issue of giving to courts the power to determine the "legal controversies" mentioned by Malcolm Sharp is a vital institutional check because the only other possibilities would either involve the legislative branch being judge in its own case, or the Executive would make a summary judgment and give the clear appearance of a power grab.

Alexander Hamilton mentions this historical experience in *Federalist 71*. Here again, the image created by his words is deeply evocative of navigational peril,

> The tendency of the legislative authority to absorb every other, has been fully displayed and illustrated by examples, in some preceding numbers. In governments purely republican, this tendency is almost irresistible. The representatives of the people, in a popular assembly, seem sometimes to fancy that they are the people themselves ... and as they commonly have the people on their side, they always act with such momentum as to make it very difficult for the other members of the government to maintain the balance of the Constitution.[76]

Clearly the elite men writing the Constitution had no desire for a proliferation of redistributive policies or laws that would weaken their rights as property owners and creditors. Here can be seen yet another example of the interests of one large numerical minority superseding the interests of the poorer masses. Ultimately, so long as the rules were applied universally, the fact that they favored the elite did not contradict the imperative to apply a consistent and just rule of law. Stability was ultimately a greater good than democracy in its pure form.[77]

---

75 Sharp, Malcolm P. "The Classical American Doctrine Of 'The Separation of Powers'." *The University of Chicago Law Review*, 2:3 (1935): 393.

76 *Federalist 71*, pp. 483–4.

77 According to Edward Levi's article, "Some Aspects of the Separation of Powers," [found in *Columbia Law Review*, 76:3 (Apr., 1976): 375] under the Articles of Confederation, "The legislatures confiscated property, erected paper money schemes, suspended the ordinary means of collecting debts. They changed the law with great frequency. One New Englander complained: '[t]he revised laws have been altered-realtered-made better-made

In *Federalist 49*, Madison justifies the primacy of stability by reminding those who would vote on ratification of a unified federal constitution that

> the people are the only legitimate fountain of power, and it is from them that the constitutional charter, under which the several branches of government hold their power, is derived; it seems strictly consonant to the republican theory, to recur to the same original authority. Not only whenever it may be necessary to enlarge, diminish, or new-model the powers of government; but also whenever any one of the departments may commit encroachments on the chartered authorities of the others.

He goes on to demonstrate why this approach does not in fact work by referring to the constitutional protections of Virginia, which require that if two out of the three branches concur the constitution needs changing or a breach of power correcting, that they can call a convention of the people to undertake the needed changes. Madison finds this procedure is well-intentioned, but flawed as a branch that was gaining in power may be able to leverage another branch into concurring with it that change is needed. It would also destabilize the government by decreasing the longevity of, and hence the respect for, its institutions and traditions, leading him to state that "The danger of disturbing the public tranquility by interesting too strongly the public passions, is a still more serious objection against a frequent reference of constitutional questions, to the decision of the whole society."[78]

Madison elaborates that constitutional revisions have thus far been successful but should not be undertaken lightly as the reframing of constitutional questions has been precipitated by extreme danger to the social order and a universal trust in national leaders who proposed principles opposite to those responsible for the unrest. He hopefully concludes that "The future situations in which we must expect to usually be placed, do not present any equivalent security against the danger which is apprehended."

Thus, rather than having a clean delineation of powers, the writers of the Constitution purposefully shared powers between the branches. Indeed, as Victoria Nourse argues,

> Every time we use the term "separation of powers," we invoke a common, yet tacit, narrative of power-a narrative constructed upon the idea of legal authority: we imagine the executive, judicial, and legislative powers divided and neatly arranged among the departments ... (A) different narrative of power, one based on the idea that power is as much constituted by the political relationships the Constitution creates as by the legal authority it bestows ... argue(s) that the separation of political power is as, if not more, vital to the continued separation

worse; and kept in such a fluctuating position, that persons in civil commission scarce know what is law'."

78 *Federalist 49*, pp. 339–41.

> of our governmental institutions as the separation of any particular function or the allocation of any particular legal authority.[79]

This is why, in defending the Constitution from detractors who decried the way responsibility for foreign affairs and other duties were shared, Madison uses *Federalist 47* to cite the man his contemporaries most respected on matters of governance, Montesquieu. Perhaps the most relevant part of Montesquieu's work to the early Americans was his examination of the English constitution and its virtues. He particularly praised the way in which power was divided between the Crown, the Parliament, and the Courts. Madison is keen to point out, however, that

> He did not mean that these departments ought to have no *partial agency* in, or no *control* over the acts of each other. His meaning … can amount to no more than this, that where the *whole* power of one department is exercised by the same hands which possess the *whole* power of another department, the fundamental principles of a free constitution, are subverted.[80]

Madison then gives examples from all the state constitutions of how separate powers have functions which overlap and support one another, but clarifies that he is not advocating any particular state constitutional model from these examples.[81]

To see how this principle works in practice, one can contrast the discussion of the judiciary in various parts of *The Federalist Papers* with writings about the negotiation and adoption of treaties, the process of impeachment, and the executive veto. In No. 71, Alexander Hamilton asks the rhetorical question "To what purpose separate the executive, or the judiciary, from the legislative, if both the executive and the judiciary are so constituted as to be at the absolute devotion of the legislative?" He continues that, "It is one thing to be subordinate to the laws, and another to be dependent on the legislative body. The first comports with, the last violates, the fundamental principles of good government; and whatever may be the forms of the Constitution, unites all power in the same hands."[82] The dichotomy between subordination and dependency can easily be understood to mean that all offices and departments in government are equally bound to follow the law, but that does not mean that those offices outside the legislative branch should be individually *financially* dependent upon the legislature.

Likewise, "It is impossible to keep the Judges too distinct from every other avocation than that of expounding the laws. It is peculiarly dangerous to place them in a situation to either be corrupted or influenced by the executive."[83] Again, the ability of any branch to bring pressure to bear on another is clearly at the forefront

79 Nourse (1996), p. 449.

80 *Federalist 47*, pp. 325–6.

81 Ibid., pp. 327–31.

82 Ibid., p. 483.

83 *Federalist 71*, p. 499.

of the founders' concerns. This particular danger is one remedied by making only the appointment of justices subject to the other branches of government. That is why they are nominated by the Executive and confirmed by the Legislative. Once appointed however, their terms are either for life, or for a fixed length of time that is not dependent upon any individual lawmaker or executive's will.

In justifying the life terms for judicial appointments during times of "good behaviour," Hamilton argues that "the judiciary, from the nature of its functions, will always be that least dangerous to the political rights of the constitution; because it will be least in capacity to annoy or injure them." By far the most passive of government branches, "(it) has no influence over either the sword or the purse, no direction either of the strength or the wealth of the society, and can take no active resolution whatever. It may truly be said to have neither Force nor Will, but merely judgment; and must ultimately depend upon the aid of the executive arm even for the efficacy of its judgments."[84]

All of these statements are fundamentally concerned with isolating the judiciary from the influence of the executive and the potential avarice of the legislature. They indicate an understanding of judicial review that is highly limited by the lack of specific powers granted to the courts, the custom of generally deferring to the popular will expressed in legislation or through the executive, and by the inherently reactive nature of courts. Justice Scalia reflects the continued dominance of this strain of thinking in contemporary conservative circles when he discusses the centrality of judicial standing in establishing jurisdiction. In order for a party to have standing to file suit and pursue a case before the courts, it is necessary for the party to demonstrate "he has sustained or is immediately in danger of sustaining a direct injury as the result of that action and it is not sufficient that he has merely a general interest common to all members of the public."[85] This standard is sufficiently high to allow only cases with demonstrable impacts on individual citizens to have much chance of ever being heard and ruled upon in open court. If the courts adhere to this view, they are greatly self-limiting the scope of their own influence.

Of course, this view of the weak judiciary is one that would be sharply challenged. Appeals to halt "judicial activism" and "legislating from the bench" are frequently heard in public discourse. Certainly, the 20th century saw a number of decisions that indicated a desire on the part of justices to pursue societal goods through the court system, such as desegregation, which simply could not be uniformly achieved through the democratic process, yet nonetheless led to a close adherence to the constitutional ideal. Interestingly, Hamilton seems to have anticipated this problem when he writes

84 *Federalist 79*, pp. 522–3.

85 Treister, Dana S. "Standing to Sue the Government: Are Separation of Powers Principles Really Being Served?" *California Law Review*, 67 (1993–1994): 689–726. Quoting Ex parte Levitt.

> In the first place, there is not a syllable in the plan under consideration, which *directly* empowers the national courts to construe the laws according to the spirit of the constitution, or which gives them any greater latitude in this respect, than may be claimed by the courts of every state. I admit however, that the constitution ought to be the standard of construction for the laws, and that wherever there is an evident opposition, the laws ought to give place to the constitution. But this doctrine is not deducible from any circumstance peculiar to the plan of the convention; but from the general theory of a limited constitution.[86]

What this statement indicates is that there is a working understanding of the constitution as an instrument that limits governmental power by its nature rather than by statute. The phrase "spirit of the constitution" that is used to describe the measure against which laws might be interpreted seems to be intentionally employed to evoke Montesquieu, yet the next sentence, in which Hamilton lays out what "ought" to be the standard used by the courts, instead used the formulation "the construction for the laws." The former phrase is clearly dealing with the fuzzier problem of interpreting the "spirit" or intent behind a law, whilst the latter focuses on the letter of the law, or its "construction." Why does he seem to give precedence to literal interpretation? Doesn't this approach lend itself less to flexible governance and more to rigid orthodoxy? To answer this question it is helpful to reference the earlier quote from *Federalist 71* in which he claims the role of the justice should be exclusively "that of expounding the laws."[87] The very practice of rendering judgment is one of intrusion into the purview of the business of the legislative and executive branches. This requires that the standard of conduct and impartiality that judges adhere to be unimpeachable. The minute this character is damaged it fundamentally undermines the legitimacy of the law itself. Similarly, once judges stray from interpreting the words "as written," it is impossible to draw the line between judging and legislating. This leads to exactly the type of conflation of powers that the framers are seeking to avoid.

Other sharing of roles between the branches is quite acceptable, indeed desirable, according to the *Federalist's* writers. On international treaties, it is the awkwardness of treaty-making itself that is the cause of the difficulty in assigning the power to any one segment of government. Alexander Hamilton explains that

> The power of making treaties ... relates neither to the execution of the subsisting laws, nor to the enaction of new ones and still less to an exertion of the common strength. Its objects are CONTRACTS with foreign nations ... agreements between sovereign and sovereign. The power in question seems therefore to form a distinct department, and to belong properly neither to the legislative nor to the executive.[88]

86 *Federalist 81*, p. 543.
87 *Federalist 71*, p. 499.
88 *Federalist 75*, pp. 504–5.

Any student of the US government is well aware that the solution to this problem was to assign a role to both the executive and legislative branches concerning treaties. The executive negotiates as a unitary actor, making it easier to achieve clarity on terms. The Senate votes to ratify or reject the treaty, adding an element of democratic accountability to any agreement between "sovereign and sovereign," which is crucial when the American sovereign is ostensibly "the people." This is furthermore appropriate because a treaty is a binding contract, which is a documentary and legal effort most closely related to legislating, whereas the implementation of the agreement in good faith is primarily an executive function.

This power-sharing arrangement was put to an early test during the Washington administration, when several mariners were captured by North African pirates. President Washington sought to create a peace treaty with the Barbary Powers. The President was highly conscious of the various checks and roles assigned to the various government branches on foreign affairs. He knew it was the Executive that conducted treaty negotiations and provided for defense, but that the House funded these endeavors, and that the Senate had to advise and consent on treaty ratification. Washington was further aware that information was a tool of power and that by providing more or less information to the public and/or the Congress he would be setting precedents for the obligations of disclosure that were not specifically provided for in the Constitution. Using the powers of his executive office to obtain information necessary for promoting the national defense, and relaying it to Congress, President Washington conscientiously avoided the appearance of imperiousness by proposing his terms in secret to Congress, incorporating their feedback, and relaying his altered plans to his diplomatic staff. Although it took several years and what amounted to a substantial bribe to appease terrorists, the end result was an enduring agreement that protected American flag ships and sailors in the Atlantic. This episode highlights that the idea of separation of powers is one in which the overlap in delineated powers means that in practice the constitution leaves tremendous room for discretion on the part of the Executive in the use of information and conduct of negotiations, and equally wide latitude for the legislature to demand information and approve or deny funds for treaty obligations as they see fit.[89]

Another sanctioned overlap of institutional responsibility concerns impeachment. One of the terms of the Constitution that came under vehement opposition was the use of the Senate as a judicial body on matters of removing executive officers, up to and including the president him or herself. In *Federalist 56*, the objections are summarized as follows:

---

89 For a detailed examination of the episode with the Barbary Powers and its implications for the Separation of Powers doctrine, see Gerhard Casper, "An Essay in Separation of Powers: Some Early Versions and Practices." *William and Mary Law Review*, 30 (1988): 242–61.

> The *first* of these objections is that the provision in question confounds legislative and judiciary authorities in the same body; in violation of that important and well established maxim, which requires a separation between the departments of power. The true meaning of this maxim … has been shewn to be entirely compatible with a partial intermixture of those departments for special purposes, preserving them in the main distinct and unconnected. This partial intermixture is in some cases not only proper, but necessary to the mutual defence of the several members of the government against each other.

Hamilton's immediate response to his critics is that,

> (The) powers relating to impeachments are … an essential check in the hands of that body (the Legislative) upon the encroachments of the executive. The division of them between the two branches of the legislature; assigning to one the right of accusing (the House of Representatives), to the other the right of judging (the Senate); avoids the inconvenience of making the same persons both accusers and judges; and guards against the danger of persecution from the prevelancy of a factious spirit in either of those branches.[90]

Although there are potentially any number of further objections that can be raised to the institutional provision for impeachments, it is obvious that the goal of placing this power in legislative hands, and further splitting it functionally between accusatory power in the House (they legally have judicial standing) and judicial power in the Senate (they have jurisdiction), is to place a powerful check upon abuses of power in the executive branch. It reinforces the principle that the same party cannot act as prosecutor and judge in the same case. To those who object that the judiciary is still available to fulfill its customary function it needs only to be pointed out that the justices who would have standing in this type of case are nominated and appointed by the executive and would therefore presumably face a blatant conflict of interest in judging cases of this type.

Finally, the issue of the veto provides what is perhaps the most straight-forward check on the dreaded potential of legislative excesses. Again writing in *Federalist 71*, Hamilton says of the Executive:

> They will consider every institution calculated to restrain the excess of law-making, and to keep things in the same state, in which they may happen to be at any given period, as much more likely to do good than harm; because it is favourable to greater stability in the system of legislation.[91]

Quite simply, the President is bound to act in the best interests of all citizens rather than any particular constituency. This negative power is limited to stifling attempts

90 Hamilton, *Federalist 56*, pp. 445–6.

91 *Federalist 71*, p. 496.

to change or write new legislation and is inherently conservative. The value of this lies yet again in preserving "stability in the system of legislation," because "the representatives of the people, in a popular assembly, seem sometimes to fancy that they are the people themselves ... and as they commonly have the people on their side, they always act with such momentum as to make it very difficult for the other members of the government to maintain the balance of the Constitution."[92] The two-thirds super-majority required to override the veto allows for cases in which there is overwhelming consensus in the legislature to overcome even executive disagreement with the law. This provides a consistent method of viewing the role of majorities in affecting government based on the presumption that it would be difficult for so large a number to agree on something inherently unjust and/or bad.[93]

Taken in its totality, the argument for ratification of the Constitution in the *Federalist Papers* is one which expresses

> two related aspects of the new American conception of politics that emerged from the experiences of the interregnum period. First, that the people, and not the institutions of government, are sovereign. The Constitution after all begins with "We, the People." Second, that no institution of government is, or should be taken to be, the embodiment of society expressing the general will of the people.[94]

Only by creating a (tri)alectic of power between the three branches of government, can the rights of minorities be reconciled with the will of the majority in a way that allows the State to navigate toward an ostensibly just destination, though it may repeatedly tack right and left to get there.

## How the West was Run—Notions of a Constitutional Civilization

> The West won the world not by the superiority of its ideas or values or religion but rather by its superiority in applying organized violence.[95]

When Samuel P. Huntington made this statement, he was referring primarily to violence of a literal, military sort. Taken in another sense, however, it could be argued that the entire development of Western governance, at least internally, is one of restricting latent violence in society and between competing groups in any given state. Whether implicitly or explicitly, it is the channeling of social energies and conflicts into an institutional framework that has been the goal of most thinking about government since at least the era of the ancient Greeks. The frameworks have grown more nuanced and complex as societies have grown in

92 *Federalist 71*, pp. 483–4.
93 See *Federalist 51*.
94 Levi (1976), p. 376.
95 Huntington (1996), p. 51.

population and diversity, but the tri-fold constitutional concerns with the Rule of Law, political and institutional authenticity, and separating the functions and forms of government power into discrete branches have remained consistently present, albeit in radically different forms. Although there are many elements of constitutionalism in the West which are not addressed here, this trinity of constitutional values creates a cohesive system which can provide the state with purpose and stability, make it representative and legitimate, and balance its need to exercise power with the peoples' need to restrain the inexorable tendency of that power to expand into ever more spheres of life. In Cicero, Montesquieu, and *The Federalist* we have three texts which are universally considered part of the Western canon, which represent distinct developments in constitutionalism, and which lend themselves to a detailed analysis of how these individual elements of constitutionalism have originated and evolved through time.

Perhaps because of this type of narrative, Western ideology has traditionally been linear and universalist in its outlook, and this is reflected not only in various national constitutions, but also in the very titles of documents like "The Universal Declaration on Human Rights." The question that remains for comparative purposes is whether these qualities are indeed unique to Western civilization. Huntington's assertion that, "The great divisions among humankind and the dominating source of conflict will be cultural. The clash of civilizations will dominate global politics," may very well be true if the West is as unique he proposes. This is not, however, a foregone conclusion. The following chapters will directly address similar constitutional principles in an Islamic context in order to ascertain the validity of Kedourie and Huntington's theses regarding the compatibility of constitutional and Islamic thought.

## Chapter 3

# From Medina to Runnymede—Comparing the Foundational Legacies of the *Constitution of Medina* and the *Magna Carta*

If the *Magna Carta* is constitutive of the Anglo-American legal tradition—and, after all nearly a thousand federal and state courts in the United States have cited the *Magna Carta* in formal decisions, and, in the half-century between 1940 and 1990, the Supreme Court cited the text in over 60 cases—it is at the same time indebted to Roman, Saxon, Norman, and Church (canon) laws, customs, and practices.[1]

Surely the *Constitution of Medina* provides valuable information on the founding of the *umma* and its nature. There is nothing in the document concerning the *umma* which contradicts what the *Qur'an* says. The two sources are mutually confirmatory in many respects, and they supplement each other. The Constitution spells out in greater detail than the *Qur'an* the political structure of the Medinan community and the agreed upon military aspects of life, such as 'neighbourly protection', blood-wit, alliances, clients, and so on. The religious nature of the *umma* is, of course, to be learned above all from the *Qur'an*, but the practical detail needed for a fuller picture must come from other contemporary documents.[2] As the quotes above illustrate, both the *Magna Carta* and the *Constitution of Medina* are formative documents in their respective legal/constitutional traditions. A vast amount of scholarship has concerned itself with the *Magna Carta* in particular, and the literature regarding the *Constitution of Medina* is also becoming more expansive. Likewise, a small corpus of literature has emerged since the attacks of September 11, 2001, describing how Muslim states work, have failed, and so on. Other books and articles concern themselves with how the West became complacent and how it can best hinder terror plots.[3] Surprisingly, little to no work has been undertaken to understand the actual roots of these disparate

1 Worcester, Kent. "The Meaning and Legacy of the Magna Carta." *PS: Political Science & Politics*, 43:3 (2010): 452.

2 Denny, Frederick M. "Ummah in the Constitution of Medina." *Journal of Near Eastern Studies*, 36:1 (1977): 39–47.

3 Examples include *The Failure of Political Islam* by Olivier Roy (Cambridge, MA: Harvard University Press, 1994), Stephen Emerson's *Jihad Incorporated* (Amherst: Prometheus Books, 2006) and Gilles Kepel's *Jihad: The Trail of Political Islam* (Cambridge, MA: Harvard University Press, 2002).

constitutional narratives and traditions, and to compare them in such a way that their commonalities and distinctive elements can be usefully employed. As the continuing protests and political upheaval throughout the Muslim world show, the conventional wisdom which portrays Muslims as politically complacent or as opposed to 'Western' constitutional norms is now largely discredited. If these events and, more importantly, their potential ramifications, are to be understood, then it is essential that more work is done in understanding how these traditions may act and interact in a world that is highly interdependent and in which cultural and historical influences are subject to constant renegotiation.

In order to appreciate the Islamic constitutional tradition, it is helpful to consider the foundations upon which the constitutional frameworks of Western and Islamic governance have developed. The story of European forms of constitutionalism begins, in a philosophical sense, in classical Athens. From a practical perspective, however, the constitutional norms still in operation are largely considered to date back to one very particular time and document, the *Magna Carta* promulgated by King John of England in 1215. This is one of the oldest documents which still has force of law under some of its provisions and it explicitly influenced many subsequent constitutional regimes in a variety of Western contexts. Although its immediate impact was minimal, the legendary legal status and legitimacy it attained can be traced as follows:

> In 1225, the court of King Henry III prepared yet another version of the document, which the king stamped with his seal "in return for a grant of taxation from his subjects sufficient to pay for war in both France and England" (Vincent 2007, 19). Within a few decades, it became "virtually inconceivable that Henry III or his successors could in any way seek to annul Magna Carta" (Vincent 2007, 20). The 1225 version was transcribed onto England's first statute roll at the end of the thirteenth century, under the aegis of Henry's formidable heir, Edward I (see Carpenter 2003 and Morris 2009). By the middle of the following century, officers of the state were legally required to pledge to observe the terms of the charter. Three of its clauses remain statutory law in England and Wales.[4]

Although there are vast quantities of scholarship that dispute the relevance, intentions, and implications of the various provisions of the charter, the position taken in the context of this chapter is one which acknowledges that "the significance of *Magna Carta* lay not only in what it actually said, but perhaps to an even greater extent, in what later generations claimed and believed it had said."[5] Whatever the limited initial intentions of its authors were, the popular and political impact that *Magna Carta* retains is undeniable. As Tom Bingham notes in his history of the

4 Worcester (2010), p. 452.

5 Tom Bingham, *The Rule of Law* (London and New York: Allen Lane, 2010), p. 12. This same type of principle is behind debates about the importance and relevance of the 'original intent' of the US Founders in their writing of the US Constitution.

rule of law, "The myth proved a rallying point for centuries to come … more than 900 federal and state courts in the United States had cited the Magna Carta … between 1940 and 1990, the Supreme Court had done so in more than 60 cases."[6] Thus, despite the fact that the secular republican United States explicitly rejected British sovereignty in its founding, an ancient charter of an ecclesiastical and monarchical England continues to exercise a powerful hold on American legal discourse and popular imagination.[7]

There is little debate that Muslim civilization came into being under the inspiration and instigation of the Prophet of Islam, Muhammad. His first foray into government dates back to the very early days of his prophetic career, after the migration (*hijra*) to Medina in 622 CE.[8] So fundamental is this event, that it marks the beginning of the Islamic calendar system, which demonstrates the utter centrality of the relationship of faith and the establishment of the Muslim community in Islam. Although the earliest accounts of his government in Medina exist outside the *Qur'an*, the reporting of Ibn Ishaq in his *Life of Muhammad* is taken to be authentic.[9] If that is the case, then the very existence of a written covenant between Muhammad and his followers, including those who were not Muslims, provides the possibility of examining the principles which formed the core of Islamic government at its conception and which, given the status of Muhammad as exemplar for present-day Muslims, arguably establishes a legitimate basis for an authentically Islamic constitutional paradigm.

The idea of an Islamic constitutional tradition can be problematic in the light of orthodox Muslim understandings of the utter sovereignty and agency of God over the entire world, governments and governed alike. Leaving the nature and extent of God's sovereignty to the theologians, this examination of Muhammad's covenant with the residents of Medina is one which argues that where there is assent and accountability, there is, at least in a practical sense, agency. The very existence of this agreement, the fact that it lays out explicit expectations of the duties of various tribes and their rights to the benefits of society, its vision of the rule of law, all indicate that practicing Muslims and non-Muslims in Islamic states must codify and negotiate the various challenges of government, within the framework of a transcendent Law (*sharīʿa*). Although this means there will be reticence on behalf of some in claiming to be establishing constitutional law, even laws generally, which are seen as the exclusive province of God, it is nonetheless accepted that day to day questions of governing will require additional statutes

6 Bingham (2010), p. 13.

7 This is particularly ironic in light of Kent Worcester's recent introduction to a symposium on the legacy of *Magna Carta* (2010) in which he notes that "Strictly speaking, the original charter was valid only for a few weeks."

8 See Montgomery Watt's discussion of the controversy surrounding the date and unity of *the Constitution of Medina*, in his *Muhammad at Medina* (Karachi and New York: Oxford University Press, 1981), pp. 225–8.

9 Denny, 'Ummah', p. 39.

to be passed. It is on this basis that the various schools of Islamic law developed their *fiqh* (Islamic jurisprudence) and it is this understanding of law which allowed Muslim rulers to 'implement *sharīʿa*' through promulgating the necessary *qānūn* (statute) or using *siyāsa* (statecraft or management).[10]

Assessing the unique constitutional characteristics of Muhammad's covenant with the people of Medina alongside King John's concessions to the English nobles will reveal that each of these documents, while not properly constitutions, do concern themselves with particular duties and rights and define their respective polities (*umma*) in sometimes surprisingly contemporary ways.[11] Thus the texts in question are being analysed in terms of the political ideas and theory that inform them and which have been subsequently shaped by them. This section will narrow its focus to the following constitutional values. Firstly, how each of these documents defines and derives its legitimacy. Secondly, how they define their respective subjects. Finally, it engages with the rights and duties actually being codified. From this initial comparison it may be possible to set the stage to identify future avenues of discourse for scholars of constitutionalism and government more generally, including Western and Islamic views of the rule of law, the character of government and governed, or the role that religion can, does, or should play within the apparatus and limits of the state.

## The Origins and Lawfulness of the *Constitution of Medina* and *Magna Carta*

Before analyzing the texts themselves it is important to understand the contexts in which they were created and the ways in which they derived their legitimacy. As it is earlier and more difficult to establish in a clear context, the Constitution of Medina will be examined first. This document, or possibly amalgamation of documents, which is recorded in Ibn Ishaq's *Life of Muhammad*, serves as the earliest known model of Islamic government.[12] More importantly, it originates from the time when Muhammad himself was leader of both the Muslim and non-Muslim communities of Medina, which makes this text an obvious potential exemplar for those wishing to govern in an Islamic fashion. It also accounts for the possibility of an Islamic pluralism that allows for peaceful religious coexistence within a Muslim state.

10 Vatikiotis, P.J. *Islam and the State*. London and New York: Croom Helm, 1987: pp. 38–9. See also *The Encyclopedia of Islam* for detailed discussions of various words associated with law and legal questions in Islam.

11 Watt, W. Montgomery. *Muhammad at Medina*. Karachi and New York: Oxford University Press, 1981, p. 228. It is important to state that this is not a historical exercise. In the case of the Constitution of Medina it is nearly impossible to confidently make historically-based arguments, as there is little agreement as to exactly when it was written, and even as to its documentary origins

12 Ibn Hisham, Abd al-Malik, Muhammad Ibn Ishaq, and Alfred Guillaume. *The Life of Muhammad*. London, New York: Oxford University Press, 1955.

Due to its longstanding existence as a document independent of the *Qur'an* and *hadith*, yet one which nonetheless is compatible with them, the *Constitution of Medina* can potentially serve as an exemplary and foundational constitutional text for even those Muslims for whom their religious identity is more cultural and historical.[13] It can accommodate a wide variety of interpretations, as to who can be included in the *umma*, what the rights and duties of the ruler and ruled are, and what the fundamental role of the state is. In other words, just as the *Magna Carta* serves a mythical role in Western jurisprudence that far outstrips the particularities of its provisions, so too might the *Constitution of Medina* provide a model of basic societal values, customs and institutions for Muslim societies.

One important caveat about the *Constitution of Medina* must be made before further discussion of its features. The works of Uri Rubin and R.B. Serjeant show that to call it a constitution at all is simply a convenience rather than an accurate descriptor. Furthermore, there is debate amongst scholars as to whether the "Constitution" was written as a unitary document. Documentary evidence supports the contention that it originates from the period just after the *hijra* to Medina, when Muhammad became judge and arbiter of that city. Furthermore, much of the text finds echoes in the *Qur'an* itself, with many passages being nearly identical. However, in his 1978 journal article, R.B. Serjeant lays out the original composition and discusses the authenticity of the *Constitution of Medina* in great detail. He makes the following claims:

> The eight documents of which it is formed are doubtless traditional in pattern and diction, not at all novel to the age, and comprise the following distinct elements.
>
> A. The confederation treaty
> B. Supplement to confederation treaty A (These two pacts A and B are to be considered as al-Sunnat al-Jdmi'ah cited in the arbitration treaty between 'Alli [*sic*] and Mu'awiyah.)
> C. Treaty defining the status of the Jewish tribes in the confederation
> D. Supplement to the treaty (C) defining the status of the Jewish tribes
> E. Reaffirmation of the status of the Jews
> F. Proclamation of Yathrib a sacred enclave (haram)
> G. Treaty concluded prior to Khandaq among the Arabs of Yathrib and with the Jewish Qurayzah, to defend it from Quraysh of Mecca and their allies
> H. Codicil to the proclamation of Yathrib a sacred enclave (haram)
>
> The two early versions of the text at present known to me are that of Ibn Ishaq which is the basis of the version given below, and that of Ab-i 'Ubayd which

13 It should be noted that this document is sometimes included in the *sunna* of the Prophet and thus carries added legitimacy for those who hold this view.

> is defective. The late copy of Isma'il b. Muhammad Ibn Kathir has also been consulted. Ibn Ishaq's text ... looks substantially reliable and correct...[14]

Contradicting this point of view, Michael Lecker contends that Serjeant's argument is unconvincing as it is based on "ethnological data relating to contemporary Yemen, in addition to comparative evidence from the primary sources."[15] The fact that the document is comprised of these complementary and contemporaneous elements, whether or not it is a unitary work, means that the discussion that follows will look at it as presented by Ibn Ishaq in the singular form which it ultimately came to possess.

The Medinan period occurred after intense persecution of Muhammad and his followers in Mecca forced them to uproot and settle elsewhere. Having heard of his gift of prophecy, he was invited to Medina to act as a judge (*hakam*) to mediate disputes between the various clans and clan chiefs.[16] In Western terms, Muhammad was *primus inter pares* (first amongst equals) and the intent of the invitation did not include changing the status quo of power relationships within Mecca beyond recognizing him as a prophet able to give rulings on behalf of God.[17]

In much the same way that the Roman Republic gradually ceded its authority quite willingly to the able and magnetic Caesar, so the Arab tribes of Medina, and eventually of the whole Arabian Peninsula, accepted the rule of a conscientious, able, and charismatic Prophet. What makes the *Constitution of Medina* so interesting to study is that it originates in a period where the political authority of Muhammad was relatively rudimentary. Although the actual document cannot be seen to have played any formative role in Muslim regimes after the time of Muhammad and the rightly guided Caliphs, one may still ask if this very early covenant's core values of limited pluralism, tolerance and minority autonomy[18] were the foundations of what would later become a framework and finally an entire politico-religious structure, one that would survive the death of its founder to eventually hold sway over most of the over 1.6 billion self-identified Muslims who still acknowledge Muhammad's authority to this day?

---

14 Serjeant, R.B. "The "Sunnah Jāmi'ah," Pacts with the Ya<u>th</u>rib Jews, and the "Taḥrīm" of Ya<u>th</u>rib: Analysis and Translation of the Documents Comprised in the So-Called 'Constitution of Medina'." *Bulletin of the School of Oriental and African Studies, University of London*, 41:1 (1978): 9. See also, pp. 5–10.

15 Lecker, Michael. *The "Constitution of Medina": Muhammad's First Legal Document*, Studies in Late Antiquity and Early Islam. Princeton, NJ: Darwin Press, 2004, pp. 3–4.

16 Berkey, Jonathan Porter. *The Formation of Islam: Religion and Society in the near East, 600–1800*, Themes in Islamic History V. 2. New York: Cambridge University Press, 2003, p. 68.

17 Watt, W. Montgomery. *Muhammad at Mecca*. Oxford: Clarendon Press, 1953, p. 238.

18 Granted, these are conditioned upon the caveat that disputes between groups be submitted to Muhammad, and presumably after his death to some idea of a higher law that is at minimum inspired by and compatible with *sharī'a*.

To begin with, Ibn Ishaq simply relates that "The apostle wrote a document concerning the emigrants and the helpers in which he made a friendly agreement with the Jews and established them in their religion and their property, and stated the reciprocal obligations."[19] This seems an odd introduction for something that could potentially be referred to as a type of constitution. In the first place, it only mentions an agreement between the "emigrants and the helpers" and the Jews, rather than with the people of Medina, as one might expect. It clearly delineates a separate identity between the Muslims and the Jews rather than a unified populace. What one may assume is that this served the purposes of Ishaq's narrative in explaining the eventual falling out between Muhammad and the Jews, an assumption bolstered by the fact that Muhammad himself went on to contradict this division when he asserted that various groups of Jews are "one community with the believers."[20] The precise nature of the community aside, the authority by which Muhammad propagated this covenant with the various Medinan communities is one which is based primarily on secular and pre-Muslim customs that are then imbued with religious meaning. The existence of clan and tribal chiefs who acted as community judges was nothing new, nor was the recognition of someone as having the gift of prophecy or the ability to transmit revelations from God. The innovative part of the equation occurs in the exclusivity of Muhammad's message. He alone was the current Prophet and his God alone was God. At first glance this would seem to primarily create division. In fact it was instead a mechanism through which the old divisions created by the worship of different deities could be overwritten and subsumed under a universal and inspirational calling to serve the one God of all people. This leads Muhammad to create a new *umma* (literally 'people') that is comprised not of blood ties but of spiritual brotherhood. Frederick Denny notes the following in his article '*Ummah* in the Constitution of Medina':

> The *ummah* of the Constitution is made up of believers and Muslims, and quite possibly Jews as well (although they may constitute a separate *ummah* 'alongside'). All the kinship groups mentioned are subsumed under this *ummah* idea, a very significant fact. But why are the believers distinguished from the Muslims? ... It is probable that *mu'minūn* throughout the document means just what it means in the *Qur'an*: 'believers'. ... This preponderance of *mu'min* may indicate an early date for much of the Constitution, before *muslim* was used as the name for the followers of Muhammad, or at least before it gained a clear technical sense limited to the followers of Muhammad. Of course, it had a deep religious sense before the time of the Constitution, describing the human approach to God pre-scribed in the Revelation.[21]

---

19 Ishaq (1955), p. 231.
20 Ibid., p. 233.
21 Denny (1977), p. 43.

This group then, constitutes another layer of identity that contains many of the same tribal obligations and expectations that existed previously, except that these obligations have gone from exclusively within one's clan and tribe to a potentially universal scope. It is particularly interesting to see that the term *muslim* was not one necessarily exclusively used for those who accepted Muhammad as prophet, but rather included all those who submitted to God in the way his and earlier prophetic traditions required. Rather than being the exclusive provenance of committed followers of Muhammad then, the community at Medina and subsequent Islamic regimes (including that of the religiously tolerant and pluralistic Mughals on the Indian sub-continent) can be legitimately described as belonging to all who show submission to God, which again is a potentially universal ideal, depending upon how submission is defined.

Ultimately, the authority which undergirds the *Constitution of Medina* is simultaneously spiritual and secular, traditional and radical.[22] Muhammad's genius is clear in the way he transformed his role as God's vessel and voice into judge, apostle, general, and exemplar of the faith. He could have, like the Christian Apostle Paul, de-emphasized temporal identities in order to place the focus solely on one's spiritual identity.[23] Instead, Muhammad was happy to keep the existing social order intact as it provided him with opportunities for mass conversions by entire tribes, an infrastructure that managed law and order within smaller more manageable groups, and a steady stream of soldiers who could assist him in defense and in his conquest of the Arabian Peninsula. His unity was also one of believers, but this did not negate their previous social relationships. Indeed, those "that have kinship by blood are closer to one another in the Book of God than the believers who are not kindred."[24]

Thus, it is unsurprising that he opens his contract by saying, "This is a document from Muhammad the prophet governing the relations between the believers and Muslims of Quraysh and Yathrib, and those who followed them and joined them and labored with them."[25] He goes on to acknowledge Jews belonging to groups like Banu al-Najjar, al-Harith, etc. Amongst Muslims he specifies the Banu ʿAwf, the Quraysh and others. The invitation to arbitrate disputes between these tribes was precisely the opening in the tribal power structure that would allow Muhammad and his message to become its centre. If God spoke through Muhammad, then who could disobey his revelation requiring all disputes between the tribes to be referred to God, and consequently to Muhammad?[26] This revelation is then codified in the *Constitution of Medina* when Muhammad explicitly states to all the Medinans,

---

22 It is important to note that this discussion of spiritual and secular authority is a modern construct. For Muhammad, this conceptual split would not have existed.

23 See for example Galatians 3:28, where Paul says "There is neither Jew nor Greek, slave nor free, male nor female, for you are all one in Christ Jesus" (NIV).

24 *Qur'an* 33:6, cited in Antony Black, *The History of Islamic Political Thought* (Edinburgh: Edinburgh University Press, 2001), p. 11.

25 Ishaq (1955), pp. 231–2.

26 Watt (1981), p. 230.

Muslim or not, that "Whenever you differ about a matter it must be referred to God and to Muhammad."[27] The authority of the state thus rests on its adherence to the message and example of Muhammad which is a direct revelation of the very word and will of God himself. A citizen could conceivably accept and follow this human example, even if he or she did not share his beliefs in whole or part.

Perhaps because it was necessitated in part by a religious dispute and a resulting crisis that at one point led to King John's temporary excommunication, the *Magna Carta* opens not by combining spiritual and secular offices, but by reaffirming the Christian tradition of assigning each power to its own unique sphere. The goals of *Magna Carta* were to allow King John to reconcile with the lords and barons who had been in revolt against his ruinous abuse of feudal taxation and land use privileges whilst at the same time reaffirming the independence of the church from the Crown and publicly affirming the King's acceptance of the Vatican's choice for Archbishop of Canterbury.[28] The essential and often overlooked function of the *Magna Carta* as a document which guaranteed the independence of the church is, according to political theorist Cary Nederman, that individual freedom is not

> ... the only way in which the language of liberty is employed in the Magna Carta. In both the first and the final articles of the charter—and at several places in between—the text refers to another sort of liberty: the liberty of the Church. Indeed, Article 1 begins with King John's declaration that he has 'in the first place granted to God and by this our present Charter confirmed, for us and our heirs in perpetuity, that the English church is to be free (*Anglicana ecclesiastica libera sit*), and shall have its rights undiminished and its liberties unimpaired.[29]

The very idea that the Church and the State could inhabit different spheres is clearly one which is in stark contrast to traditional Islamic notions of the State, which conceive of State and Religion as conjoined twins that are utterly inseparable. There is however, a commonality in the concern that secular power not be allowed to infringe upon the higher prerogatives of religious authority. Indeed, it could even be argued that the Medieval Church, in some respects, aspired to exactly the same type of political-religious fusion of power and universal domination that traditional views of proper Islamic governance espouse.[30]

27 Ishaq (1955), p. 232.

28 See the excellent overview of the historical context of Magna Carta at the website of the British Library.

29 Nederman, Cary J. "The Liberty of the Church and the Road to Runnymede: John of Salisbury and the Intellectual Foundations of the Magna Carta." *PS: Political Science & Politics*, 43:3 (2010): 457.

30 A classic example of a Muslim juristic view of the state can be seen in Mawardi's *The Ordinances of Government*. Likewise, the Catholic Church is replete with examples of popes who exercised substantial temporal power, for instance Julius the 'Warrior Pope'.

King John's (1215) opening statement gives a clear indication of the authority on which its legitimacy rests. "JOHN, by the grace of God King of England, Lord of Ireland, Duke of Normandy and Aquitaine, and Count of Anjou..." God's grace is superficially acknowledged before the King's titles and the power they reveal over various lands are placed on display. He is King, Lord, Duke, and Count (at least in name) over a sizeable kingdom. These titles are not those of prophet, priest, or judge, but of raw earthly power and each of them denote his status at the top of the feudal pecking order. Perhaps because the text to follow was really a series of compromises and capitulations to the Church on one hand (the King had recognized the Pope as overlord in a successful bid to gain church support for his rule) and the barons on the other, King John felt it necessary to begin the document with a show of strength. This show is short-lived however, for in the very next paragraph he acknowledges that the terms were largely dictated to him by the "advice" of "our reverend fathers Stephen, archbishop of Canterbury, primate of all England, and cardinal of the holy Roman Church, Henry archbishop of Dublin ... [various other bishops] ... Master Pandulf subdeacon and member of the papal household, Brother Aymeric master of the knighthood of the Temple in England, William Marshal earl of Pembroke, William earl of Salisbury ... [and several other lords and barons] ... and other loyal subjects." One can only imagine how much pride he had to swallow to call rebellious lords his "loyal subjects."[31]

Clause 1 of the *Magna Carta* is one of the few parts of the document that still retains legal force; it serves to reinforce the King's role as sovereign in ordering his kingdom but at the same time contains the strongest possible assertions of the rights of the Church and of all "free men." In it, John says that "We have granted to God ... that the English Church shall be free, and that it shall have its rights undiminished, and its liberties unimpaired." Even though the whole clause is an affirmation of rights that the King cannot transgress, he claims that it is he, King John who "has granted to God" that these rights will be respected. This could be because even though Christianity itself does not make claims to temporal authority or have an explicit legal or political program, it does assert that "there is no authority except that which God has established."[32] Indeed, the Church of the Middle Ages was both political and powerful and was content to flex its might through the muscle of whatever local king was in authority. The monarchs themselves had little choice to resist since their faith taught them that the Church held the one and only key to the salvation of their souls. What ultimately sets the legitimacy of the *Magna Carta* apart from the *Constitution of Medina* is that the religious power undergirding the document is willingly subverted to the secular legal power even while it is simultaneously the implicit force behind the King's authority and arbiter of his eternal destiny.

---

31 King John, 1215. *Magna Carta* (Preamble). British Library Treasures Online, [Online], Available at: http://www.bl.uk/treasures/magnacarta/index.html [accessed 17 August 2009].

32 See Romans 13:1.

Of course, constitutional documents are never merely statements of authority or legitimacy. They are traditionally conceived as social contracts between both *ruler* and *ruled* or the *government* and the *governed.* In order to assess the legacies of these foundational texts it is therefore vital that one ascertain exactly which groups in society are being addressed. Who are the subjects or citizens who will be bound by the constitution?

### *Defining the Subject: The Object(s) of Authority in the* Constitution of Medina *and* Magna Carta

As alluded to earlier, the *Constitution of Medina* is a document that subverts, elevates, and recreates tribal identities and obligations by placing them largely intact under a new umbrella identity. Uri Rubin argues that "the name of the new unity declared by the 'Constitution' is '*umma*'. Western scholars ... were aware of the fact that it must be examined according to its meaning in the *Qur'an*, where, in most relevant cases, it has a pure religious connotation."[33] Rubin goes on to point out that in the opening of the constitution it states that "They are one *umma* to the exclusion of all men", which in its original form joins *umma* with *waḥida.* In all nine instances where the phrase *umma waḥida,* or singular people, occurs in the *Qur'an* it always "denotes people united by a common *religious* orientation." In other words, the Muslims and the Jews of Medina comprise a unified body that shares the same religion in distinction to those who practice other faiths.[34] So, in the first instance, the people with whom Muhammad makes his covenant are qualified for "citizenship" based upon their faith.[35]

Lest one doubt the inclusion of the Jews, he continues by saying "To the Jew who follows us belong help and equality. He shall not be wronged ... The peace of the believers is indivisible."[36] Those who are not of the monotheistic Abrahamic

33 Rubin, Uri. "The "Constitution of Medina" Some Notes." *Studia Islamica*, 62 (1985): 12.

34 Ibid., p. 13. It is unclear how the status of *dhimmi*, or protected peoples, applies to this passage. It could be that because this is prior to the definitive split between Muhammad and the Arab Jews, their monotheism and tacit acceptance of his leadership were enough to consider them part of the *umma* without additional distinction. Alternatively, the fact that many of the Jews were already clients of Arab tribes would make such a distinction redundant.

35 The use of *umma* in the sense of spiritual brotherhood being emphasized prior to political brotherhood is not intended to contradict claims that *umma* "is basically a political confederation", but rather highlights the further point that these confederations were "usually theocratic." See R.B. Serjeant (1978), pp. 4–5. Serjeant makes the further point that "The Jews, when Muhammad made the confederation pacts after his arrival in Yathrib, were included in the ummah; 'through the peace (sulh) which took place between them and the Mu'miniin "Believers" they became like a collective body (jami'ah) of them, with a single word and hand'."

36 Ishaq, *Life of Muhammad*, p. 232.

faiths are *not* included in the social contract and regardless of their tribal ties to those within Mecca exist definitively outside of the protection of the community at large. Muhammad could not be any clearer on this point when he writes that "Believers are friends one to the other to the exclusion of outsiders."[37]

In addition to being a community or *umma* based upon faith, Medina was also a polity based upon the establishment of sacred territory, or *haram*. This basis finds echoes in the West in Hobbes and others who locate the basis of obligation between a citizen and the state in the state's role in protecting and preserving the lives of its citizens. Thus Rubin notes that some traditions hold that Muhammad declared Medina to be sacred, therefore elevating it to the same religious status as Mecca, before the crucial battle against Mecca just two years after the *Hijra*. This would mean that the natives of Medina, or *Yathrib*, would be expected to protect and defend their sacred ground in the same manner that the Quraysh would protect the holy precincts of Mecca.[38] This basis of community originating from a desire to band together for the common defense is a regular feature of constitutional documents. What is interesting is that Muhammad's declaration of *haram* endows it with religious significance it would not otherwise have and reasserts the centrality of religious belief and faith in the formation of his polity. He goes on to assert:

> The Jews must bear their expenses and the Muslims their expenses. Each must help the other against anyone who attacks the people of this document ... The Jews must pay with the believers as long as war lasts. Yathrib shall be a sanctuary (*haram*) for the people of this document.[39]

Like any other constitution then, this document creates an *us* and a *them*, allowing for the new *umma* to express itself not only by its positive affirmation of monotheism and residence in Medina, but also in its opposition to polytheism and its defence against outsiders and attackers.[40]

The emphasis on common religion and territory in the *Constitution of Medina* should not completely obscure its continued recognition of pre-existing family and tribal relationships, which continued to be relevant well after Islam became the established faith of Arabia. As mentioned previously, it consistently refers to groups based on tribal identity, particularly when it discusses Jewish clients of various Arab tribes.[41] The Quraysh and Tha'laba are distinguished from other tribes. In essence, the polity Muhammad sought to establish could be expressed in

37 Ishaq (1955), p. 232.

38 Rubin (1985), p. 11.

39 Ishaq (1955), p. 233.

40 It is important to note that a large number of henotheists remained unmolested in Medina, provided that they not foment rebellion with their co-religionists against the Muslims.

41 Rubin (1985), pp. 5–9.

three iterations, a tribal polity, a territorial polity, and finally and most importantly, a religious polity.[42]

Once again, the *Magna Carta* proves to be more monolithic in its definition of polity. After reaffirming the independence of the church the rest of the document lays out the rights of "all free men." Left out of the protections are the peasants who had feudal bonds to their lords that required them to work without compensation, and kept them in a state of perpetual near slavery. The basis of the community falling under his protection as king is one that is purely territorial, as is made clear when "all free men" is followed by the further stipulation that they are "of my kingdom."[43] Though ostensibly free, in essence nobody in the feudal framework was free of the rigid social hierarchy that extended from king to peasant with its corresponding set of duties and honors owed to those higher up the chain. Even the barons were required to provide military service or a quota of troops from their manors financed at their own expense upon the king's request. It was only under King John and his unprecedented abuse of this system that the lords felt the need to rebel and to assert that even the rights of the king himself came with their attendant duties. It is this dichotomy along with the fact that the *Magna Carta* makes law supreme over even the king that makes it a constitutional document rather than simply a royal decree.

## Rights, Duties, and Their Respective Parties

The rights and duties spelled out in each of these documents range from the specific and time-bound to the universal and timeless. In Muhammad's contract there is far less emphasis on the duties imposed on Muhammad than on those required of the people of Medina. Instead the obligations spelled out are primarily those owed by one particular group within society to another. The duties and rights spelled out here can be split into those dealing with internal disputes and crimes and those dealing with external threats and war. The definition of internal and external is, as already discussed, both territorial and spiritual and both requirements must be met for the provisions of this document to be in force.

Internal duties include payment of blood money, avenging those wrongfully killed, providing hospitality and taking unresolved disputes to Muhammad. These imply the right of individuals to be recompensed for damages or deaths regardless of cause, along with the rights of people to obtain hospitality when in need and to have access to a judge to resolve disputes.[44]

---

42 Although tribal identities remained intact, the new stipulation that arbitration was taken out of the tribal context and that instead disputants had recourse to Muhammad and the Quran gradually affected the tribal dynamic and arguably subverted this identity to a Muslim identity.

43 *Magna Carta*, Clause 1.

44 Ishaq (1955), pp. 232–3.

In reference to outsiders, the Constitution states "A believer shall not slay a believer for the sake of an unbeliever, nor shall he aid an unbeliever against a believer" (a negative duty). No matter what tribal affinities one may have, that of belief supersedes any other. In a similar manner, "believers must avenge the blood of one another shed in the way of God" (a positive duty). This defensive obligation extends to a territorial definition when Muhammad specifies that the "contracting parties are bound to help one another against any attack on Yathrib." The focus on war extends to raiding parties and offensive battles which present the opportunities for spoils from which "everyone shall have his portion from the side to which he belongs."[45]

If this document is to be considered truly constitutional, however, it must place some sort of restraint upon the ruler so that the contract itself is truly binding and cannot simply be changed by the will of the ruler. This criterion is clearly not met in the text itself. Aside from requiring Muhammad to fulfill his role as judge, the only other requirement placed upon him is to give his permission for parties to go out to war and by inference to protect 'the good and God-fearing man' since God is their protector and he, Muhammad, is 'the apostle of God'.[46] However, one could easily argue that this restraint is implicit and must be understood in the context of the ruler being subject to the *Qur'an*, and therefore limited in many substantive ways. At the very least, the *Constitution of Medina* certainly does not advocate autocracy and its nod to minority autonomy limits power implicitly, much as the authors of the *Federalist Papers* argue that the very division of power into different branches acts as a check upon potential abuse of that power in any one of the branches.

Unfortunately for King John, he did not inspire the same level of devotion that Muhammad did. His tyrannical actions cost him the trust of his people and so his charter primarily restricts his power and obligates him to respect a wide range of rights and privileges, all the while gaining nothing more than a reaffirmation of long-established duties from his nobles. In the interest of brevity, only the clauses which remain in force will be discussed here. First amongst the rights specified is that of the English church to be free from influence by the Crown.[47] Secondly Clause 13 states that, "The city of London shall enjoy all its ancient

45 Ibid.

46 Ibid., p. 233.

47 *Magna Carta*, Clause 1: "FIRST, THAT WE HAVE GRANTED TO GOD, and by this present charter have confirmed for us and our heirs in perpetuity, that the English Church shall be free, and shall have its rights undiminished, and its liberties unimpaired. That we wish this so to be observed, appears from the fact that of our own free will, before the outbreak of the present dispute between us and our barons, we granted and confirmed by charter the freedom of the Church's elections—a right reckoned to be of the greatest necessity and importance to it—and caused this to be confirmed by Pope Innocent III. This freedom we shall observe ourselves, and desire to be observed in good faith by our heirs in perpetuity."

liberties and free customs, both by land and by water. We also will and grant that all other cities ... shall enjoy all their liberties and free customs." This can be broadly interpreted to support the right of localities to self-determination on local issues. It also demonstrates reluctance to micro-manage the affairs of the state and affirms the legitimacy of the layers of government that exist below the level of the monarch or head of state. The king could have qualified this statement with the addition of a phrase such as, "so long as these liberties do not impinge upon the good of the realm," but he chose not to do so and went so far as to call these liberties "ancient," which would seem to bolster their legitimacy even further.

Finally, Clause 39, which deals with the fundamental right of *habeas corpus*, is perhaps the most relevant and important of the clauses still in effect. Tom Bingham's book *The Rule of Law* refers to this writ as "the most effective remedy against executive lawlessness that the world has ever seen."[48] This clause protects all free men from being "seized or imprisoned, or stripped of his rights or possessions, or outlawed or exiled, or deprived of his standing in any other way." He points out that originally, *habeas corpus ad subjiciendum* simply meant that a person in custody had to be made available to a judge.[49] It was only later that this practice was used to ensure that the lawfulness of a person's detention was examined or to protect individual liberty. However, the evolutionary process which produced *habeas corpus* as it is now conceived nonetheless is traceable to the belief that it is an essential precept in *Magna Carta*.[50] No less a legal luminary that Sir Edward Coke, who was involved in the seventeenth century effort to rebuke monarchical abuses of judicial power, argued in favor of Parliament's 1628 *Petition of Right* on the basis that detention was forbidden by the charter without "due process of law," and that the only way to ensure such due process was through the mechanism of the writ of *habeas corpus*.[51] It also enshrines the institution of jury trials in that punishment may only occur "by the lawful judgment of his equals or by the law of the land."[52] To all of these guarantees is added the extra protection of Clause 40 which states: "To no one will we sell, to no one deny or delay right or justice," thus protecting the citizen and the state from the corrosive effects of corruption and indefinite detention without charge. The totality of these clauses provides a substantial bulwark for the protection of individual liberty, even if the scope of that liberty was highly restricted at its conception. Thus, while the attribution of *habeas corpus* and its related protections may not be due to *Magna Carta* in

48 Bingham (2010), p. 14.

49 Literally, "you may have the body subject to examination."

50 Bingham (2010), pp. 13–14.

51 Wert, Justin J. "With a Little Help from a Friend: Habeas Corpus and the Magna Carta after Runnymede." *PS: Political Science & Politics*, 43:3 (2010): 476.

52 The clause reads in full: "No free man shall be seized or imprisoned, or stripped of his rights or possessions, or outlawed or exiled, or deprived of his standing in any other way, nor will we proceed with force against him, or send others to do so, except by the lawful judgment of his equals or by the law of the land."

a strictly historical sense, they are clear developments upon the clauses of the original document and were advocated as such by those who strengthened and codified these protections in subsequent generations. Here it is helpful to consider Justin Wert's concluding remarks on the myth of *habeas corpus* and jury trial as latent in *Magna Carta*:

> Nevertheless, the very fact that the substantive and procedural due process rights that both the Magna Carta and habeas corpus have protected through the centuries have varied considerably—even in negative directions—is proof enough of their liberty-regarding potential. In this sense, our acceptance of less than accurate histories is, at the very least, testament to our normative preference for more capacious notions of personal rights and liberties.
>
> In his 1914 article critiquing Whiggish accounts of Magna Carta, Charles McIlwain came to the conclusion that while some modern rights, like trial by jury, were never implied in the document in the way that we imagine today, "we may still hold, as our fathers did, that the law of the land is there" (McIlwain 1914, 51). Intentional or not, then, the wisdom of the barons who managed to secure feudal rights at Runnymede was present in the framing of procedural rights—like *legem terrae*—that were specific enough to protect their most immediate substantive concerns but, fortuitously, general enough to remind us that there is still work left to be done.[53]

It would seem then, that the emphasis on the rule of law as an ideal that exists above and apart from the head of state, becomes in *Magna Carta* an inherent characteristic of the state itself and of the nation it governs. The reciprocal duties and rights it lays out are important not merely because their codification is binding, but also because they define the scope of the state and the limits of the ruler's power. It is little wonder then, that despite its very specific context, that *Magna Carta* is considered *the* founding document for the establishment of individual rights as being a fundamental part of the constitutional order. From it, one can trace the key principles enshrined in the United States' *Bill of Rights* and its subsequent emulators in various states and international institutions.

## From Medina to Al-Azhar: Is Qur'anic Government an Open Book? Ali 'Abd al-Raziq and the Argument for Muslim Self-determination

In direct contrast to this argument that one can directly trace the constitutional values both explicit and implicit in most of the world's constitutions to *Magna Carta*, is Ali 'Abd al-Raziq's argument about the relationship (or lack thereof) between the *Qur'an* and the state. It may therefore seem somewhat counterproductive to

53 Wert (2010), pp. 477–8.

entertain al-Raziq's notions of this relationship in an analysis of the *Constitution of Medina* and *Magna Carta*. His 1925 *Islam and the Bases of Power* caused an immediate stir and encountered criticism from a variety of quarters, even from Muslim modernists like Rashid Rida, and in the process lost him his post and judgeship at al-Azhar.[54] However, despite the fact that his argument revolves around emphasizing Muhammad's role as Prophet, and delegitimizing arguments that he was also a ruler, its general contours dovetail nicely with the constitutional values latent in the Medina document and it also illustrates the way in which the document could be seen to advocate certain values, without necessarily arguing for religiously-based institutional arrangements.

In direct contrast to what many Orientalists claim about the nature of Muhammad's leadership, and indeed what many Muslim thinkers also claim, al-Raziq creates a dichotomy of power before analyzing the particular type of power Muhammad exercised, saying that study to determine whether or not Muhammad was a king or not "falls outside the area of those beliefs which the *'ulama* have treated and on which they profess well-established opinions. It belongs more to the area of scientific research than to that of religion. Let the reader follow us without fear and with a tranquil soul."[55] What is clear is that this scholar from the renowned al-Azhar is well aware that his audience may view this parsing of power as heretical and/or unorthodox. Placing political discussion in the realm of science, rather than as a social or religious concern is essential because it places the conversation back within the bounds of independent reasoning and means that any solutions proposed are simply contingent ideas for a very particular time and place, avoiding any claims or competition with the timeless *sharī'a*. One may be tempted to think that his discussion will obscure the historical record of Muhammad's leadership or that he will be forced to deny certain events, but instead he fully embraces the *Qur'anic* and the *hadith* accounts of his life. He argues that Muhammad's primary role was as a Messenger from God, and that "The Message also requires its carrier to have the kind of strength, which will prepare him to influence the minds of the people so that they will heed his call ... 'We have sent no apostle but that he should be obeyed by the will of God' (*Qur'an*, Sura 4, Verse 64)."[56] In other words, it is obvious that as one who would convey God's final and perfect revelation Muhammad would have to have many attributes of leadership. Indeed,

> The Messenger may tackle the politics of his people as a king would, but the Prophet has a unique duty which he shares with no one, namely to communicate with the souls embedded in bodies, and to remove visual obstacles in order to

54 Kurzman, Charles. *Liberal Islam: A Source Book*. New York: Oxford University Press, 1998, p. 29.

55 Al-Raziq, Ali 'Abd. *Islam and the Bases of Power*, in Donohue, John J., and John L. Esposito. *Islam in Transition: Muslim Perspectives*. New York: Oxford University Press, 1982, p. 29.

56 Al-Raziq, in Kurzman (2004), p. 30.

> look upon the hearts embedded in chests. He has the right, nay, he must open up the hearts of his followers in order to reach the sources of love and hate, of good and evil, the passages of thought, the places of obsessions, the origins of intentions, the repository of morality … He directs the politics of the worldly living and that of the next world.[57]

What al-Raziq does in this passage is to elevate the role of Messenger above any other earthly role, including that of king, which means that anyone who ascribes political roles to Muhammad is consequently diminishing his status. This is augmented by his claim that Muhammad's call was "a religious call, full of religiosity, untainted by a tendency to kingship or a call for government."[58] Given that the Caliphate had become a rather obvious contrivance by the time it was abolished in the year prior to this book's publication, it is not surprising that al-Raziq would view government as a taint. In many respects, this line of logic makes perfect sense if someone wished to protect a perfect revelation from dilution or infection. Once one begins to mix kingship with the role of Prophet, one is very possibly mixing the sacred and the profane. The one exception to this, according to al-Raziq, is the leadership of Muhammad because he had qualities that far surpassed those of kings, whilst at the same time subsuming the roles of a king within a larger religious duty. However, this does not mean that those who came after him maintained this same calling from God. In effect, the general focus on al-Raziq's advocacy for a completely open approach to government in Muslim states and his denial of a political role for Muhammad misses the larger point that he is delegitimizing the very idea of deputyship or the Caliphate. Muhammad is no longer in the world or of the world, and so his leadership has passed and his special role as Prophet and lawgiver cannot be replicated.[59]

Lest one be tempted to doubt the religious bona fides of his argument, he marshals a vast assortment of verses from the *Qur'an* to support his contentions, as seen in the following passage:

> The Glorious *Qur'an* supports the view that the Prophet, peace be upon him, had nothing to do with political kingship. *Qur'anic* verses are in agreement … "He who obeys the Messenger obeys God; and if some turn away (remember) we have not sent you as a warden over them." (Sura 4, Verse 80) … "So follow what is revealed to you by your Lord, for homage is due to no one but God, and turn away from idolaters. Had He willed it, they would not have been idolaters.

57 Ibid., pp. 30–1.

58 Ibid., p. 29.

59 Ibid., pp. 30–1. See especially, Sections 3 and 4, which include the statement that "The Messenger's trusteeship over his people is a spiritual trusteeship whose origin is faith from the heart, and the heart's true submission followed by the submission of the body. On the other hand, the trusteeship of the ruler is a material one. It depends on subduing bodies without the heart."

> We have not appointed you their guardian, nor are you their pleader." (Sura 6, Verses 106–107)... "Say: 'O people, the truth has come to you from your Lord, so he who follows the right path does so for himself, and he who goes astray errs against himself, and I am not a guardian over you'." (Sura 10, Verse 108)... "We are cognizant of what they say; but it is not for you to compel them. So keep on reminding through the *Qur'an* whoever fears my warning." (Sura 50, Verse 45) "Remind them: you are surely a reminder. You are not a warden over them, other than him who turns his back and denies, in which case he will be punished by God with the severest punishment." (Sura 88, Verses 21–24)[60]

This laundry list of scriptural verses may not be the typical manner of conducting a political philosophy debate, but al-Raziq is clearly engaging with an audience he knows will be critical on their home turf. He is more than able to summon the authority of the *Qur'an* to make his points, as his opponents are able to summon other verses that may contradict him. In either case, he creates a win-wins scenario for himself because one must conclude that either he is right and that Muhammad was a Messenger, and a very special one, but not a king, or one must conclude that the *Qur'an* leaves the issue of the nature of Muhammad's authority up for debate, even as it very consistently locates the source of that authority in God. This is an essential result for al-Raziq's argument for two reasons. Firstly, it demonstrates that the authority of the state is not bound with its religion, and as such leaves open the possibility of popular sovereignty as a source for government legitimacy. Secondly, it relegates the political to a lesser sphere subject to the religious rule of God, which would make it tantamount to heresy for a ruler to claim to be God's or Muhammad's deputy.

On the off chance that he hadn't made his point thoroughly enough, al-Raziq continues by relating a compelling story from Ahmad bin Zayni Dahlan's *Biography of the Prophet* in which a man fearfully approaches Muhammad and is told by him, "Be calm, for I am no king nor a subduer, for I am the son of a woman of Quraysh who used to eat dried meat in Mecca."[61] This story is filled with pathos and a reminder that what sets Muhammad apart from other figures is his *lack* of a claim to personal authority. He resolutely and consistently insists authority and sovereignty are not his possessions and this story communicates a view of himself as a social equal with this man, even if he was his superior in religious terms. Interestingly, it also includes a reminder of his tribal identity, which is another signal that one need not abandon all references to identity outside of his or her faith. Immediately following this recounting from the *sunna*, al-Raziq relates the *hadith* that Muhammad was given a choice between being a king-prophet or a worshipping prophet. After the angel Gabriel signaled that he should be humble, he chose to be a worshipping prophet, leading al-Raziq to conclude that "this

60 Al-Raziq (2004), pp. 32–3.

61 Ibid., p. 34.

makes it very clear that the Prophet, peace be upon him, was not a king, and did not seek kingship, nor did he, peace be upon him, desire it."[62]

In assessing the relevance of al-Raziq's work to present debates about the relationship between Islam as a religion and the proper role of the state in Muslim societies, it is helpful to look at what some relatively early commentators had to say. His work is generally mentioned only in passing and it would be a worthwhile undertaking, albeit well beyond the scope of this work, to give it a more sustained and methodical analysis. However, based on rather limited secondary material, the following observations can be made. Firstly, that the "significance of Raziq's theory lies in permitting the heads of Muslim states to conduct foreign relations in accordance with rules and practices not necessarily derived from the sacred law, since this matter lay outside the domain of religion."[63] Whatever one may think of his ideas, Muslim leaders have more or less been acting in *de facto* agreement with this point, the primary exception of course concerning the state of Israel and its advocates. Secondly, according to Gudrun Kramer, the very outrage and rejection provoked by his argument spurred other thinkers to reformulate and clarify what they meant by claiming that Islam was both "religion and state (*al-islam din wa dawla*)." This led to broad consensus amongst otherwise quite divergent thinkers that there are "two differentiated spheres of human life and activity: one revolving around faith and worship and the other revolving around worldly affairs, both of them subject to the precepts of Islam." What is perhaps most surprising and closely related to the aim of al-Raziq's work is that she argues they further agree that "the hallmark of the truly Islamic system (*al-nizam al-islami*) is the application of the *sharīʿa* and not any particular political order—the historical caliphate included."[64] It appears that al-Raziq may have lost the ideological battle and failed to convince his fellow scholars that Islam was a religion and *not* a system of government, yet that he still managed to win the war simply by "causing a sensation" and provoking such a fierce response.[65] Some would take this reaction to mean that al-Raziq's work represents "a radical reinterpretation" of the *Qur'an*, but the subsequent, seemingly unconscious, agreement with some of his key points on the part of his critics suggests that this is not a radical departure from established understandings, so much as an unusually frank account of the state of Muslim political thought as actually practiced.[66]

---

62 Al-Raziq (2004), p. 34.

63 Khadduri, Majid. "Islam and the Modern Law of Nations." *The American Journal of International Law*, 50:2 (1956): 369.

64 Kramer, Gudrun. "Islamist Notions of Democracy." *Middle East Report*, 183 (1993): 4.

65 See Ziadeh, Nicola A. "Recent Books on the Interpretation of Islam." *Middle East Journal*, 5:4 (1951): 505.

66 As discussed in Black, Antony. "Religion and Politics in Western and Islamic Political Thought: A Clash of Epistemologies?" *The Political Quarterly*, 81:1 (2010): 121.

## Conclusion

When analyzing the *Constitution of Medina* and the *Magna Carta* side by side, it is clear that they are texts which emerge from fundamentally different contexts. They are documents that address the particular concerns of a particular people in a particular place and time. Despite this, both of these documents retain a remarkable degree of relevance to present constitutional discourse as founding documents of Western and Islamic protections of the rights and duties of individual citizens. In regards to the *Constitution of Medina*, as the discussion of al-Raziq's work shows, it has the potential to highlight the unique nature of Muhammad's role, while simultaneously pointing out how his example of leadership relied more on persuasion than coercion, and that there is a great deal of latitude in how one structures a Muslim state so long as that structure exists within the larger sphere of the values and commands of the *Qur'an*.[67] In a similar vein, the fact that some of the *Magna Carta* is still in effect in legal terms demonstrates its lasting impact, as does the fact it is cited in court decisions even outside the United Kingdom as having the power of moral and legal precedent.

The power of the *Constitution of Medina* mainly lies in its constituent parts being authored by Muhammad himself. One can see that the symbiosis of religion and political power existed from the very origins of Islam, but that in its earliest form its definition of *umma* was far more inclusive and pluralistic. No matter how hard one looks, it is impossible to find in the *Constitution of Medina* a ready-made system of government that would work today, but one does find well-established, time-tested principles that have achieved wide acceptance and legitimacy amongst diverse groups of Muslims. This can be seen historically in the millet system of minority autonomy operated by the Ottomans and more recently in the religious freedom and political rights given to Copts in Egypt. Furthermore, when paired with modern thinkers like al-Raziq, the *Constitution of Medina* points to the possibility that what many Western scholars have seen as a shocking lack of political theory within early Muslim writing and philosophy is perhaps instead an intentional oversight designed to emphasize the sacredness of the Message of Islam and the distinctness of the Messenger of Islam so that no subsequent revelations or revealers could claim their full mantle of authority.

Likewise the *Magna Carta* highlights the tension in Christendom and its successor states between the need to govern this world using secular and even violent forms of power, while acting in accordance with the respect for individual rights that some would argue Christian teaching advocates. In neither case will one find a ready-made system of government that would work today, but one does find well-established, time-tested principles that have achieved wide acceptance and legitimacy amongst the societies they represent. By understanding the areas in which these civilizational foundations overlap, it may be possible to continue

67 Indeed, thinkers like An-Na'im assert that this need to adhere to the Quran when paired with the vast assortment of its interpretations

the comparison into the nature of specific constitutional ideas in a way that can encourage greater understanding between these two traditions as the peoples they represent try to negotiate the best possible common future.

Furthermore, and more practically, the comparison of the *Magna Carta* and the *Constitution of Medina* is important if only for the fundamental reason that all majority Muslim states are part of the United Nations. This means that they are likewise signatories of the Universal Declaration of Human Rights and various other international charters which enshrine the very same values of individual liberty, right to fair trial, recourse to *habeas corpus* and other protections that are grounded in the nature of the *Magna Carta*. This has established the *Magna Carta* as the cornerstone of modern law for the entire globe in the context of international law. As people in Tunisia, Egypt and Libya grapple with how to best institutionalize their values, goals and societies in new constitutional regimes, they will undoubtedly grapple with the dual demands of preserving the Islamic nature of their identities whilst simultaneously ensuring that their constitutions adhere to international law and the entirety of its attendant requirements. Without this type of fundamental comparison, one is either forced to advance the very tenuous position that each civilization is based upon fundamentally different norms and values which may be irreconcilable and bound for a clash, or to argue that Western norms have won the ideological struggle for survival and that we have arrived at some kind of "end of history."

Neither of these positions seems tenable in light of the overwhelming evidence that, from the very earliest times, people have borrowed ideas from one another based on a very practical desire to create stable governments for their respective societies. Additionally, there can be no ignoring the demands for Muslim states to in some way enshrine Islam in their constitutions, or that these demands are being made in many cases with representative, accountable and responsive government as an end goal. Much more work needs to be done in non-Muslim states to address the need for minority groups to exercise their fundamental rights, which may include providing for family and private law courts that conform to Jewish Talmudic law or Muslim *sharīʿa*. Sadly, progress seems to be rather absent on this front as governments in both the United States and the United Kingdom have denied recognition or even restricted the very mention of Islamic norms in court rulings.[68] For better or for worse, issues of religion and its role in the state seem to be wedded for the foreseeable future. Perhaps this discussion will provide a model of political and religious engagement, rather than denial, and better elucidate how they can negotiate a stable and harmonious marriage of the values they embrace.

68 See for example Lady Cox's Arbitration and Mediation Services Equality Bill, recently tabled in the House of Lords (Available at: http://services.parliament.uk/bills/2010-11/arbitrationandmediationservicesequalityhl.html) and the Oklahoma constitutional amendment banning the use of Islamic law in court (discussed amongst additional state measures in Andrea Elliott's 'The Man Behind the Anti-Shariah Movement,' *New York Times*; 30 July, 2011, available at http://www.nytimes.com/2011/07/31/us/31shariah.html?pagewanted=all.)

Naturally, it is also vital to see how those who came after Muhammad wrestled with the meaning and implications of his example, especially because the agreement between him and his relatively small group of followers in Medina was born of a situation so dramatically different from the Islamic empire that was to develop over the next few centuries and which would expand from the control of some Arab cities to a sphere of influence that spanned the wide swaths of Europe, the Middle East, North Africa, and South and Southeast Asia. Examining the effect of this expansion in a philosophical and practical sense is what the next chapter will undertake through an analysis of various Islamic texts, including al-Farabi's work *On the Perfect State*, ibn Khaldun's *Muqaddimah*, and the Ottoman *Tanzimat* reforms of 1839 and 1856.

# Chapter 4
# Comparing Constitutionalisms—Is there an Islamic Constitutionalism?

> The danger I think is when the United States or any country thinks that we can simply impose these values on another country with a different history and a different culture … Democracy, rule of law, freedom of speech, freedom of religion—those are not simply principles of the West to be hoisted on these countries, but rather what I believe to be universal principles that they can embrace and affirm as part of their national identity.
>
> President Barack Obama[1]

The question of whether there are indeed "universal" principles, as President Obama contends in the above quote, is one that is contentious and difficult to answer in a rigorous fashion. Rather than arguing that any particular constitutional values are universal and directly transferable between various states and cultures, this chapter seeks to examine strains of Islamic political thought that have applicability to constitutional issues. The goal of this examination is to ascertain to what degree these ideas may be comparable in any meaningful way, to highlight areas of broad agreement between the civilizational histories of Western and Islamic regimes.

Just as the chapter on the Western constitutional tradition drew from a few key thinkers to discuss the principles of Rule of Law, National Character, and Limits on Government Power, so too will this chapter look primarily at similar discourses in the works of al-Farabi, ibn Khaldun, and the Ottoman *Tanzimat* reforms of the mid-19th Century. Additional relevant works will be briefly discussed, for instance Mawardi's *The Ordinances of Government* and the experiences of the Young Ottomans and their early experiments in constitutionalism, where they can further illuminate the core concepts. The constitutional principles in question take on a distinctive character in these works, yet it may be possible to elaborate broad comparisons between the two constitutional narratives in order to understand to what degree Islam itself is compatible with what Western scholars consider to be constitutionalism, and to what extent the constitutionalism represented is compatible with Western notions of these norms and values.

---

1 This can be found in his BBC Interview of 1 June, 2009; available on the BBC website at: http://www.bbc.co.uk/blogs/thereporters/justinwebb/2009/06/an_interview_with_president_ob.html.

## Al-Farabi's *On the Perfect State* and the Personification of the Rule of Law

Ironically, despite the genius of Muslim philosophers, their impact on Islamic thought was marginal. If the use of reason in scholastic theology had been suspect, how much more was philosophy, which, in contrast to theology, took reason and not revelation as its starting point and method ... more often than not they were viewed as rationalists and non-believers. Philosophy never established itself as a major discipline. In contrast, Muslim philosophy had a major impact on the West. By transmitting Greek philosophy to medieval Europe, it influenced the curriculum of its universities and the work of such scholars as Albertus Magnus, Thomas Aquinas, Duns Scotus, and Roger Bacon.[2]

Given the rather disappointing junction of Islamic philosophy and political-theological acceptance mentioned above, one could be forgiven for questioning the inclusion of al-Farabi in a discussion of Islamic constitutionalism. If his and his colleagues' impacts upon Islamic jurisprudence and politics were so minimal, why is there such enthusiasm for studying their work on the part of Western scholars? Indeed, Patricia Crone, in her substantial study, *God's Rule: Government and Islam*, says of al-Farabi:

> A historian of mainstream Islam is apt to dismiss all philosophers as marginal ... One does not often encounter the philosophers or their 'political science' in sources written by these scholars. In fact, one does not encounter al-Farabi anywhere at all. But after al-Farabi's time, attempts to fuse philosophy with the religious sciences began to be made ... and though some rejected such efforts as attempts to undermine Islam from within, there can be little doubt that the appeal of philosophy widened. Even religious scholars and theologians took to reading it, be it for purposes of instruction or refutation.[3]

Although these questions are certainly valid, particularly in the case of those claiming to be presenting an "Islamic view" of a matter, the aims of this chapter are substantially humbler. Rather than presenting a constitutional discourse that represents itself as valid in Islamic terms, this and the following sections will simply state a case for the types of concepts and thinkers that could be included in a constitutional discourse that is derived from Islamic sources and geared towards local needs, which may include tacit or explicit nods to Islam in the constitution of the state and its values and institutions. It is also useful to look at thinkers whose work shares some vocabulary and background knowledge with those common in Western political thought. As the person who is arguably the most directly responsible for introducing ancient Greek thought back into European scholarship,

2 Esposito, John L. *Islam: The Straight Path.* 3rd ed. New York and Oxford: Oxford University Press, 1998, p. 74.

3 Crone, Patricia. *God's Rule: Government and Islam.* New York: Columbia University Press, 2004.

al-Farabi is an ideal candidate for comparative analysis.[4] By examining his work *On the Perfect State* (*Ahl al-Madina al-Fadila*), it will be possible to draw direct comparisons to classical conceptions of the good life, virtuous ruler, and the ultimate aim of the state in relationship to creating and sustaining virtuous citizens. Furthermore, by following up this examination with a complementary analysis of Muslim jurist al-Mawardi's *The Ordinances of Government*, it will be possible to make an initial assessment of the compatibility and relevance of Muslim philosophy with more prevalent forms of political thinking found in the jurists and the mirror of princes literature.

Before examining his work in detail, a brief biographical sketch of Abu Nasr al-Farabi is necessary to put his work in context. He was born in Turkestan (modern day Kazakhstan) in circa 870 AD and was most likely an Imami Shiite. He was brought up and educated in Baghdad, was taught philosophy by a Christian, and "was friendly with the Christian Aristotelian and translator, Mata ibn Yunus. He lived in Baghdad, but did not belong to the court, bureaucracy or any literary group; he worked on his own."[5] This may explain why his work retains a distinctive quality to this day, and why he is considered the founder of Islamic *al-'ilm al-madani* (political science).[6]

Eventually, he did take up a place at court in Aleppo in the court of the Imami Hamdanids and produced, amongst other works, the *Ahl al-Madina al-Fadila* during this time (942/3 AD).[7] His work is essentially Aristotelian but is heavily influenced by Platonic ideals and the neo-Platonism of late antiquity and early Christian thought. As Patricia Crone (and others) sees it, the fascination al-Farabi held with Plato was largely due to its apparent commonalities with Islamic assumptions. In Plato, he could compare the colonizing experience of the Greeks and the early followers of Muhammad, and view Muhammad himself through the lens of a founder or lawgiver. "Moreover, the early Greeks shared the early Muslim view that membership of a particular polity … was a precondition for human perfection/salvation."[8] She also contends that his work equates the Prophet with "the lawgiver," the *sharī'a* as "the law (*namus*), or constitution (*sira, siyasa*),

4 See for example Robert Hammond's *The Philosophy of Al Farabi and Its Influence on Medieval Thought*, which lays out passages from al-Farabi and Thomas Aquinas in parallel, showing how the earlier writings of Farabi were often borrowed wholesale by Aquinas. This includes even passages which describe the means by which God may be known and described. Given their theological differences, this provides some intriguing avenues for questioning the essential differences of these two traditions.

5 Black, Antony. *The History of Islamic Political Thought: From the Prophet to the Present*. Edinburgh: Edinburgh University Press, 2001, p. 61.

6 Crone (2004), p. 167. This may also explain his aforementioned attractiveness to Thomas Aquinas. The neo-Platonist streak in Farabi's writings is strong and would have been appealing to many early Medieval Christian thinkers.

7 Black (2001), p. 61.

8 Crone (2004), pp. 171–2.

the Muslim community as his polity (*madina*), and not least, of the philosophers as the true legatees of its founder."[9]

*Al-Farabi's Ideal Ruler, The Incarnate Rule of Law*

The beginning of al-Farabi's discourse *On the Perfect State* begins, like many philosophical works, with definition of key terms. Crucially, the subject of this inquiry, the *medina* or city/state, is defined as thoroughly Islamic, even sharing a common root with the word Muslim (one who submits) and Islam (submission or peace). He reminds his reader of the definition given the term by the popular and trusted reporter,

> Abu Ishaq—may God give him support—(who) has said: The word *al-Madina* is derived from a root which denotes submission, obedience, compliance, and concurrence <of people> in obeying a strong ruler who governs them fully while upholding their rights and accepting the obedience which they owe to him.[10]

It is important to note that the rule of law presented here is deeply personified. This is in keeping both with Shiite proclivities to emphasize the role of the Imam in salvation, and with a Platonic ideal of philosopher-king. It also uses the constitutional dichotomy of rights and obligations in describing the relationship of the ruler as one who "governs fully while upholding their rights." The personification of the rule of law and the state is carried further in Chapter 15 of his work (the previous chapters are largely concerned with metaphysics, the "First Cause," etc.) as seen below:

> The excellent city resembles the perfect and healthy body, all of whose limbs co-operate to make the life of the animal perfect and to preserve it in this state. Now the limbs and the organs of the body are different and their natural endowments and faculties are unequal in excellence, there being among them one ruling organ, namely the heart, and organs which are close in rank to that ruling organ, each having been given by nature a faculty by which it performs its proper function in conformity with the natural aim of that ruling organ … The same holds good in the case of the city. Its parts are different by nature, and their natural dispositions are unequal in excellence: there is in it a man who is the ruler, and there are others whose ranks are close to the ruler … these are

9 Ibid., p. 172. Although *dustur* is the more common Arabic term used today to translate constitution, it was not used in this way in al-Farabi's time. *Siyasa* simply means government or policy, but given his classical influences Crone's contention that his use of *siyasa* indicates a meaning more like constitution seems perfectly reasonable.

10 al-Farabi, Abu Nasr, and Richard Walzer. *Al-Farabi on the Perfect State: Abu Nasr Al-Farabi's Mabadi Ara Ahl Al-Madina Al-Fadila: A Revised Text with Introduction, Translation, and Commentary*. Oxford: Oxford University Press, 1985, p. 51.

> the holders of the first ranks ... the limbs and organs of the body are natural, whereas, although the parts of the city are natural, their dispositions and habits, by which they perform their actions in the city, are not natural but voluntary...[11]

This biological anthropomorphism of the city is familiar in its acceptance of social hierarchies as natural and in its assumption that the manner in which these hierarchies are composed is based on natural variation in "excellence." Importantly, this is qualified by a nod to human agency in the promulgation of and obedience to the law, as indicated by his claim that "their dispositions and habits, by which they perform their actions ... are not natural but voluntary."[12] This means that society is not simply composed of structural/institutional components, but that it is also socially constructed and dependent upon the accumulated acts of its individual members for its creation and maintenance.[13]

The ruler, in particular, is absolutely vital to the state:

> In the same way (as the heart rules the body) the ruler of this city must come to be in the first instance, and will subsequently be the cause of the rise of the city and its parts and the cause of the presence of the voluntary habits of its parts and of their arrangement in the ranks proper to them; and when one part is out of order he provides it with the means to remove its disorder.[14]

In his commentary on this work, translator Richard Walzer points out that al-Farabi is following Plato in making the primary object of his political science the definition of the "right ruler."[15] This is because, for al-Farabi, the ruler is the very genesis of the state and all of its subsequent parts and social relationships. One point Walzer omits in this brief comment, is that the ruler is also given the ongoing duty of providing for public order through correction of any elements that

11 al-Farabi (1985), pp. 231–3.

12 One cannot help but be reminded of the similarity of this idea to Plato's *Republic*.

13 Here one may be reminded of the frontispiece of Hobbes' *Leviathan*, which features an anthropomorphized State rendered in the likeness of an all-powerful Sovereign who looms over the surrounding territory, endowed with the symbols of state power, the Sword and the Scepter. Crucially, this figure is composed of a multitude of individual people who all cooperatively subject themselves to the will of their Head of State. This imagery is very much in keeping with traditional Muslim emphases on submission to God and authority along with a focus on the community over the individual. As if to take this even further, Hobbes writes his work's title as "Leviathan, or 'The Matter, Forme, and Power of a Common Wealth Ecclesiasticall and Civil'." This leaves no doubt that the intent of his work is for State and Church to be closely intertwined, much as Muslim jurists and *falsafa* argue State and Mosque must be.

14 Farabi (1985), pp. 235–7.

15 Walzer (1985), p. 436.

would throw the apparatus of state out of proper balance. This power could even be interpreted to include that of deciding on the life or death of a subject.[16]

Furthermore, the ruler is on-going exemplar for his subjects and establishes the overall aims of the state as a whole.[17] The question remains as to what qualifications confer legitimacy and ability on the ruler to undertake such an ambitious task of founding, maintaining, and ruling a state rightly. Here al-Farabi states that, "(r)ulership requires two conditions: (a) he should be predisposed for it by his inborn nature, (b) he should have acquired the attitude and habit of will for rulership which will develop in a man whose preborn nature is predisposed for it."[18] Again, the importance of both nature and nurture can be seen, although in this case, the nurture would appear to be self-nurture in the form of consistently acting virtuously. The art of the ruler "must be an art towards the aim of which all the other arts tend, and for which they strive in all the actions of the excellent city."[19] What exactly this art is, is never stated, but from later passages it becomes clear that it is the art of fulfilling one's role in society, and the subsequent acts and attitudes this requires (which are discussed further on). Nowhere in this passage does al-Farabi state how this ruler is to acquire power over those less virtuous, or indeed whether this power is a pre-requisite for the virtuous man to also be Lawgiver and Ruler. Ann Lambton mentions that in his other works, including his *Philosophy of Plato and Aristotle*, he says that "The prince or the *imam* is prince and *imam* by virtue of his skill and art, regardless of whether or not, anyone acknowledges him ... whether or not he is supported in his purpose by any group."[20] Though the idea that a leader could exist without any followers is one that is certainly odd in some respects, al-Farabi seems to view this possibility as one that is at minimum beneficial to this philosopher-king.[21]

> Thus he is ... a wise man and a philosopher and an accomplished thinker who employs an intellect of divine quality, and through the emanation from the Active Intellect to his faculty of representation a visionary prophet: who warns of things to come and tells of particular things which exist at present.

---

16 Although cryptic, the phrase "means to remove its disorder," does have at least the implication that executions may be necessary for the protection of society.

17 See al-Farabi (1985), where he states "The excellent city ought to be arranged in the same way: all its parts ought to imitate in their actions the aim of their first ruler according to their rank." p. 239.

18 Al-Farabi (1985), pp. 239–41.

19 Ibid., pp. 241.

20 *Alfarabi's philosophy of Plato and Aristotle*, quoted in Ann Lambton (1981), *State and Government in Medieval Islam*. Oxford: Oxford University Press, p. 72.

21 This is certainly a marked contrast with the view of Machiavelli that gaining and maintaining power is largely the end and means of being a ruler and that doing so may require the ruler to possess qualities that are anything but virtuous in private citizens. See for example *The Prince*, Chapter XVII.

> This man holds the most perfect rank of humanity and has reached the highest degree of felicity ... He is the man who knows every action by which felicity can be reached. This is the first condition for being a ruler. Moreover, he should be a good orator and able to rouse [other people's] imagination by well-chosen words. He should be able to lead people well along the right path to felicity and to the actions by which felicity is reached. He should, in addition, be of tough physique in order to shoulder the tasks of war.
>
> This is the sovereign over whom no other human being has any sovereignty whatsoever; he is the Imam; he is the first sovereign of the excellent city, he is the sovereign of the excellent nation, and the sovereign of the universal state (the *oikumene*).[22]

Here can be seen an explicitly Islamic reference to the *Imam* and one which clearly identifies the *imam* with the Platonic ruler. Walzer makes a point of mentioning that the term had a variety of uses in the intellectual debates of al-Farabi's day. Amongst the identifications given to it were the Prophet Muhammad and his successor, the Caliph.[23] The usefulness of this dual meaning is that the righteous ruler need not be immortal for the continued existence of the excellent city. His successors can utilize his teachings and examples, particularly his "representation" of truth as given in his role of "visionary prophet," to maintain right rule.[24]

Following a discussion of the 12 essential qualities of a founding ruler, Al-Farabi goes on to explore the six qualities found which must exist in subsequent sovereigns. These are as follows:

> (1) He will be a philosopher. (2) He will know and remember the laws and customs (and rules of conduct) with which the first sovereigns had governed the city, conforming in all his actions to their actions. (3) He will excel in deducing a new law by analogy where no law of his predecessors has been recorded, following for his deductions the principles laid down by the first Imams. (4) He will be good at deliberating and be powerful in his deductions to meet new situations for which the first sovereigns could not have laid down any law; when doing this he will have in mind the good of the city. (5) He will be good at guiding the people by his speech to fulfill the laws of the first sovereigns as well as those laws which he will have deduced in conformity with their principles

22 Al-Farabi (1985), pp. 245–7.

23 Walzer (1985), pp. 442–3.

24 Here is seen an echo of Cicero's contention in *Republic* Book III, that "a state should be organized in such a way as to last for ever. And so the death of a state is never natural, as it is with a person, for whom death is not only natural but also frequently desirable."

> after their time. (6) He should be of tough physique in order to shoulder the tasks of war, mastering the serving as well as the ruling military art.[25]

Importantly, all these qualities need not be present in one person alone. Rather, when there is "philosophy in one man and the second quality in another man and so on, and when these men are all in agreement, they should all together be the excellent sovereigns."[26] Many of the existing practices of Muslim societies can also be seen in this passage.[27] Notably, the ability to "know and remember the laws" when combined with "deducing a new law by analogy" is in conformity with conventional Islamic jurisprudence. It also injects the potential for dynamism and change in what could otherwise be a very static society. If the successors of the ideal ruler are also philosophers, which is, after all, requirement number one on his list, then al-Farabi is confident they will be able to face "new situations" for which no law could exist as they were unforeseen. For present-day political theorists, this opening for innovation is one that could potentially answer many doubters of Islam's ability to adapt to changing times and social conditions. In other words, under Farabi's scheme the gates of *ijtihad* would never be closed so long as societies exist because they will necessarily face novel situations and conundrums which will need to be reconciled with the ongoing fundamental values and goals of that society.

Ralph Lerner observes that this passage is indicative of the fact that:

> for Farabi as for Plato, the possibility of a succession of such true princes remains doubtful at best. Yet the confluence of such rare qualities—in an individual or in a small number—is the condition for the perpetuation of the founder's handiwork. One may say of such a group or series of fully qualified princes that they form, as it were, a single soul, a single prince.[28]

If one allows that al-Farabi did in fact believe that the existence of the excellent city was, in fact, possible, and if one agrees with Walzer that his ideal city is largely based upon the premise that Muhammad is such a lawgiver and communicator of transcendental truth to the masses, then the fact that he absolutely requires continued rule by wise philosophers could lend itself to an argument for a government based upon consultation and assent. The Islamic idea of *shura*, or consultation, is one which is complemented by the act of *bay'a*, or "pledging allegiance," in which

25 Al-Farabi (1985), pp. 251–3.

26 Ibid., p. 253.

27 See Ralph Lerner's (1987) "Beating the Neoplatonic Bushes," in *The Journal of Religion*, 67:4. In this review of Walzer's translation of al-Farabi, he points out that, "This absorption of the religious notion of prophet into the secular notion of philosopher-legislator-and its import-was first remarked on by Leo Strauss in a series of studies published in 1934–36."

28 Lerner (1987), p. 512.

new rulers must be legitimized through public acclamation after a process in which the elders and/or wise confer to select a ruler. This longstanding tradition, placed in a more modern context, could easily be coupled with this philosophical argument from al-Farabi to provide both a historical and theoretical justification for democratic, or at least democratically accountable, government.[29]

### *The Universal Mandate of the Excellent City*

The need for the co-existence of innovation and application of the principles of excellent rule is seemingly anticipated by al-Farabi. This can be demonstrated in his view that the excellent city is potentially one that is universal and eternal because he takes the unorthodox view that all of the excellent rulers, even those living at the same time, are "like one single soul … they are all of them in the same way like one single king and their souls like one single soul."[30] Rather than some type of relativism or imperialism, the motivation and justification for his universalizing tendencies could result from what Patricia Crone refers to as "al-Farabi's belief in the universal nature of philosophy (which) accounts for his strangely context-free presentation." Some could see this as a flaw in his work, but it has the advantage of offering a high degree of intellectual freedom and interpretation to the reader. Indeed, "one is free … to envisage him (the Lawgiver/Prophet) as Muhammad, but one can also identify him as Moses or any other prophet familiar to Islam, or as a past or future philosopher."[31]

With all this emphasis on the ruler, it is fair to ask, "What of the ruled?" The continuation of the rule of law within the excellent city is achieved by the inhabitants embracing two complementary identities. They "have things in common which they all perform and comprehend, and other things which each class knows and does on its own. Each of these people reaches felicity by … what he has in common with the others and what the people of his class to which he

29 Similarly, Bodin's account of sovereignty in Book 1, Chapter 8 of *Six Books of the Commonwealth*, argues that power, even absolute power, is only conferred upon a person or people for a finite amount of time. "Hence the people did not divest itself of sovereignty when it established one or more of its lieutenants with absolute power for a definite time." The need for the ruler to conform to the higher dictates of natural law as established by God is one which places a sovereign who is otherwise not opposable in a position where "the prince has no advantage over the subject except that, if the justice of a law he has sworn to uphold ceases, he is no longer bound by his promise, as we have said, which is a liberty that subjects cannot exercise with respect to each other unless they are relieved [of their obligations] by the prince." This principle matches nicely with the Islamic custom of abrogation in which later revelation is given more validity than earlier revelation in determining the rightness of an action or idea because the morality of the act is ultimately based upon conformity to a timeless and transcendent sense of justness in particular temporal circumstances.

30 Al-Farabi (1985), p. 261.

31 Crone (2004), p. 174.

belongs have on their own."[32] This would seem to be a lesser happiness than that experienced by the *imam*, but happiness nonetheless and the best such people can hope to attain. He does not address whether it is free will alone, or also coercion, which provides the impetus to keep each of these people in their proper social sphere. There is also no justification for why what they share in common with others in their class provides happiness, so one must reason that al-Farabi assumes commonality to lead to social understanding on a more profound level, which would in turn lead to increased happiness. Likewise, the exclusive properties that distinguish each class also provide them with a type of joy and fulfillment. This could be a simple recognition that people like to feel unique, and yet part of some larger group, or it could be an answer to the question of what force keeps people in line. In this case, it could be that social groups like their distinctions and take such comfort in their internal relationships, that these distinctions become both mutually constituted and self-reinforcing.

### *The Transcendental and Eternal Nature of the Rule of Law*

Al-Farabi's view of the rule of law's centrality to existence extends, as seen previously, to the metaphysical and spiritual. For the citizens blessed enough to belong to the "excellent city," he envisions an afterlife in which the following occurs:

> The enjoyment which results from that disposition of the soul (to do what is right) grows in strength and the delight which he feels in himself at having it increases and his love for it expands. The same is true of the actions by which felicity is attained: the more they increase … the stronger and more excellent and more perfect becomes the soul whose very purpose is to reach felicity, until it arrives at that stage of perfection in which it can dispense with matter so that it becomes independent of it, neither perishing, when matter does, nor requiring matter to survive.[33]

This transcendental state is one that is not merely non-physical, but one in which perfection exists in degrees. At first glance, the concept of perfection being more or less perfect seems to be an oxymoron. If one thinks of logic from a mathematical perspective however, as many philosophers have done, a simple analogy presents itself. This conception of Farabi's is much like that of differing degrees of infinity. All infinity is infinitely large, yet it is still logical to argue that the distance from one to infinity is greater than the distance from 10 to infinity, even though both differences are infinitely large. The great difference of course, is that for mathematicians this line of reasoning does not carry any type of normative weight. For al-Farabi and other philosophers, it is a crucial means by which the idea of a perfect vision of the afterlife can be reconciled with the idea of rewards

32 Al-Farabi (1985), p. 261.

33 Ibid., p. 263.

based upon how one lived temporally. Although on certain points he is unorthodox in terms of traditional Muslim understandings of the afterlife, al-Farabi does still situate his musings within the general beliefs in eternal reward for a life well lived, and in differing degrees of eternal bliss.[34]

Interestingly, he also ascribes a very communal idea of "felicity" to the afterlife that is arguably in keeping with the Islamic ethos of emphasizing the *umma* over the individual. As he sees it,

> When one generation passes away, their bodies cease to exist and their souls are released and become happy and when other people succeed them in their ranks, these people take their place and perform their actions. When this generation passes away as well and is released [from matter], they occupy in their turn the same ranks in felicity as those who passed away before, and each joins those who resemble him in species, quantity and quality … The more similar separate souls grow together and join one another—in the way that one intelligible joins another intelligible—the more increases the self-enjoyment of each of them. Whenever any member of a later generation joins them, the enjoyment of the new arrival increases when he meets those departed before him, and the joys of the departed increase when the new arrivals join them, because each soul thinks its own essence and thinks the like of its own essence many times, and thus the quality of what it thinks increases.[35]

Immediately notable in this passage is the absence of God and divine judgment. This perfect state seems to be a self-regulating and perpetuating system of pure enlightenment. Does this mean the excellent city is likewise a type of perpetual motion machine, which when put into operation creates a structure in which its residents, so long as they do not rebel against it, are pre-destined to eternal felicity?[36] Note how his vision includes class distinctions that persist into eternity because of how physical life shapes the soul, and how he assumes that similar

34 See for instance, Chapter 16.3 (p. 265) where he says, "since these souls … were before in various matter and since it has become clear that the dispositions of the souls depend on the temperament of the bodies … it follows necessarily that these dispositions differ, because the bodies they were in differed. And since the differences of bodies cannot be determined in number, the differences of souls are equally indeterminable in number." See also 16.5 (p. 267), where he says "The kinds of felicity (so not only the souls but the happiness they experience) are unequal in excellence and differ in three ways, in species, quantity and quality; this is similar to the difference of arts in this world of ours."

35 Al-Farabi (1985), p. 265.

36 This vision of the afterlife is highly reminiscent of that found in the famous *Dream of Scipio* passage in Book 6 of Cicero's *Republic*. Here, Scipio is reassured in a dream, "for everyone who has saved and served his country and helped it to grow, a sure place is set aside in heaven where he may enjoy a life of eternal bliss." Although the Roman version of this paradise is more individualistic, with an emphasis being on personal happiness and prestige, it nonetheless claims that to God, "nothing is more welcome than those companies

souls will associate, and implies that dissimilar souls will not. Is this an inherently non-egalitarian vision of perfection? Perhaps it is not. It is relatively simple to see how if one bases equality on equal enjoyment rather than equal rank or status, that eternal felicity could be more or less enjoyed as much as one is capable of enjoying it. Does this serve to provide especially strong motivation for the ruler/lawgiver to strive for the very highest forms of perfection since he will presumably be joined *in aeternum* to souls of similar "quality"? This seems more likely. After all, what ruler would not wish to think himself worthy of continued exalted capabilities and rank in the afterlife? However, the question remains as to what happens to the people of the other cities that do not meet the standard of "excellent"?

The blunt verdict al-Farabi enters on the destiny of those who live outside the bounds of the excellent city is that "Since the actions of the people in the other cities are bad, they produce bad dispositions of the soul in them … the more a man persists in those actions, the more deteriorates the disposition of his soul."[37]

It is noteworthy that once again he does not rely upon the judgment of God as a mechanism of punishment or correction. Depending on one's point of view, his perception of the soul of the inhabitant of the non-excellent city is conceivably even harsher than that of more orthodox Islamic conceptions of God's wrath and punishment, or it could be viewed as even more cynical about the opportunity such people have for redemption. His view of the symptoms of the diseased soul is that it leads to a situation in which

> They often *enjoy* (emphasis mine) the dispositions which they acquire from those actions. People who are physically ill, like many of those smitten with fever, their sense-perception being spoiled, enjoy flavors which are not normally enjoyable and feel discomfort at things which are normally pleasant, or fail to taste the flavor of sweet things which are normally pleasant: in the same way people whose soul is diseased, their faculty of representation being spoiled by will and habit, enjoy bad dispositions and bad actions and either feel discomfort at good dispositions and actions and excellent things in general or do not have them within the grasp of their faculty of representation at all.[38]

Al-Farabi uses an analogy any medical doctor would find familiar, describing how

> There are among the physically diseased some people who are unaware of their illness and some who fancy in addition that they are in good health; they fancy this so strongly that they do not listen at all to the words of a doctor. In the same way people whose soul is diseased are unaware of their illness or fancy in addition that they are virtuous and healthy in their souls and hence do not listen

and communities of people linked together by justice that are called states. Their rulers and saviors set out from this place, and to this they return."

37 Al-Farabi (1985), p. 269.

38 Ibid., pp. 269–71.

> at all to the words of a man who leads them in the right path, teaches them and puts them straight.[39]

Clearly, even in the presence of the virtuous lawgiver or prophet, these people would be unable to accept the corrective measures he would propose and consequently are thoroughly unredeemable. They are also, to al-Farabi's mind at least, delusional in their self-perception, which means that the state of their soul is one of deterioration and their state of mind is fundamentally one of ignorance about the all-important state of their souls.

What is the destiny of these sad, depraved souls? Eschewing traditional accounts of eternal punishment and Hell, al-Farabi argues instead that because the souls of people from bad cities are not perfect, they "necessarily require matter for their preservation, since no trace of truth whatsoever except the first intelligibles has been imprinted on them." This leads to a cycle of metaphysical decay that mirrors the process of decay experienced in a dead body until, in the end, the best possibility remaining for these people is that the material matter of which they were composed becomes part of a human being once again. Their souls however, are a lost cause. "These are the men who perish and proceed to nothingness, in the same way as cattle, beasts of prey and vipers."[40]

How is this relevant to an Islamic view of the rule of law? It demonstrates an orthodox acceptance that the fate of individual souls is based upon individual merit and right conduct, but these individuals exist in a state where God is ultimately and thoroughly sovereign, causing each and every action in the world to occur, good or ill. Each individual is judged and rewarded or punished according to his or her acts. This means that despite al-Farabi's very unconventional representation of the afterlife, it is still in general philosophical accordance with wider streams of Islamic thought. It also crucially gives a nod to the idea that the real rule of law is the will of God, which is likely to give his thought at least some additional credibility in Muslim quarters.

There does seem to be one class of person for whom al-Farabi foresees a fate worse than non-existence, and that is for the ruler of "people of the cities which have gone astray: the man who led them astray and turned them away from felicity … is himself one of the people of the wicked cities; therefore he alone … will be wretched." This seems to be some sort of state of eternal misery that could be equivalent to a type of Hell, especially when he continues by saying that "the

39 Al-Farabi (1985), p. 271.

40 Ibid., pp. 271–3. The fate of the soul lacking virtue again brings to mind Cicero's comment that such people, who "are impelled by lusts that serve pleasure to violate the laws of gods and men—those souls, on escaping from their bodies, swirl around, close to earth itself, and they do not return to this place (heaven) until the have been buffeted about for many ages." It is also important to note that this position is Farabian, but not in line with *Qur'anic* or mainstream Muslim teaching. This may be one reason some of his thought would be suspect to those of a more orthodox persuasion.

others will perish and ultimately dissolve in the same way as the people of the ignorant city."[41]

One final possibility for the afterlife, that is both intriguing and less determinist, is mentioned in al-Farabi's discussion of what happens to "people of the excellent city" when they are "compelled and forced to act like people of the ignorant city." Because they are aware of the fact they are being forced to do something bad, and because they feel discomfort and are acting against their will, the commission of these non-virtuous acts "will not harm" them. This situation occurs either when "the man under whose rule (the virtuous man) lives is one of the people of the cities opposed to the excellent city or when he is compelled to live in the places of the people of the non-excellent cities."[42]

What seems to be represented here is an affirmation of the traditional Shiite doctrine of dissimilation (*taqiyya*), which allowed them to act as though they were Sunni for the sake of their own protection, so long as they were compelled to do so, without incurring guilt. There is also a recognition that it is possible for a virtuous person to exist within a context which is not "excellent." This clearly demonstrates that although the community to which people belong has an extremely influential role in their temporal and eternal well-being and happiness, it is ultimately the individual who does or does not attain true knowledge and excellence. Here again, broader Islamic tradition is reflected, which undoubtedly places a heavy emphasis upon the benefits and relative ease of living in a Muslim society for one who wishes to live lawfully, yet which does not preclude the possibility of individual believers being able to live rightly outside of that context. What al-Farabi achieves in this schema is a remarkable balance in weighing the influences of nature and nurture, the individual and society. This vision is one which is thus steeped in the ethos reflected from the earliest times of the Muslim community in which the people were both one *umma* accountable for their public acts and maintaining an Islamic society and simultaneously individuals accountable for their private deeds and inward belief.

Al-Farabi's contentions on the afterlife and how it is attained are thus arguably more just than many fundamentalist visions because one is neither guaranteed eternal joy, nor is one bound for non-existence merely based upon the accident of where he or she was born. It also places his thought well within classical Western philosophy and political thought, which is no surprise given his profound admiration and detailed study of Aristotle's work, and in light of the role he personally played in reviving Greek thought for the Arabic-speaking world in a manner that would eventually lead to its reintroduction in Europe thanks to the Moorish conquest of Spain.[43]

---

41 See pp. 273–5, for a discussion of how the misery of the willfully bad city increases infinitely.

42 Al-Farabi (1985), p. 277.

43 For a very interesting discussion of exactly what texts were available to medieval European scholars at various places and times, and how these were transmitted via assorted

### *General Observations on a Farabian Rule of Law*

Ultimately, for al-Farabi as for many ancient thinkers, the presence of the rule of law is one that exists on a metaphysical and essential level of reality, which then determines the shape and form and operation of laws in the physical and social worlds. This is a classical view of natural law, which finds that a lack of rule of law is one that occurs not in fact, because the law is transcendental, but rather in apprehension, because people are not able to reason clearly enough to discern the truth of its existence and the individual mandates it requires of the one who wished to live well and earn "eternal felicity." The Islamic twist on this concept that gives his thought unique merit and distinguishes it from the Greeks that he clearly admires and imitates, is the emphasis on the individual lawgiver as embodied in the person of the prophet (and by extension The Prophet, Muhammad) and the apprehension of true law by the masses as occurring symbolically through a simplified version of the truth delivered by the prophet as "revelation."[44]

Unusually, al-Farabi does not believe that this revelation needs to be the same in all places and times for its truth-revealing potential to work. Indeed he recognizes the individuality of different nations and peoples and makes the following case in regards to their particular revealed truths:

> The philosophers in the city are those who know these (truths) through strict demonstration and their own insight ... But others know them through symbols which produce them by imitation, because neither nature nor habit has provided their minds with the gift to understand them as they are. Both are kinds of knowledge, but the knowledge of the philosophers is undoubtedly more excellent ... Now these things are produced by imitation for each nation and for the people of each city through those symbols which are best known to them. But what is best known often varies among nations, either most of it or part of it. Hence these things are expressed for each nation in symbols other than those used for another nation. Therefore it is possible that excellent nations and excellent cities exist whose religions differ, although they all have as their goal one and the same felicity and the very same aims.[45]

The argument that different revelations, so long as they have the "same aims" and "felicity" as their goal, can lead a people on the path to excellence is one that would not necessarily be expected by an observant Muslim. Whether or not

---

Arabic/Islamic thinkers see Josep Puig's (1994) "The Transmission and Reception of Arabic Philosophy in Christian Spain (Until 1200)," in Butterworth and Kessel (eds), *The Introduction of Arabic Philosophy into Europe*. Brill: Leiden, New York, Cologne, pp. 7–30. In particular, note his assertion that Europeans had access to al-Farabi's work by the end of the 12th Century and his brief discussion of Farabi's work on pp. 15–16.

44 See al-Farabi (1985), pp. 277–85.

45 Ibid., pp. 279–81.

his co-religionists agreed, as many undoubtedly did not, al-Farabi opens up an important philosophical door which strongly contradicts claims that Islam and Western thought are bound for any sort of "clash." Taken further, it could, in fact, open the door for a state that is both Islamic and pluralist, which is one of the biggest objections raised by people who both advocate and abhor the idea of an Islamic state.

Another potential application of al-Farabi's thought would be in recognizing the distinctions within what is traditionally referred to as the House of Islam (*Dar al-Islam*) and to give validity to the variations that exist in Islamic belief and practice, which vary radically from one another. Islamic government in Saudi Arabia looks very little like Islamic government in Malaysia or Pakistan, yet each of these states is a self-proclaimed "Islamic" state. Perhaps the use of natural law doctrines could be helpful in explaining how regimes could take on different forms and yet still conform to the overarching dictates of justice required by the *sharīʿa*. Al-Farabi clearly sees revealed law as a more readily understandable and palatable form of the law of God and nature. The law of the land could be seen as simply a further distillation of the essential justice and goodness needed to maintain the state. Al-Mawardi, on the other hand, approaches the creation of the good state from the opposite tack of a juristic/institutional approach that de-emphasizes the personal qualities of the ruler in exchange for placing a much stronger spotlight on the role of law, custom, and religious practice. The next section of this chapter looks at his work in order to assess a more prevalent form of Muslim political thought and also to place al-Farabi in a wider context in order to ascertain to what extent the philosophical model exists either in tandem or in opposition to the juristic model of state and societal organization.

## Al-Mawardi's Ideal Regime in the Real World—An Analysis of The Ordinances of Government

> Al-Mawardi has said: "Praise the Lord, who has clarified the faith and favored us with the comprehensive Book, who has issued us His commands and so delineated the boundaries of right and wrong that they have become the ultimate ordinance in this world, whereby the welfare of men is assured and the foundations of truth are firmly established. It is He who has entrusted leaders with the implementation of His just rules and with the conduct of affairs in the manner He has so magnificently planned..."[46]

> The market supervisor should exercise his discretion regarding what is harmful or harmless, because that belongs to reasoning based on custom rather than

46 Mawardi, Ali ibn Muhammad, and Centre for Muslim Contribution to Civilization. *The Ordinances of Government: A Translation of Al-Ahkam Al-Sultaniyya W'al-Wilayat Al-Diniyya*, The Great Books of Islamic Civilization. Reading: Garnet, 1996, p. 1.

> juridicial reasoning. The difference between the two kinds of reasoning is that juridicial reasoning is that in which a principle is observed which has been established by canon law, while customary reasoning is that in which the principle observed is established by custom ... The market supervision office is one of the bases of religious affairs. The sovereigns used to attend to it in person owing to the public good and rich personal reward it brings. However, when the Caliph turned away from it, and delegated it to the insignificant, so that it became open to profiteering and corruption, it became less important and lost the respect of the public. Still, a rule does not become invalidated because it has been violated. Scholars have failed to detail its rules which should not have been so inadequately treated. Most of this book we have written contains matter that has been either omitted or inadequately covered by other scholars. So, we have mentioned what they ignored and detailed what they only casually dealt with.[47]

In stark contrast to the free-form and highly abstracted language of al-Farabi's treatise, al-Mawardi begins and ends his work on government with a solid grounding in the day to day running of the Muslim state as seen in the passage above. This is no attempt to derive right rule by observation of the cosmos or one's innermost musings. Mawardi's work is thoroughly steeped in references to the *Qur'an*, the life of Muhammad, and to the work of various jurists in each of the main Sunni legal schools. As this analysis will show, Mawardi's writing is also infused with a concern for the derivation, use, and delegation of power. This power preoccupation is the foundation of his vision for a timeless rule of law that can undergird the multitude of constantly shifting regulations and political actors in any real state. His own doctrine is of the *Shafi'ite* school, but this does not prevent him from mentioning Hanafi, Hanbali, Maliki, and other interpretations throughout his work.[48] Furthermore, there is an unrelenting concern with the practical and mundane affairs of the daily business of governing that permeates his writing, constantly connecting eternal and transcendent truth to the fine details of society and how it does business, entertains itself, defends itself, and cares for its least fortunate. For Mawardi, the devil is not in the details. Rather, the devil is in not giving detail its due respect and ensuring that the requirements of the eternal law are firmly fixed within the interpretation of that law in everyday life.

As evidenced in the passage above, Mawardi's conception of the relationship between the ruler and religion is well within the "medieval Sunni tradition." This tradition posits that "the state provides for the necessary legality and material conditions for the religion to flourish."[49] Here again is a conception in which the

47 Mawardi (1996), p. 280.

48 Calder, Norman. "Friday Prayer and the Juristic Theory of Government: Sarakhsī, Shīrāzī, Māwardī." *Bulletin of the School of Oriental and African Studies*, 49:1 (1986): p. 44.

49 March, Andrew F. "Taking People as They Are: Islam as a "Realistic Utopia" in the Political Theory of Sayyid Qutb." *American Political Science Review*, 104:1 (2010): 204.

rule of law as conceived politically is one which is made subject to a transcendent rule of law as represented by the *sharīʿa*. Mawardi had the intellectual luxury of having experienced no rule outside nominal caliphal rule, meaning that his conception of political legitimacy could not admit of the possibility that it may cease. That being said, he nonetheless knew very well that an overwhelming number of claims had been made on the part of would-be caliphs and that it was impossible for all of these rivals to be equally legitimate.

Interestingly, Abu al-Hasan al-Mawardi lived merely one century after al-Farabi. Born in 974AD and living until 1058AD, he was the son of a rose-water merchant in Basra during the reign of the Abbasid Caliphate in Baghdad.[50] His life was one immersed in the power struggles of this time, with near constant political upheaval arguably wielding a particularly strong influence upon his thought. The following assessment of his work will discuss Mawardi's conception of the institutional nature of the Caliphate and its preeminent position in his formulation of power, making note of his emphasis on the need for the Caliphate to continue in order for any government to claim the mantle of Muslim and "legal," in the sense of complying with the eternal dictates of *sharīʿa*.

### *Mawardi's Institutional Caliph—The Agent of Sovereignty*

As is the case with many works on government, a great deal can be gleaned from the structure of Mawardi's argument. His primary goal in every section of his work is to enshrine the contention that the Caliphate, or Imamate, is "a main point laid down by the principles of the creed ... all public matters are guaranteed by it ... Its rules must then be given priority of mention over other statutes of government..."[51] If one were to put a Foucault-style gloss on this statement, it could be said that the Caliphate is the channel through which all power moves in the Muslim state. Power is not quantified in the sense in which modern realists like Morgenthau would visualize it, but rather it derives from God and is meant to be used in accordance with His design for society. The settled nature of the debate on power's origins means that the process by which power is exercised is placed at the forefront of Mawardi's discussion. Much as government functions in constitutional monarchies are undertaken in the name of a titular head of state, it is the Caliphate alone, which is the "focal point of the Islamic governmental, constitutional, and legal system, all important functions of the state are derived from it."[52] Thus this work begins by laying out the qualifications of electors, followed by those for one who would be Caliph, along with the mechanisms by which the Caliph may be legitimately chosen and remain in power.

The qualifications for electors in Mawardi's scheme are simultaneously idealist and practical. In an ideal sense, electors must evidence three qualities:

50 Wahba, W.H. in Mawardi (1996), p.xiii.

51 Mawardi (1996), pp. 1–2.

52 Ibid., p. xv.

probity, knowledge leading to recognition of those qualified to be a candidate, and prudence and wisdom to "choose the best candidate and the most capable and knowledgeable in managing state affairs."[53] On a practical note, he mentions that though there is no legal reason for it, residents of the capital city are customarily given precedence in selection of a new ruler simply because they are first aware of the death of the previous Caliph and are most likely to be acquainted with the candidates qualified to take on the post.[54] Mawardi's formulation thus incorporates the ideal of a virtuous elite citizen qualified to find and elect a capable ruler alongside the reality that this group will likely be limited to those in the closest proximity to power.

This list of qualifications would seem to open the possibility of being an elector to virtually any well-educated and devout member of the community. It is not difficult to envision even this very traditional juristic approach to electing a new ruler being amenable to reinterpretation along constitutional, even democratic, lines. One could simply advocate that the public goods of education and well-ordered society would prepare most people for such a role as responsible citizens. Likewise, with modern communication capabilities, virtually all people have the chance to observe and judge those in power. However, there are significant qualifications that must be made in such an observation. Mawardi's system itself is not one which is democratic or which aspires to be. This, much like the appropriation of concepts of *shura* and other Muslim terms by liberal thinkers of the 19th and 20th centuries, would be a deliberate attempt to reinterpret and recontextualize a more venerable and respected concept or thinker.

The conservatism of Mawardi's thought comes to the forefront in his list of the ten public duties required of the caliph. These are delineated as follows:

> First, he must guard the faith, upholding its established sources and the consensus of the nation's ancestors, arguing with emerging heretics or suspicious dissenters ... administering to them the legal penalties, so that the faith should remain pristine ... Second, he must enforce law between disputing parties ... Third, he must protect the country and the household ... Fourth, he must dispense the legal punishments ... Fifth, he must strengthen border posts (by both equipment and soldiers) ... Sixth, he must fight those who resist the supremacy of Islam ... until they convert or sign a treaty of subjection, so that God's claim to have a faith superior to any other is established ... Seventh, he must collect the legal taxes and alms ... Eight, he has to estimate payments and allocations ... and pay them neither before nor after the appointed time ... Ninth, he must appoint men who are reliable and sincere and of good counsel to ... take care of the funds he charges them with in order to ensure efficiency ... Tenth, he has personally to oversee matters and study the conditions of the people in order

53 Mawardi (1996), p. 4.

54 Ibid.

> to manage public policy and guard the faith instead of relying on delegation of authority while he is preoccupied with pleasure or worship...[55]

Taking these stipulations in turn, what emerges is a sort of Leviathan figure who must, above all else, avoid civil strife. Hence, the ruler's first role is to "guard the faith." His authority is thus derived from his duties, the foremost being a religious duty to ensure the protection of the sacred in the midst of the mundane. Notice too that this faith is singular and unitary, and no mention is made of variants of Islam, let alone other religions that may be practiced by his subjects. The second through fifth points are largely concerned with the more traditional contention that legitimacy is maintained, if not derived, from the successful protection of life, limb, and property of one's subjects. The sixth point comes back to religious duties, being a statement of a kind of *jihad* and a reminder that non-Muslims will be subject to *dhimmi* status and its attendant *jizya*. The seventh through ninth points are very practical concerns with the efficient and just administration of the state and a reminder that the paying of alms is not merely a social but a religious duty.

Most interesting for the present discussion of the rule of law is his tenth stipulation. Here, Mawardi creates what is effectively a duty imposed on the ruler himself, as opposed to a duty he enforces through the coercive power of the state. Namely, "personally to oversee matters and study the conditions of the people in order to manage public policy and guard the faith instead of relying on delegation of authority while he is preoccupied with pleasure or worship." This implies several important things. First, the Caliph is ultimately responsible for what occurs in his domains, thus he must be personally involved in their day to day affairs. Secondly, he rules not only on God's behalf, but also on behalf of his fellow Muslims and other subjects, making it attendant upon him to know the "conditions of the people." Thirdly, this management of public policy and protection of the faith are to take absolute priority over his own personal good, whether the mundane good of pleasure or the sacred good of worship. One can see in this statement that Mawardi's approach to rulership and power bears more than a passing resemblance to Hobbes, yet predates him by several centuries. The reason this is worth pointing out is that just as Hobbes has been used variously to justify despotism and liberalism, so too can Mawardi's description of caliphal duty be used to further despotic or constitutional ends. If one considers that the Caliph does not rule by hereditary right, but by the will of God and the expressed will of electors, and that his duties to guard the faith and the faithful supersede his prerogatives for personal pleasure, then what emerges is a system which simply accommodates itself to the political realities on the ground, whilst simultaneously mustering all the gentle and not so gentle reminders of the duties and obligations of rule that it can. All of this, again, is marshaled in the effort to ensure that the

55 Mawardi (1996), p. 16.

overarching good of Muslim unity and purity of faith are maintained at virtually any cost.[56]

Indeed, Mawardi's advocacy for the primacy of the power of the sultan (by virtue of his legitimation by the caliph) extends beyond those who would elect the caliph, beyond the duties of the caliph, which could be seen as a mundane political activity by some thinkers, and includes even the conduct of Friday prayers in the mosques. Calder relates that "He distinguishes between the post of prayer leader in relation to communal prayer, Friday prayer and supererogatory prayer:"

> The appointment of an *imam* to lead the communal prayer is dependent on the type of mosque in which prayer is held. There are two types: *masdjid sultdniyya* and *masdjid 'dmmiyya* [government mosques and public mosques]. The *sultdniyya* mosques are those ... for the supervision of which the *sultan* is responsible. No-one may be appointed *(intiddb)* to the imamate [in such a mosque] except one appointed *(nadab)* and invested *(qallad)* by the *sultan* ... Once someone has been invested [in a post] he has more right than any other to lead the prayer *even if others are better or more knowledgeable than he.*[57]

Thus, in Mawardi's formulation of the rule of law, even in its cosmic sense, all social practices, even those which are part of the Five Pillars of Islam, must be stamped with the worldly legitimacy of the caliphal institution in order to be valid. Ironically, this rather dogmatic assertion of the sultan's ultimate authority to appoint imams, and the further insistence that they be given priority over any other prayer leader in a given mosque is meant to cut through the inevitable disputes as to the proper conduct of prayer depending upon which school of *fiqh* one subscribed to. Briefly, the immediate aim of unity and peace within a Muslim state took priority over sorting out doctrinal disputes. This end justified the means of achieving it, even if those means amounted to little more than despotism.

From the appointment of electors, to the assumption of caliphal duties, to the just administration of the market place and the mosque, Mawardi's vision of power is one which permeates every layer of society, and one in which that power itself is permeated with the divine, the execution of divine commands and the prevention of what is divinely forbidden. This rule of law is one which is inherently concerned with binding Muslims together under one political power, even one which is admittedly nominal, and which seeks to subvert doctrinal disputes to the larger good of unity in order that the Message of Islam can be more effectively spread and lived in the real world. It bears remarkably strong resonances with those of Hobbes, who lived through similar times of social, political, and religious

56 This even includes conditions under which a usurper caliph can legitimately be installed once his predecessor is shown to be no longer capable of exercising his office. See Mawardi (1996), pp. 20–1.

57 Calder (1986), p. 44.

upheaval, and like Hobbes, his primary concern is the stability of the state, in this case the meta-state that was the House of Islam.

Mawardi can be a bit of a political philosophy Rorschach test. Conservative religious thinkers can easily point to his juristic focus and advocate a traditional approach to the enforcement of *sharīʿa* and the need to reestablish a universal Caliphate. Liberals could likewise point to his various admonitions that the Caliph had to protect and look after his religion and his subjects, and could even argue this is a very basic type of social contract (albeit one without recourse to elections or other means to get rid of a poor Caliph unless this be brought about through invasion or another type of demise).

The desire to understand the rise and fall of these various states, the characteristics of their peoples and leaders, and in particular the role played by cultural identity and cohesion in gaining and maintaining political power is what motivated the work of Ibn Khaldun, whose encyclopedic examination of the known world, particularly of the medieval Islamic world, was unprecedented in scope and insight, leading many present-day scholars to refer to him as not merely a historian, but also as "the father of sociology." It is his distinctive views of the bonds and characteristics that create and bind nation and state to which this chapter next turns.

## Ibn Khaldun and the Centrality of *Asabiyya*—The Role of "Group Feeling" in Creating, Ruling, and Sustaining the State

In his recent book *African Constitutionalism and the Role of Islam*, Abdullahi An-Naʿim laments the treatment of non-Western thinkers in the global scholarly canon, saying, "In contrast to the foundational significance of Plato, Marx, or Vico as theorists of society, politics, or history in general and not just of or in the West, this level of recognition is not given to Ibn Khaldun as a philosopher of history." Not only is he not necessarily recognized as a key philosopher of history writ large, but "to the few who know his work at all in the global academy, Ibn Khaldun is seen as a sociologist of the Arab world."[58] An-Naʿim's concern may be partly ameliorated by the work of Western scholars like Antony Black, whose *The History of Islamic Political Thought* actually concludes with the sentence: "Ibn Khaldun should be read by every modern social scientist of his understanding of the kind of society that existed in the Islamic world from the seventh to seventeenth century, and to some extent beyond."[59] Although this call for wider study of Ibn Khaldun is surely justified, it is unfortunate that even it finishes with a reminder of the "Islamic" nature of his work. Indeed, commentators like Mahmoud Dhaouadi have noted that like Western sociologists, Ibn Khaldun uses "a dualist typological

58 An-Na'im, Abdullahi Ahmad. *African Constitutionalism and the Role of Islam*. Philadelphia, PA: University of Pennsylvania Press, 2006, pp. 19–20.

59 Black (2004), p. 354.

approach (Bedouin/sedentary)."[60] This examination of his work, and specifically of his use of the concept of *asabiyya* or "group feeling" as an explanatory element in the legitimacy, power, and survival or fall of political actors and groups, seeks to redress in some small way the relative lack of study he has received in the global academy. From a close look at his *Muqaddimah*, or Introduction, to his much larger work which sought to be a universal *History*, it may be possible to derive new insight into the characteristics of a ruler or ruling group that allow them to achieve a degree of constitutional legitimacy, be it in a Muslim context or otherwise.

### *Ibn Khaldun's Dualistic Approach to the Study of History and Society*

Ibn Khaldun's opening words in *The Muqadimmah* are startling when one considers that he was writing during the 14th Century AD, a time characterized by social and cultural stability and massive political upheaval, violence, and instability.[61] He begins his *History* with a categorical critique of history as it had been done to date and with an explicit definition of his own view of what history is and was as follows:

> Analogical reasoning and comparison are well known to human nature. They are not safe from error ... Often, someone who had learned a good deal of past history remains unaware of the changes that conditions have undergone. Without a moment's hesitation, he applies his knowledge (of the present) to historical information, and measures such information by the things he has observed with his own eyes, although the difference between the two is great. Consequently, he falls into an abyss of error.[62]

> It should be known that history, in matter of fact, is information about human social organization, which itself it identical with world civilization. It deals with such conditions affecting the nature of civilization as, for instance, savagery and sociability, group feelings, and the different ways by which one group of human beings achieves superiority over another .... And with all the other institutions that originate in civilization through its very nature.[63]

---

60 Dhaouadi, Mahmoud. "Ibn Khaldun: The Founding Father of Eastern Sociology." *International Sociology*, 5:3 (1990): 319–35.

61 For an excellent description of the social and political milieu of Ibn Khaldun's day, especially at the time of his writing his *History*, see Allen Fromherz, *Ibn Khaldun Life and Times*, pp. 4–32.

62 Khaldun, Ibn. NJ Dawood (Ed.); Franz Rosenthal (Transl.). *The Muqaddimah*. London: Routledge and Kegan Paul, 1987, p. 26.

63 Ibid., p. 35.

Here can be seen his view of how not to do history, and conversely a dual approach to how history should be studied. Prior to beginning his own account, he attacks the use or misuse of historical information in drawing lessons from a past that is inherently different from the present to which they are being applied.[64] Indeed, he reasons that "Times differ according to differences in affairs, tribes, and group feelings, which come into being during those (times). Differences in this respect produce differences in (public) interests, and each (public interest) has its own particular laws."[65]

Aside from its intended audience of fellow historians, Ibn Khaldun's statement could certainly also serve as a cautionary element for politicians seeking to justify their acts with the drawing of historical parallels. (The overuse of World War II metaphors immediately comes to mind.) On the issue of how history should be undertaken, what comes first is an examination of personal and group characteristics that cause a group to become superior. Second is an analysis of institutions and how they originate. It is not difficult to see the immediate application of such an approach to a consideration of constitutional issues, Western, Islamic, or otherwise.

For present purposes, Ibn Khaldun's division of history into these two categories will be utilized in order to assess to what degree he offers an original view of the constitution of the state and its leadership, and what the significance of his thought is for constitutional thought in an Islamic sense. Does his work remain bound to a highly personified vision of law in the vein of al-Farabi, or is his view of legitimacy and rule one that is more broadly applicable to societies and leaders that would not qualify for al-Farabi's seal of excellence? If so, that certainly makes his work potentially more applicable to practical politics and takes it out of the purely theoretical and philosophical realm. Likewise, the original insights he offers the thinker of constitutionalism and the state more generally speaking will also be considered.

### *The Centrality of* Asabiyya *in Ibn Khaldun*

Any discussion of Ibn Khaldun's thought necessarily centers on the concept of *asabiyya*, which has been rendered as "group feeling" in the translation of his text used here, and is otherwise also translated as "tribal affiliation."[66] For Ibn Khaldun, this quality is one that is absolutely essential politically and it is literally the cohesive force, or social glue, that holds families, tribes, and regimes together. Hayden White points out that this central concern is also strongly rooted in an examination of the relationship between the physical and social environments people inhabit. He claims that "The first part of the Muqaddimah is devoted to the

64 One is reminded here of the work of Quentin Skinner on the philosophy of history, which comes 500 years after Ibn Khaldun wrote these words.

65 Khaldun (1987), p. 169.

66 This is the preferred translation of the term for Fromherz and others as it gives perhaps a more precise vision of the type of group affinity being described.

most thorough examination of the relation between environment and society in historical literature between Herodotus and Montesquieu."[67] On his use of *asabiyya* in relation to the rise of a group and its leaders, several interesting insights emerge.

The violent nature of political maneuvering is emphasized in the writing of Ibn Khaldun. Indeed, he argues that "Nothing can be achieved in these matters without fighting for it, since man has the natural urge to offer resistance. And for fighting one cannot do without group feeling, as we mentioned from the beginning."[68]

Using the work of an earlier historian as a foil, he highlights the centrality of *asabiyya* in successful conquest:

> At-Turtushi mentions that one of the reasons for victory in war is that one side may have a larger number of brave and famous knights than the other ... The side that has more (according to him), even if only one more, will be victorious ... but he is not right. What is the fact proven to make for superiority is the situation with regard to group feeling. If one side has a group feeling comprising all, while the other side is made up of different numerous groups, and if both sides are approximately the same in numbers, then the side with a united group feeling is stronger than, and superior to, the side that is made up of several different groups.[69]

Group feeling in this view is at least partly a matter of unity in social identity. This unity, he argues, is far more powerful than historians have thus far given it credit for. Indeed, in critiquing At-Turtushi, Ibn Khaldun said that "he too failed to 'verify his statements or clarify them with the help of natural arguments' and so 'did not realize his intention'."[70] In contrast, he offers an illustration of how his assertion works in practice, he gives the example of the earliest Muslim conquests, reminding the reader that:

> The members of the dynasty they attack may be many times more numerous as they ... They are overpowered by them and quickly wiped out, as a result of the luxury and humbleness existing among them ... This happened to the Arabs at the beginning of Islam during the Muslim conquests. The armies of the Muslims at al-Qadisiyah and at the Yarmuk numbered some 30,000 in each case, which the Persian troops at al-Qadisiyah numbered 120,000, and the troops of Heraclius, according to al-Waqidi, 400,000. Neither of the two parties was able to withstand the Arabs, who routed them and seized what they possessed.[71]

67 Hayden V. White, "Ibn Khaldûn in World Philosophy of History," *Comparative Studies in Society and History*, 2:1 (1959).

68 Khaldun (1987), pp. 97–8.

69 Ibid., p. 230.

70 Malik, Mufti, "Jihad as Statecraft: Ibn Khaldun On the Conduct of War and Empire," *History of Political Thought*, 30:3 (2009), 395–6.

71 Khaldun (1987), p. 126.

Clearly, if history demonstrates that armies can prevail against odds of 4:1 and nearly 10:1, then Ibn Khaldun believes his contention should be taken seriously.[72] He sees a lack of *asabiyya* as one of the greatest threats to any political order and goes to great lengths and much repetition in offering examples of its utility and necessity.[73] One result of this is that he often glorifies and elevates the character of groups that would typically be treated as more primitive and uncivilized than those in settled urban kingdoms. Stephen Dale argues that Ibn Khaldun's view of society is one which sees an ongoing antagonism between the Bedouin (and similar groups) and the sedentary urbanites. These groups are "natural" in the sense that they unavoidably arise from human association.[74] As Ibn Khaldun sees it the reason these tribal groups are so tremendously powerful as conquerors is due to the fact that:

> The restraining influence among Bedouin tribes comes from their shaykhs and leaders. It results from the great respect and veneration they generally enjoy among the people ... Their defense and protection (of their settlements) are successful only if they are a closely knit group of common descent. This strengthens their stamina and makes them feared, since everybody's affection for his family and his group is more important (than anything else). Compassion and affection for one's blood relations and relatives exist in human nature as something God put into the hearts of men. It makes for mutual support and aid, and increases the fear felt by the enemy.[75]

These societies are not only bound in a sort of social contract; they are bound in ties of blood and familial obligation. This is important because Ibn Khaldun sees these qualities as part of the very fabric of human existence, noting that they are "something God put into the hearts of men." He affirms this elsewhere saying that "It is clear that it is in the nature of human beings to enter into close contact and to associate with each other, even though they may not have a common descent. However, such association is weaker than one based upon common descent, and the resulting group feeling is proportionally weaker too."[76]

72 It is important to keep in mind Ibn Khaldun's background in Muslim Spain and North Africa at a time of political upheaval and decay. This view of violence as crucial to gaining power would resonate with a thinker such as Machiavelli. See for example, *The Prince*, Chapter 8.

73 Montesquieu's definition of political virtue makes similar arguments for the effectiveness of group feeling, although without using the term itself. In Book 5 of *The Spirit of the Laws* he writes, "Virtue in a republic, is a very simple thing: it is the love of the republic; it is a feeling and not the result of knowledge ... Love of the homeland leads to goodness in mores, and goodness in mores leads to love of the homeland."

74 Dale, Stephen Frederic. "Ibn Khaldun: The Last Greek and the First Annaliste Historian." *International Journal of Middle East Studies*, 38:3 (2006): 431–51.

75 Khaldun (1987), p. 101.

76 Ibid., p. 292.

Not only is it woven into human nature, it is also highly useful as it "increases the fear felt by the enemy." It could be argued that the enemy discussed here is nearly always couched in terms of Bedouin vs. city-dweller. This relationship is not only antagonistic, but also evolutionary and teleological. The Bedouin, according to him, is prior in existence, but more than that, is necessary for the existence of the settled population. This is because these conquering tribes are forced to rule their conquests and take on the qualities of the very urban dwellers they defeated in prior generations. This is a fate they are seemingly unable to escape however, as it is their very purpose to seek dominion, which forces them to become "civilized."[77]

*On the Decline of* Asabiyya

In direct contrast to this characterization of the Bedouin, is his account of how urban regimes evolve and decay. The first thing that occurs is that power is consolidated, and the victorious tribe itself cedes power to its leaders, and eventually to *a* leader.

> Thus the aspirations of various group feelings are blunted. People become tame and do not aspire to share with the leaser in the exercise of control. Their group feeling is forced to refrain (from such aspirations). The leader takes charge all by himself, as far as possible. Eventually, he leaves no part in his authority to anyone else. He thus claims all glory for himself and does not permit the people to share in it … it is something unavoidable in a dynasty.[78]

Again, there is a highly deterministic view inherent in Ibn Khaldun's thought that does not envision any type of alternative path for those in power. Success is its own worst enemy.[79] One could easily question why he is so deterministic on the

77 Dale (2006), p. 437. The only possible alternative he suggests is one based on non-tribal *asabiyya*: The consequences of common descent, though natural, still are something imaginary. The real thing to bring about the feeling of close contact is social intercourse, friendly association, long familiarity, and the companionship that results from growing up together, having the same wet nurse and sharing the other circumstances of death and life. If close contact is established in such a manner, the result will be affection and co-operation. Observation of people shows this to be so.

78 Khaldun (1987), p. 132.

79 The tenuous nature of power as perceived by Ibn Khaldun is reminiscent of Augustine's discussion of the Roman Empire in *The City of God* (Book 4, Chapter 3), where he writes that "the Romans always lived in dark fear and cruel lust, surrounded by the disasters of war and the shedding of blood … the joy of such men may be compared to the fragile splendor of glass." A key difference of course is that his work largely condemns such violence because the blood that was shed is "human nonetheless" and Christian teaching advocates non-violence, whereas even in the days of Muhammad, the Muslim empire accepted and embraced the necessity of warfare for its expansion, viewing the use of force in encouraging people to enter the House of Islam as entirely legitimate.

question of power being taken over by individuals. Why is there no legitimacy or credence given to government by the few or by the whole tribe? It seems ironic that the cohesion of the group is so crucial to his thought, and yet the group is subsequently tossed aside in favor of strongman rule. Of course, it may simply be a reflection of the extent to which the idea of the Caliphate had permeated social thought, but in a thinker as original as Ibn Khaldun, this should not necessarily have meant his vision of rule would be constrained by this idea. Lest one doubt his insistence on this occurring, it is merely necessary to look again at his text, where he says that "Moreover, politics requires that only one person exercise control. Were various persons, liable to differ among each other, to exercise it, destruction of the whole could result."[80]

### Asabiyya *as Legitimacy and the Dangers of Dynastic Rule*

It may be that his obsession with one man rule is simply a result of the society and time into which he was born. This is certainly why Allen Fromherz cautions his readers not to see Ibn Khaldun as "modern," despite the many modern types of ideas that could be seen in his writings.[81] The regimes he encountered were those run by men who claimed royal titles and privileges, sometimes based on family ties, at other times based on religious titles, but always centered on consolidation of power, at least in a formal sense, into the name and hands of individual rulers. This being the case, it is noteworthy that Ibn Khaldun has a philosophical and historical justification for this political arrangement that goes beyond merely accepting the status quo. His historical account states:

> Leadership exists only through superiority, and superiority only through group feeling. Leadership over people, therefore, must, of necessity, derive from a group feeling that is superior to each individual group feeling. Each individual group feeling that becomes aware of the superiority of the group feeling of the leader is ready to obey and follow him.[82]

What he observes then, is that *asabiyya* is a force that exists within people individually as well as socially. Each individual person has agency and has to choose to assent to the rule of an *asabiyya* that is in some way "superior" to his own. This then could illuminate more constitutional applications of Ibn Khaldun's thought because, despite the despotic nature of his rulers, they are nonetheless obeyed willingly, at least at first. What makes one *asabiyya* superior to another though? To answer this question, Ibn Khaldun conceives another concept, namely "royal authority" which he derives from the following:

80 Khaldun (1987), p. 94.
81 Fromherz (2010), p. 4.
82 Khaldun (1987), p. 101.

By dint of their nature, human beings need someone to act as a restraining influence and mediator in every social organization, in order to keep its members from (fighting) with each other. That person must, by necessity, have superiority over the others in the matter of group feeling. If not, his power cannot be effective. Such superiority is royal authority. It is more than leadership. Leadership means being a chieftain, and the leader is obeyed, but he has no power to force others to accept his rulings. Royal authority means superiority and the power to rule by force.[83]

Viewed in this manner, royal authority[84] is "a goal to which group feeling leads."[85] It is not enough to have a stronger *asabiyya*, however. The ruler with royal authority also has the "power to rule by force."[86] This power is not simply exercised; it is divinely derived and causes the ruler to become a mirror of the divine presence on earth, which (it needs not be said) makes it difficult to oppose.[87] At this stage, the germ of a social contract present in the tribal assent to rule by one of their own is obliterated in pursuit of raw power.[88]

Dynastic rule is problematic for starters because "Islam does not consider preservation of (the ruler's) inheritance for his children the proper purpose of anointing a successor. Succession to the rule is something that comes from God who distinguishes it by whomever He wishes."[89] In other words, there is no proper mechanism in this type of regime to ensure that the ruler has been tested and thus

83 Khaldun (1987), pp. 107–8.

84 This appears to be translated from the word *mulk*, which could alternatively be translated as authority based on position or institutional position. See Sidani, Yusuf M. "Ibn Khaldun of North Africa: An Ad 1377 Theory of Leadership." *Journal of Management History*, 14:1 (2008): 81.

85 Dale, Stephen Frederic. "Ibn Khaldun: The Last Greek and the First Annaliste Historian." *International Journal of Middle East Studies*, 38:3 (2006): 431–51.

86 Again one cannot help but think of the general argument of Machiavelli on the effectiveness of the use of force in maintaining internal stability and external defense.

87 In Ibn Khaldun (1987), p. 112 he continues: "Furthermore, political and royal authority are God's guarantee to mankind and serve as a representation of God among men with respect to His laws … He who thus obtained group feeling guaranteeing power, and who is known to have good qualities appropriate for the execution of God's law concerning his creatures, is ready to act as His substitute and guarantor among mankind."

88 See also Ibn Khaldun (1987), p. 132, where he uses a metaphor very much like the Western conception of the ruler being the sword of God, writing: "Royal authority exists through group feeling … The secret here is that a group feeling extending over the entire tribe corresponds to the temper in the things that come into being. Temper is the product (of the mingling) of the elements. When the elements are combined in equal proportions, no mixing can take place. One (element) must be superior to the others, and when (it exercises) its superiority over them, mixing occurs. In the same way, one of the various tribal group feelings must be superior to all, in order to be able to bring them all together, to unite them, and to weld them into one group feeling comprising all the various groups. All the various groups are then under the influence of the superior group feeling."

89 Khaldun (1987), p. 169.

educated and approved for rule by God. Should anyone doubt his belief on the matter, he reiterates by saying, "Leadership must of necessity be inherited from the person who is entitled to it, in accordance with the fact, which we have stated, that superiority results from group feeling."[90] Only the possession of superior *asabiyya* is a legitimate claim to rule. Bloodline succession is explicitly rejected as the sole means of deciding succession, though it is important to recognize that it is not utterly forbidden should the descendant ruler actually possess the requisite character.[91]

This dynastic civilizing process is so destructive that Ibn Khaldun declares that it absolutely limits the life cycle of any dynasty. The deterministic element of his thought comes to the forefront yet again in his explanation of why the typical regime will only last for a few generations before it inevitably declines and is overthrown. His somewhat long generic account relates that:

> The fourth generation, then, is inferior to the preceding ones in every respect. Its member has lost the qualities that preserved the edifice of its glory. He despises (those qualities). He imagines that the edifice was built through appreciation and effort. He thinks that it was something due his people from the very beginning … and not something that resulted from group (effort) and (individual) qualities. For he sees the great respect in which he has is held by the people … He imagines that it is due to his descent and nothing else. He keeps away from those in whose group feeling he shares, thinking that he is better than they. He trusts that they will obey him because he was brought up to take their obedience for granted, and he does not know the qualities that made obedience necessary. Such qualities are humility (in dealing) with (such men) and respect for their feelings. Therefore, he considers them despicable, and they, in turn, revolt against him and despise him. They transfer leadership from his and his direct lineage to some other related branch, in obedience to their group feeling, after they have convinced themselves that the qualities of the (new leader) are satisfactory to them.[92]

According to Michael Brett, this means that "Without deeds, the masses themselves are ignored, although it is their civilization that is the cultural achievement of the political adventure, and the subject of analysis in the *Muqaddima.*" Rather than

90 Khaldun (1987), p. 101.

91 This view of succession is in keeping with earlier Greek traditions from both Aristotle and Plato that describe rulers not in terms of bloodline, but in terms of innate character. It could be argued that just as Plato thinks a philosopher-king would know best what something ought to be, including a society, so too would Ibn Khaldun's ideal ruler have the best sense of the intangible ties that bind and empower social groups. For further discussion of Plato's view of the ruler, see Peter Steinberger's excellent article "Ruling: Guardians and Philosopher-Kings" in *The American Political Science Review*, 83:4.

92 Khaldun (1987), p. 106.

focus on the benefits and achievements of this civilization, "Ibn Khaldun turns instead to the Bedouin rejected by that civilization, as the new nation growing up in the wilderness to eclipse the old, and bring the work back to its original starting-point in the Maghrib."[93] The important dynamic here is one in which the superior *asabiyya* of the ruler actually sets him apart from his group to such an extent that he loses touch with them and their values, causing him to make the deluded conclusion that it is his descent, rather than the innate quality of his ancestors, which legitimates his expectation of obedience.[94]

### Asabiyya *as Popular Assent, Potential Constitutional Implications*

Although a constitutional, representative view of government may not be present in latent form when Ibn Khaldun argues that the qualities of a legitimate ruler are "humility in dealing with such men and respect for their feelings," his work could be used by modern thinkers to advance that cause. Even more significant is the fact that the mutual distaste the 4th generation ruler generates causes his subjects to revolt and to subsequently "transfer leadership from his and his direct lineage to some other related branch, in obedience to their group feeling, after they have convinced themselves that the qualities of the (new leader) are satisfactory to them." Despite his determinism and acceptance of despotism, Ibn Khaldun is ultimately adamant that rule is only sustainable by those who have some form of popular acceptance.[95]

This principle even applies to religious leaders, especially those who take on political functions.

> Every mass political undertaking by necessity requires group feeling. This is indicated in Muhammad's saying: "God sent no prophet who did not enjoy the protection of his people." If this was the case with the prophets, who are among human beings those most likely to perform wonders, one would (expect it to

93 Brett, Michael. "The Way of the Nomad." *Bulletin of the School of Oriental and African Studies*, 58:2 (1995): 225.

94 Ibn Khaldun undertakes a more theological and Shiite oriented discussion of legitimate rule when he discusses the speculated overthrow of the "Antichrist" at the end of the world. He says: "If it is correct that a Mahdi is to appear, there is only one way for his propaganda to make its appearance. He must be one of them, and God must unite them in the intention to follow him, until he gathers enough strength and group feeling to gain success for his cause and to move the people to support him. Any other way—such as a Fatimid who would make propaganda for (the cause of the Mahdi) among people anywhere at all … by merely relying on his relationship to the family of Muhammad—will not be feasible or successful, for the sound reasons we have mentioned previously."

95 See Ibn Khaldun (1987), p. 112, where he lays out the moral argument that: The existence of group feeling without the practice of praiseworthy qualities would be a defect among people who possess a 'house' and prestige. All the more so would it be a defect in men who are invested with royal authority, the greatest possible kind of glory and prestige.

> apply) all the more so to others. One cannot expect them to be able to work the wonder of achieving superiority without group feeling.[96]

*Every* political undertaking requires *asabiyya*. This statement is not followed immediately by another about political rule, but instead is succeeded by one dealing with the legitimacy of prophets. Here can be seen a distinctive element in Ibn Khaldun's work, that advocates the fusion of the roles of prophet and politician. Earlier he writes:

> Another sign (that a person has been chosen by God to reveal truth and lead people) is the prestige they have among their people ... That means that (such a man) has group feeling and influence which protect him from harm at the hands of unbelievers, until he has delivered the messages of his Lord and achieved the degree of complete perfection with respect to his religion and religious organization that God intended for him.[97]

A religion, then, is not merely about revelation and belief; it is also an "organization." In other words, it too is a political institution. It is an institution that is mandatory for the ultimate success of the state because "Religious coloring does away with mutual jealousy and envy among people who share in a group feeling, and causes concentration upon the truth. When people come to have the (right) insight into their affairs, nothing can withstand them, because their outlook is one and their object one of common accord."[98] This statement recognizes the inherent danger in the idea of *asabiyya*, and offers religion and its corresponding morality as antidotes.[99]

*Blunting the Double-edged Sword,* Asabiyya *in the Context of Shared Faith*

Oddly, Ibn Khaldun himself offers up a strong religious critique of his advocacy of *asabiyya*, a critique from none other than Muhammad himself. He admits:

> We find that Muhammad censured group feeling and urged us to reject it and leave it alone ... We also find that Muhammad censured royal authority and its representatives ... He enjoined friendship among all Muslims and warned against discord and dissension...[100]

---

96 Khaldun (1987), p. 127.

97 Ibid., p. 71.

98 Ibid., p. 126.

99 An early Islamic example of this principle can be seen in the way Muhammad recognizes and subverts various tribal identities in the covenant referred to as "The Constitution of Medina."

100 Khaldun (1987), p. 160.

According to his own account, Muhammad asked his followers not simply to be careful with the exercise of group feeling, but rather "censured it" and "urged (them to reject it." This would seem to leave little room for the type of advocacy Ibn Khaldun undertakes countless times in his *Muqaddimah*. Even here, however, he has a ready answer to the dilemma put before him; an answer based partly on an assumed ability to interpret the Prophet's intent, and partly upon logic.

> When Muhammad forbids or censures certain human activities or urges their omission, he does not want them to be neglected altogether. Nor does he want them to be eradicated, or the powers from which they result to remain altogether unused. He wants those powers to be employed as much as possible for the right aims. Every intention should thus eventually become the right one and the direction of all human activities one and the same ... when the religious law censures group feeling ... (it) is directed against a group feeling that makes a person proud and superior .... On the other hand, a group feeling that is working for the truth and for the fulfillment of the divine commands is something desirable.[101]

What the reader is left with, following this discussion, is a matter of prioritizing the ends over the means, and intention over orthopraxy. If one could only ensure that his or her motives were rightly aligned by obeying the religious regulations given in Muhammad's revelation, then it would be possible to channel the power of *asabiyya* for good rather than evil. Ibn Khaldun makes no apologies for it, succinctly claiming that "Group feeling is necessary to the Muslim community. Its existence enables (the community) to fulfill what God expects of it."[102] This would presumably include its mission to preach Islam to the rest of the world and to set an example of Muslim unity to make this message more powerful and attractive.

The task of a community fulfilling "what God expects of it," comprises the next section of this book, which will look at the Ottoman *tanzimat* reforms of the 19th Century and the ways in which they fostered a constitutional conception of limiting government power and sharing power amongst various stakeholders in the population.

## The Tanzimat Reforms and the Rise of the Young Ottomans—Reformism and Modernization of Political Power

### *The Tanzimat in Context*

One of the most intriguing periods of Islamic thought for constitutional purposes stems from 19th Century modernization and reform movements that occurred

101 Ibid., pp. 160–1.

102 Ibid.

throughout the Islamic world, particularly in those provinces nominally part of the Ottoman Empire. This vast realm, known colloquially by Europeans as "The Sick Man of Europe," was under threat not only from European colonial encroachments and capitulations on the rights of foreigners within its bounds, but also from overwhelming internal atrophy in even the most basic government functions of tax collection, military defense, and burgeoning local nationalism that undermined the universalist and more traditional Ottoman notions of being the legitimate heirs of an Islamic empire. This identity was one that did not necessarily require particular citizens to be Muslim, but did anchor its claim for legitimacy on the caliphate and *sharīʿa*. In answer to the various threats to its survival, the bureaucrats running the Ottoman Empire promulgated a series of modernizing and sometimes liberalizing reforms aimed at using European technology and industrial advances to strengthen the economy and military of the Empire. These reforms, collectively called *Tanzimat*, were undertaken over a period of roughly 50 years (from 1826 to 1877) under the leadership of Grand Viziers including Reshid Pasha, who promulgated the Hatt-i Sherif of Gülhane, and Ali and Fuad Pasha, who together instituted the Hatt-i Humayun of 1856.[103]

The focus of this section will be upon these two edicts, as it is these two sets of reforms in particular that are addressed in the later work of another eventual Ottoman Grand Vizier, Khayr al-Din Pasha (al-Tunisi). In assessing these brief documents it is important to bear in mind that for most of Ottoman history the Empire had been run as a loose bureaucracy funded by successful conquests. Once these ceased, revenue was raised via tax farming, an inefficient means of collecting money that was riddled with opportunities for abuse and corruption. On the political side of the Empire, the Sultan was the nominal successor to the earthly rule of Muhammad himself and wielded power that can only be described as despotic. It is only in this context that the radical nature of these reforms in defining, and thereby limiting the scope of Imperial power, can be fully appreciated.

### *An examination of the 1839 Hatt-i Sherif of Gülhane*

As if to underline the despotic past just mentioned, the 1839 Hatt-i Sherif of Gülhane begins with the statement:

> All the world knows that since the first days of the Ottoman State, the lofty principles of the Qur'an and the rules of the Sheriat were always perfectly observed. Our mighty Sultanate reached the highest degree of strength and power, and all its subjects [the highest degree] of ease and prosperity.[104]

---

103 Weiker, Walter F. "The Ottoman Bureaucracy: Modernization and Reform." *Administrative Science Quarterly*, 13:3 (1968): 451–70.

104 Hatt-i Sherif of Gülhane or *Hatt-ı Hümayun of Gülhane* (1839), paragraph 1.

Although the perfect observation of the *sharīʿa* is clearly aspirational at best, this text reveals that, at a minimum, the idea that the Empire observes Islamic law and fulfills its earthly purpose is central to its identity and mission. This is then linked with the Sultanate reaching "the highest degree of strength and power." The question naturally arising from this is why, if it is also true that "all its subjects (have reached) the highest degree of ease and prosperity," is reform necessary. Of course, the simple answer is that Ottoman subjects were far from the top of the world's wealthiest citizens, and that there was general unease about the state of the Empire and a lack of prosperity. The document continues by acknowledging the following:

> in the last one hundred and fifty years, because of a succession of difficulties and diverse causes, the sacred Sheriat was not obeyed, nor were the beneficent regulations followed; consequently, the former strength and prosperity have changed into weakness and poverty. It is evident that countries not governed by the laws of the Sheriat cannot survive.[105]

Notice that there is no admission of responsibility for this state of affairs on the part of the Sultan. The poor fortunes of the Empire are due to a lack of obedience to the *sharīʿa* and "beneficent regulations," rather than due to simple mismanagement and corruption. Regardless of the lack of admission of culpability, Ottoman elites had no illusions as to the seriousness of the need for major change. As Ira Lapidus comments, "Russian advances in the Caucasus, the rise to power of Muhammad ʿAli in Egypt, and the Greek wars for independence again made the need for reform urgent.[106] Ironically, the initial push for reform was one that sought to centralize government to make it more efficient, which was also meant to strengthen the Sultan's power to move beyond the largely nominal roles of Caliph and Commander of the Faithful, and to turn him into something resembling a European absolute monarch. This involved dismantling the janissary corps and co-opting religious courts and schools into the state.[107] Nonetheless, these reforms ultimately led to several liberalizing strains of thought, which guaranteed basic rights to all Ottoman subjects regardless of their religious or national background, which in turn made these subjects more like citizens in the modern and legal sense than they had ever been before.

The Hatt-i Sherif of Gülhane reorganized and limited state power in four crucial and constitutional ways. Firstly, it established security of one's person and private property for all of its subjects. Secondly, it created and defined the purposes of various state institutions that would collect taxes in a regulated and fair manner to ensure a reliable revenue stream. Next, it regulated military service to

105 *Hatt-ı Hümayun of Gülhane* (1839), paragraph 1.

106 Lapidus, Ira M. *A History of Islamic Societies*. Cambridge: Cambridge University Press, 1988, pp. 597–8.

107 Ibid., p. 598.

limited terms and in consideration of the numbers of soldiers individual localities could realistically be expected to contribute. Finally, it established the principle that criminal trials and sentencing should be held publicly and that punishing crime could only occur after due process. In each of these aims it is apparent that discontent and a lack of stability threatened the survival of the regime and these are all attempts to address the most pressing of those threats.

This first task of creating and securing private property rights is one that would be familiar to any constitutional thinker in the Western tradition.[108] Commerce and trade, along with hospitality, also form the backbone of Islamic culture. The edict recognizes this urgent need, reasoning that

> If there is an absence of security for property, everyone remains indifferent to his state and his community; no one interests himself in the prosperity of the country, absorbed as he is in his own troubles and worries. If, on the contrary, the individual feels complete security about his possessions then he will become preoccupied with his own affairs, which he will seek to expand, and his devotion and love for his state and his community will steadily grow and will undoubtedly spur him into becoming a useful member of society.[109]

There is a sense in this statement that subjects must become citizens and see themselves as stake holders in the Empire if it is to command their loyalty and support. Much as the bureaucrats running the affairs of the Empire had a vested interest in sustaining it, and as the janissary officers had an interest in expansion via conquest, it was hoped that people would see the Empire as a protector and benefactor, a sphere within which a person could pursue wealth with the reasonable expectation that it would be protected from arbitrary theft.

Closely related to this protection of property is the regulation of taxes. The edict bluntly states that "Tax assessment is also one of the most important matters to regulate." Stanford Shaw's article entitled "The Nineteenth-Century Ottoman Tax Reforms and Revenue System" gives a compelling account of why this was one of the areas in urgent need of rethinking. This is because the "tax system inherited by the Tanzimat was basically that developed during the sixteenth century in accordance with traditional Islamic financial practices."[110] These included a tithe on agricultural produce collected from *timur*, or fiefs, and *iltizam*, or tax farms

108 See John Locke's *Second Treatise of Government*, Chapter IX (pp. 350–1), in which he writes, "And 'tis not without reason, that he seeks out, and is willing to joyn in Society with others who are already united, or have a mind to unite for the mutual *Preservation* of the Lives, Liberties and Estates, which I call by the general Name, *Property* … The great and *chief end* therefore, of Men's uniting into Commonwealths, and putting themselves under Government, *is the Preservation of their Property.*

109 Hatt-i Sherif of Gülhane (1839), paragraph 5.

110 Shaw, Stanford J. "The Nineteenth-Century Ottoman Tax Reforms and Revenue System." *International Journal of Middle East Studies*, 6:4 (1975): 421.

in addition to fees for entering or leaving territories and towns, using the market, customs duties, and for non-Muslims, the *jizya* or head tax given in exchange for military protection and exemption from conscription.[111]

In contrast to the earlier language deflecting blame for the Empire's failures from the Sultan, this particular section of the edict is uncharacteristically direct in castigating the existing practice of tax farming as "harmful" and something which "amounts to handing over the financial and political affairs of a country to the whims of an ordinary man and perhaps to the grasp of force and oppression, for if the tax-farmer is not of good character he will be interested only in his own profit and will behave oppressively." Obviously, the lack of consistent tax revenue and complaints of subjects from various corners of the Empire had led the Grand Vizier and Sultan to conclude that the system was irreparably corrupted and unfair.[112] Although the document is vague on the level of taxation and system of calculating taxes due, it does promise that everyone "should be taxed according to his fortune and his means, and that he should be saved from any further exaction." In practice, this meant that taxation was made more urban and things like profit from one's trade and craft were taxed, which necessarily meant that taxes would be more proportional to one's ability to pay them than they were under the previous system of paying fees for simply using the marketplace or travelling.[113]

Although this tax reform plan is one that could easily be used to enhance the despotic power of the Sultan, this centralizing vein of reform brings to mind a key constitutional idea, which is that before tackling the problem of tyranny in government, it is vital for a government to legitimize itself by protecting its subjects/citizens from the tyranny of a Hobbesian State of Nature in which life, limb, and property are all at constant risk of attack.[114] Only once some type of

---

111 Shaw (1975), p. 421. Note that at this stage, subjects of the Empire are not equal before the law as non-Muslims are obligated to pay the head tax and forbidden military service. They are, however, allowed a high degree of religious and communal autonomy and many groups, such as the Jews, fared better historically under this system, than they did in Christian Europe.

112 In fact, the system of reform was difficult to enforce in the countryside and the old *iltizam* system had to be temporarily restored in order to take advantage of local connections and the self-interest of the tax farmers themselves. This was finally reformed in 1847 by giving tax farmers longer 5-year leases on their taxation rights, which encouraged long-term thinking. Additionally, they had to provide for the welfare of individual farmers, providing them with very low interest loans for basic supplies, waiting to collect revenue until after the harvest and they were only able to charge the tax based on market rates. This greatly protected peasants from the most flagrant abuses of the system's past. See Shaw (1975), p. 423.

113 Shaw (1975), pp. 422–3.

114 Of course Hobbes is only one of many thinkers who make the argument that state legitimacy is based first and foremost on protection of life. The addition of property protection however can trace its roots back to ancient Roman thought in Cicero's Republic, and continues to be a mainstay of present-day Conservative thought.

uniform definition of justice and protection of personhood and property are achieved can citizens participate in the creation of institutions to administer the state and in limiting the power these institutions exercise.[115]

Likewise, the necessity of protecting one's citizens and maintaining a military had led to the unintended consequence that conscription had become an extremely onerous burden on certain segments of the population. Muslim tradition did not allow for non-Muslims to serve in the military, which reduced the number of men eligible to fight. Furthermore, those in military service were not given a clear idea as to when they could expect their obligation to have been met. This is evident from the wording of the decree which admits:

> legislation will put an end to the old practices, still in force, of recruiting soldiers without consideration of the size of the population in any locality, more conscripts being taken from some places and fewer from others. This practice has been throwing agriculture and trade into harmful disarray. Moreover, those who are recruited to lifetime military service suffer despair and contribute to the depopulation of the country.[116]

Clearly, if particular towns were losing substantial numbers of their young men to the military, especially in agricultural areas, it would be difficult for entire communities to survive, let alone prosper. Once again, this particular set of reforms strengthened the Sultan by allowing the government to regulate conscription according to its needs and to do so in a way meant to foster domestic stability. It does however, carry the latent promise that individual citizens and localities matter and should have a voice in the conduct of the state's affairs.

Finally, a very brief section of the document focuses upon the criminal justice or penal system. All subjects are promised that "every defendant shall be entitled to a public hearing, according to the rules of the Sheriat, after inquiry and examination; and without the pronouncement of a regular sentence no one may secretly or publicly put another to death by poison or by any other means."[117] Although not exactly a liberal beacon, the wording of the protections given to those accused of a crime would seem to establish something very much like the Western concept of habeas corpus because an accused must be presented to a public court and cannot be secretly sentenced if found guilty. The mechanisms available to the courts and their composition are not specified here, but nonetheless this does represent a

115 In the Edict itself, there is already a limit on this power in the form of an admission that "It is also necessary that special laws should fix and limit the expenses of our land and sea forces." This tackles the spending side of the government budget equation, ensuring that the state cannot recklessly pursue wars that would unnecessarily strain the resources of its citizenry.

116 Hatt-i Sherif of Gülhane (1839), paragraph 7.

117 Ibid., paragraph 9.

substantive check on state power simply by requiring a level of transparency in the justice and penal systems.[118]

The closing section of this early *Tanzimat* edict gives further tantalizing promises of reforms yet to come, saying that other "decisions must be taken by majority vote."[119] However, the crucial caveat is that this majority is not of voters, adult males, propertied male voters, nor of any citizen group, but rather simply of a council of advisers chosen by the Sultan and his Vizier. Though not an enormous restraint, it does still allow for the leadership to consult one another and to potentially direct the sovereign will towards the public good.

## An Analysis of the Hatt-i Humayun of 1856

In 1856, yet another round of reforms were launched, some of which bring to fruition earlier promises only hinted at in the Hatt-i Sherif of Gülhane. These largely follow the earlier set of reforms in terms of subject matter and aims, focusing on reorganizing the tax code, modernizing the military, standardizing the process of creating a state budget and using it for infrastructure, and enhancing equality before the law of non-Muslim subjects. These reforms, particularly those relating to the status of non-Muslims, are far more radical in their moves away from traditional notions of *sharīʿa* compliance and toward a Westernized conception of liberal equality.

The tax reforms of 1839 attempted to overthrow the tax farming system in favor of one in which government agents would be directly responsible for collecting an established percentage of profits from urbanites and of the harvest yield from rural subjects. This had to be abandoned in the countryside, as discussed previously, and the tax farming system was temporarily reinstated. By 1856, the new system of direct collection had been refined and consolidated to the point where the government was prepared to move at last to abolish tax farming, stating:

> The system of direct collection shall gradually, and as soon as possible, be substituted for the plan of farming, in all the branches of the revenues of the State. As long as the present system remains in force, all agents of the Government and all members of the Meclis shall be forbidden, under the severest penalties, to become lessees of any farming contracts which are announced for public competition, or to have any beneficial interest in carrying them out.[120]

What is notable in this passage is the direct language aimed at rooting out potential conflicts of interest and corruption from within the corps of tax collection

118 See Tom Bingham's *The Rule of Law*, for an excellent discussion of habeas corpus rights and their development from *Magna Carta* to the present.

119 Hatt-i Sherif of Gülhane (1839), paragraph 10.

120 Hatt-i Humayun (1856), paragraph 23.

officers already in government employ. While this goal is laudable, it is largely a continuation of earlier reform. The innovation in this particular set of tax reforms is found just prior in the section dealing with the taxation of non-Muslims. Here, for the first time in the Ottoman Empire, it is declared that, "The taxes are to be levied under the same denomination from all the subjects of my empire, without distinction of class or of religion."[121] This represents a substantial break from tradition as the *jizya* tax levied on non-Muslims in exchange for military protection and exemption from military duties is one of the most venerable in Islamic tradition, tracing itself back to the days of Muhammad himself.[122] The reason behind this change will become clear as the corresponding military reforms are examined.

Like the *jizya*, the prohibition on non-Muslims serving in the military of an Islamic state is one which has long-standing acceptance dating back to Muhammad.[123] The Hatt-i Humayun of 1856 makes a radical break from this tradition when it announces the following:

> The equality of taxes entailing equality of burdens, as equality of duties entails that of rights, Christian subjects and those of other non-Muslim sects, as it has been already decided, shall, as well as Muslims, be subject to the obligations of the Law of Recruitment. The principle of obtaining substitutes, or of purchasing exemption, shall be admitted. A complete law shall be published, with as little delay as possible, respecting the admission into and service in the army of Christian and other non-Muslim subjects.[124]

The connection between the tax reforms for non-Muslims and the reform of the military is thus made perfectly clear. It is also written in language that would find itself comfortably at home in the Western philosophical tradition of speaking of government in terms of reciprocal rights and duties. The appearance of the word rights itself should not be underestimated, as it implies that subjects of the Empire are not bound to arbitrary rule, but to an expectation of rule of law. Again, this reform like so many others acts as an important curb on the potential abuse of state power and acknowledges that individual and community rights are part of

121 Ibid., paragraph 23.

122 See Qur'an, Sura 9:29, which mentions the *jizya* as a means of humbling People of the Book who have not accepted Islam. It seems it was initially meant to be a tax that would motivate people to convert to Islam by both ostracizing and penalizing their decision to remain outside the *umma*.

123 Interestingly, as the *Constitution of Medina* indicates, even Muhammad did allow non-Muslims to fight in the earliest days of his political leadership, so long as they were monotheists and willing to submit to his political rule. It could be argued that the situations of both Muhammad's Medina (Yathrib at this time) and of the Ottoman Empire were dire enough to be considered in a struggle for their very existence, which could provide a justification for contradicting this well-established point of *sharīʿa*.

124 Hatt-i Humayun (1856), paragraph 20.

the social contract. For the first time, non-Muslims can serve in the military, and for the first time they are subject to recruitment quotas previously only applied to Muslims. This did not mean in practice that Christians were truly treated as equals once they entered the military. Roderic Davison notes that the idea of serving under Christian officers caused many Muslim military men to take umbrage.[125] This state of affairs may not have been satisfactory to all parties as some inequalities can be personally beneficial (i.e. if one is a pacifist not wishing to fight in war). However, what is not clear in this passage is whether the "principle of obtaining substitutes, or of purchasing exemption," applies to Muslims as well as to the non-Muslims who traditionally had this option. If the equality of burdens was truly being shared by this reform, then one would have to assume this was possible.

This set of military reforms, was only one of many changes to the law designed to provide a greater sense of Ottoman identity and citizenship. Another basic, but essential, reform was the passage of a law which published and publicized the annual government budget.[126] This corruption-fighting measure was twinned with a promise to ensure that public works "receive a suitable endowment, part of which shall be raised from private and special taxes levied in the Provinces, which shall have the benefit of the advantages arising from the establishment of ways of communication by land and sea."[127] This particular set of reforms accomplishes two important aims. Firstly, it ensures that Ottoman subjects have a clear idea of what their state is raising in taxes and spending on the public's behalf. This type of information provides a means with which a person or group could usefully comment upon or perhaps even oppose the way in which the government is either taxing or spending. It also makes it less likely that various actors down the chain of command will be able to raid government coffers.[128] Secondly, it brings disparate corners of the Empire together (or at least seeks to) by using well-tested means to create new avenues of commerce and communication, such as "the formation of roads and canals to increase the facilities of communication and increase the sources of the wealth of the country. Everything that can impede commerce or agriculture shall be abolished."[129] It could be argued that in present-day terms, the Ottoman Empire thus saw itself as a sort of Islamic type of European Union, a commercial and cultural union of distinct nations, and like the EU, it sought to

125 Davison (1954), p. 859.

126 See Paragraph 26 of the Hatt-i Humayun: "A special law having been already passed, which declares that the budget of the revenue and expenditure of the State shall be drawn up and made known every year, the said law shall be most scrupulously observed. Proceedings shall be taken for revising the emoluments attached to each office."

127 Hatt-i Humayun (1856), paragraph 25.

128 This type of occurrence was widespread in some Ottoman provinces and plays a key part in the biography of Khayr al-Din al-Tunisi, whose work will be examined later.

129 Hatt-i Humayun (1856), paragraph 22. Of course, the section which promises to abolish "everything which can impede commerce or agriculture" would seem to be rather aggressive and unlikely, but the overall aim could not be clearer.

enhance the larger sense of Ottoman identity and to emphasize the various benefits of cooperation and union in terms of not only commerce, but also defense and international power.

The tension between the need to maintain a distinctly Islamic identity and to find a way to include its non-Muslim subjects in a way that would ensure their loyalty was a vexing problem for an empire on the wane. Eastern European parts of the Ottoman domains were already host to friendly overtures from various Christian states, and other more distant parts of the Empire in North Africa were facing the threat of Western colonial expansion. This might explain why the vast majority of the 1856 reforms were focused on the status and rights of non-Muslims. These reforms were of paramount importance in light of the massive number of non-Muslims, the majority of whom were Christians, living under Ottoman rule. Roderic Davison estimates that out of 35 million total subjects, fully 14 million of them were non-Muslims.[130] This represents 40 percent of the total population. Davison assesses the importance of these particular *Tanzimat* reforms by saying "It is, therefore, one of the most significant aspects of Ottoman history in the nineteenth century that the doctrine of equality did, in fact, become official policy."[131]

The actual details of this equality are sketched out throughout the text and are relevant to each of the other sets of reforms already discussed. In fact, the document begins by reminding readers of the earlier Hatt-i Sherif of Gülhane and promising to uphold and more fully manifest its promises to all of the Ottoman Empire's subjects, "without distinction of classes or religion."[132] Again, this is a radical departure from the entire legacy of the Ottoman Empire in promoting itself as a primarily Islamic state and shows that a more modern conception of the nation state as a secular entity was already forming well before Ataturk created Turkey as we know it today. The document continues in the next paragraph by promising to uphold the traditional autonomy of various religious minorities as represented in the ancient millet system, but adds to this a promise that these each of these groups will be invited "to examine its actual immunities and privileges, and to discuss and submit to my Sublime Porte the reforms required by the progress of civilization and of the age."[133] Although these representatives are not directly elected or chosen by any sort of democratic process, the fact that the Sultan is inviting feedback and consultation is a departure from despotism.

In addition to the new military rights/duties and the change in tax status for non-Muslims that have previously been discussed, the reforms seek to realize their equal opportunity rhetoric[134] by opening up the bureaucracy, which is often

130 Davison, Roderic H. "Turkish Attitudes Concerning Christian-Muslim Equality in the Nineteenth Century." *The American Historical Review*, 59:4 (1954): 844–64.

131 Davison (1954), p. 846.

132 Hatt-i Humayun (1856), paragraph 1.

133 Ibid., paragraph 2.

134 See Hatt-i Humayun (1856), paragraphs 10 and 11, which read as follows: "Every distinction or designation tending to make any class whatever of the subjects of my

considered to be the real power behind the Ottoman state, to members of any nation.[135] The new meritocracy would theoretically make a relatively prosperous lifestyle available to vast new swaths of the population, although, as later discussions of the *Tanzimat* in Khayr al-Din's work will show, this was not necessarily a move that endeared the majority Muslim populations to the new reforms.

The other sector of the state that is specifically mentioned in regards to minority rights is the court system, both civil and criminal. In order to protect the rights of both parties in a dispute, the Hatt-i Humayun establishes that when the religions of the parties are not the same, they will be given a public hearing before a "mixed tribunal." When the parties share the same faith, they will be given the option of having their cases tried within their own communities, according to their own customs. This is very much like the Jewish, and in some cases *sharīʿa*, courts that are operating in some of today's Western liberal democracies. This reaffirms traditional Ottoman rule in the sense of local autonomy,[136] and establishes a new principle that recognizes that communities may become more mixed as equality and commerce measures come into force, which will require a legal and justice system that has come to terms with this possibility.[137] Additionally, as subjects are treated more like citizens and become accustomed to thinking in terms of personal rights, the enforcement of those rights and the restriction of government powers

Empire inferior to another class, on account of their religion, language, or race, shall be for ever effaced from the Administrative Protocol. The laws shall be put in force against the use of any injurious or offensive term, either among private individuals or on the part of the authorities.

As all forms of religion are and shall be freely professed in my dominions, no subject of my Empire shall be hindered in the exercise of the religion that he professes, nor shall be in any way annoyed on this account. No one shall be compelled to change their religion."

135 The language used here in paragraph 12 is distinct. It says that employment in the state apparatus will be based not on nationality, but on merit. This reveals that the reforms are again aiming to create a more cohesive sense of Ottoman nationality to combat and compete more localized nationalities that were coming to the fore.

136 Starr, June. *Law as Metaphor: From Islamic Courts to the Palace of Justice*. Albany, NY: State University of New York Press, 1992. She begins her book by quoting Serif Mardin's observation that "For much of the population [in the Ottoman Empire], nomad or settled, rural or urban … cultural separation was the most striking feature of its existence on the periphery."

137 To this effect, paragraphs 16 and 17 create new safeguards for all subjects, Muslim and non-Muslim, saying: "Penal, correctional, and commercial laws, and rules of procedure for the mixed tribunals shall be drawn up as soon as possible, and formed into a Code. Translation of them shall be published in all the languages current in the Empire.

Proceedings shall be taken, with as little delay as possible, for the reform of the penitentiary system as applied to houses of detention, punishment, or correction, and other establishments of like nature, so as to reconcile the rights of humanity with those of justice. Corporal punishment shall not be administered, even in the prisons, except in conformity with the disciplinary regulations established by my Sublime Porte, and everything that resembles torture shall be entirely abolished."

to impede upon them become crucial. The penal reforms mentioned towards the end of this document are important not only because they go so far as to say that "everything that resembles torture shall be entirely abolished," but the following paragraph makes the pointed assertion that "Infractions of the law in this particular shall be severely (punished) … in conformity with the Civil Code, of the authorities who may order and of the agents who may commit them."[138] It is only by holding government agents to account in this manner, that the government can consolidate the legitimacy of its rule and reforms.

Given the highly segregated nature of religious groups and nationalities in the Empire, legitimacy of these reforms would also be highly dependent upon their endorsement by the relevant authorities.[139] When the regime promised that "Proceedings shall be taken for a reform in the constitution of the Provincial and Communal Councils, in order to ensure fairness in the choice of the deputies of the Muslim, Christian, and other communities, and freedom of voting in the councils,"[140] they were taking yet another key step in providing new avenues of political participation and representation. Both of these forces empower the government by giving it legitimacy and popular reach, but also limit its power by tethering its acts in some way to the will of the people. Again, this was not anything like representative democracy, but was a type of communal representation and would have allowed all Ottomans to feel they had a voice.[141]

Although not directly related to the rights of minorities, or to limiting government power, one final note on this set of reforms is necessary. It is impossible to appreciate the goals and necessity of these types of reforms without recalling the extreme pressure European development and expansion were placing upon the Empire. Under pressure, the edict also includes the following provision:

> As the laws regulating the purchase, sale, and disposal of real property are common to all the subjects of may empire, it shall be lawful for foreigners to possess landed property in my dominions, conforming themselves to the laws and police regulations, and bearing the same charges as the native inhabitants, and after arrangements have been come to with foreign powers.[142]

---

138 Hatt-i Humayun (1856), paragraph 18.

139 This actually forms a key audience for Khayr al-Din in his defense of the *tanzimat* since he spends a great deal of time addressing the ulama in his work and essentially selling them on the Islamic virtue of reform.

140 Hatt-i Humayun (1856), paragraph 22.

141 This idea is taken yet further in paragraph 27, which requires "The heads of each community and a delegate designed by my Sublime Porte … to take part in the deliberations of the Supreme Council of Justice on all occasions which might interest the generality of the subjects of my Empire." They also serve one-year terms, which could either make it easier for the regime to oust members whose opinions were less welcome, or could make the advisors more accountable to the groups they were representing.

142 Hatt-i Humayun (1856), paragraph 23.

This capitulation to foreign pressure would result in further compromises that eventually allowed foreigners to escape Ottoman jurisdiction for criminal matters,[143] and the property rules eventually led to fiscal disaster.[144] Although the many reforms and rights being made by the Ottomans in the 19th Century placed them more firmly within the European model of political thought and within the European political orbit, the relationships between the Ottoman Empire and various European powers were dominated by colonial designs and Ottoman decline, sped along by rapid industrial and military advances in Western Europe.

*Assessing the Mixed Legacy of the* Tanzimat *in 19th Century Reform Movements*

Although the *Tanzimat* reforms were not ultimately successful in saving the Ottoman Empire from collapse, or perhaps reformulation may be a better term, it is worth pointing out that they nonetheless inspired a sea-change in the political aspirations of a whole variety of political thinkers and actors within the Ottoman orbit. In fact, there is a surprisingly close relationship between some of the leading figures of these movements and the Ottoman court.

One of the best known of these Muslim modernists is Jamal al-Din al-Afghani. Despite protestations to the contrary, evidence seems to suggest that Afghani was not courted by Sultan Abdul-Hamid, so much as he himself sought to be brought into the sultan's inner circle, even castigating reformers in his writing to curry favor.[145] An alternative argument is that Afghani opposed the particular brand of Young Ottoman constitutionalism because it was secular and did not reflect the Muslim character

143 See p. 6 of Yannis Stivachtis' chapter, "The Politics of Power and Identity in European-Turkish Relations," in Müftüler-Bac, Meltem, and Yannis A. Stivachtis. *Turkey–European Union Relations: Dilemmas, Opportunities, and Constraints*. Lanham, MD: Lexington Books, 2008. He points out a major cultural misunderstanding in the way the capitulations were perceived by the Europeans and Ottoman Turks. While the Ottomans saw the capitulations giving European trading rights and powers of jurisdiction over their own nationals living within Ottoman domains as something which would only last for the life of the Sultan who agreed to them, European powers saw them as binding in a non-personalized sense that made them permanent barring mutual agreement to change or repeal them.

144 See Davison (1954), p. 850, where he claims that the two reform edicts being discussed here were both a response to external pressures as much or more than internal ones. "The Hatt-i Sherif of 1839 was proclaimed at a time when Muhammad Ali of Egypt threatened the empire's integrity and when the Ottoman government sorely needed the European support which such a promise of reform might help to secure. The Hatt-i Humayun of 1856 was issued under diplomatic pressure as a means of avoiding foreign supervision of Ottoman reform after the Crimean War."

145 For discussion of the relationship between Afghani and Abdul-Hamid, see Keddie, Nikki R. "The Pan-Islamic Appeal: Afghani and Abdülhamid Ii." *Middle Eastern Studies*, 3:1 (1966): 46–67.

of the majority of the Turkish and Ottoman people.[146] In either case, his idea of an Islam-based nationalism was an alternative constitutional response to what were seen to be fundamental flaws in the *Tanzimat*. Firstly, the rights expressed in these reforms are granted to the subjects by the ruler. They are neither "God-given" nor "inalienable" but rather a gift, and one which could potentially be revoked at that. Additionally, many of the Turks in the Ottoman court felt that the reforms were only beneficial to non-Muslims and thus found it impossible to support them.[147]

Attempts to rectify these problems were proposed by the Young Ottoman constitutionalists, who brought about their own revolution within the system and managed for a time to implement a fairly liberal institutionalized government based upon the core value of liberty.[148] A glance at their core constitutional argument is instructive in the manner in which they used the spirit of the *Tanzimat* as a platform to create what they felt was a balanced approach to personal liberty and the preservation of the Muslim nature of the Ottoman state. Their contentions were:

> A constitutional government meant a government run according to a fundamental law. The Ottoman state was an Islamic state, that is, its government was based on and regulated by the Seriat. As such, it was basically constitutional; but, because of the non-observance of the Seriat, it had turned into an absolutism. The *ummet* should restore government and its rulers to a constitutional condition. This could be done only by making the *ummet* the supreme controller of the government, that is, by institutionalizing and assembly representing the people. The duties of this assembly were; (a) to supervise the revenues and the expenditures of the state; (b) to see to the full execution of the Seriat and the laws; and (c) to demand the modification of laws harmful to the interests of the country. The assembly, therefore, was not a body to make laws, or to execute them. Its members were rather "the defense lawyers of the people, so to speak." The duty of the assembly was only to watch, check, and defend the interests of the people against the improper execution of the laws. It was a body to enlighten the ruler against the tyranny of the government, and the only means through which to voice the needs of the people and to check the government. This function of the assembly did not curtail the sovereign rights of the ruler. The enforcement of the Seriat, and the approval and execution of laws were within the authority of the ruler. The institution of this assembly with non-Muslim members was not contrary to the Seriat, because the assembly was not constituted to discuss or decide upon religious affairs ... Muslims and non-Muslims were equal in terms of law.... In introducing the constitutional regime, there was no need to imitate the systems

146 Berkes Niyazi. *The Development of Secularism in Turkey*. New York: Routledge, 1998, p. 240.

147 Ibid.

148 See for example Black (2001), pp. 292–5. Also Berkes (1998), pp. 223–50.

> of European countries because the Muslim Seriat provided all the necessary principles amply and comprehensively.[149]

Comparing this set of constitutional contentions to the two reform decrees promulgated in previous decades shows a remarkably similar set of concerns. Both the original *Tanzimat* reforms and the constitutionalist response to them are concerned with somehow incorporating non-Muslims more fully into the state whilst protecting the Islamic nature of the state. Likewise, there is a fundamental understanding that basic economic justice and non-corrupt management of state coffers are essential for legitimacy and stability. Perhaps most interestingly, even the "secular" constitutionalists couch their diagnosis of the state's ills in terms of non-compliance with the letter and spirit of *sharīʿa*. Thus it is clear that those on all sides of the reform debate, the relevant parties saw the preservation of at least a nominally Muslim state identity as absolutely crucial. Furthermore, both also hearken back to an idealized past in order to claim that all the tools needed in structuring this new constitutional regime can be reclaimed from within the Muslim historical and political tradition. In a time of waning empire and European encroachment and domination, the Caliphate represented "a self-confident Muslim ruler, independent of all foreign influences and interventions ... he fostered everything that preserved, glorified, and justified tradition."[150] What emerges then is a picture of reform itself becoming an effort to preserve tradition against colonial and cultural imperialism, but the ideological nature of this reform was not up to the task of changing the material conditions that would actually determine the continued viability of the Ottoman state.[151]

## Assessing the Contours of Islamic Constitutionalism—Distinctives and Commonalities

Having looked at the Islamic interpretations of the rule of law, national character, and limiting government power in the works of al-Farabi, Ibn Khaldun, and the Ottoman *Tanzimat* reforms, respectively, it is clear that these thinkers have much in common with their Western counterparts. It is also clear that an Islamic

---

149 Berkes (1998), pp. 240–1.

150 Ibid., p. 255.

151 There are numerous examples of interesting thinkers from this period who deserve detailed study as constitutionalists. The include Muhammad Abduh, Rashid Rida, the Young Turks, and those involved in the Iranian Constitutional Revolution of 1909, amongst many others. A good starting point for an overview of their ideas can be found in Najjar's (2004) "Ibn Rushd (Averroes) and the Egyptian Enlightenment Movement," Berkes' (1998) *The Development of Secularism in Turkey*, Black's (2001) *The History of Islamic Political Thought*, and of course Hourani's (1983) now classic *Arabic Thought in the Liberal Age*.

constitutional narrative uses its own distinct vocabulary and historical points of reference in its effort to create meaning and legitimacy for its ideas.

Assessing al-Farabi's legacy alongside that of thinkers like Cicero or Aquinas is perhaps the most straightforward of all. As mentioned above, his work was crucial in reintroducing ancient Greek texts that had largely been lost after the fall of Rome back into European scholarship. His conception of the afterlife and its relationship to properly fulfilling one's role in society is notable for its emphasis on social rather than individual life, and it employs almost identical imagery to that found in Cicero's Dream of Scipio. In the case of Aquinas, it has been shown that much of his work is borrowed wholesale from al-Farabi, begging the question of whether Islamic thinkers need to Islamicize Western thought, or whether, in fact, Western thinkers as early as the Middle Ages were Westernizing political thought that had already been interpreted and mediated by its Arabic translators and torch bearers.[152] His conception of the rule of law fits comfortably within the Western natural law tradition, yet contains enough distinct elements as regards the role of the Prophet/Lawgiver and adhering to the sovereign order embodied by nature and symbolized by God, that it remains true to many of the core tenants of Islam (at least on its surface).

Ibn Khaldun, on the other hand, is a thinker whose departure from the established norms of doing historical and political analysis makes him a truly rare revolutionary, at least in scholarly terms. On the question of assessing people groups as nations, rather than as a united *umma*, and in regards to his association of climate to national character, his thought closely aligns with Montesquieu's, though it predates it by a few centuries. The revolutionary aspect of his work, at least from the perspective of constitutionalism, is his concept of *asabiyya* and the central role it plays in both the cohesion and rise of social groups, along with the eventual downfall of comfortable urbanized regimes. His deterministic approach does seem to limit the possibilities for escaping the cycle of rise and fall, but if one assesses his work aside from its predictive elements, political rulers could potentially draw a variety of lessons about the sources of legitimacy for an Islamic regime. However, if one takes *asabiyya* outside its purely tribal origins and transplants it onto a faith group, then this unity by faith can be maintained through a close observance of the values and norms of that faith. This could be especially useful in post-conflict settings because his work does not shy away from discussing the role of violence, but it does provide a conceptual framework in which the Bedouin warrior ethic can be translated into a political movement. In fact, in looking at instances in which groups formerly involved in terrorist activity transitioned into peaceful political movements, most of them do not entirely dissociate from their earlier violent terminology, but they do demilitarize and make the fight one of political justice carried out through the institutions of the state.

152 See for instance, Hammond, Robert. *The Philosophy of Al Farabi and Its Influence on Medieval Thought.* New York: Hobson Book Press, 1947. This book conveniently lays out passages between the two philosophers in parallel for extremely efficient comparison.

The Ottoman Empire is an institution that in some ways perfectly embodies and proves the argument of Ibn Khaldun. It was founded by a group of fierce warriors whose success on the battlefield sustained its growth and prosperity for hundreds of years. It was urbanized in terms of its political leadership and bureaucracy, especially after winning Constantinople, but it was also still tribal and militaristic. Its class of janissaries maintained their influence in the state for as long as they proved mighty in way. The mamluk civil servant/slave class facilitated the maintenance of these hard-won lands by ensuring that taxes were levied, and that Muslim leaders adhered to the party line of the sultans in their role as caliph. It also kept the tribal *asabiyya* of its conquered subjects alive by allowing various national, linguistic, and religious groups to attend to their own private and local community matters through the millet system. Once the machinery of conquest began to break down, the social fault lines that had been papered over by general prosperity and tolerance reemerged and, though it took far more than the four generations predicted by Ibn Khaldun, the Ottoman Empire which stretched across North Africa, parts of Southern and Eastern Europe, and modern-day Turkey, began its descent in earnest.

It was in an effort to reverse this decline that the 19th century sultans promulgated the *Tanzimat* reforms, which because of European military, economic, and political pressures necessarily reflected European ideas of equality before the law, fair taxation, and to an extent, participation. Oddly enough, though the *Federalist Papers* were written by men seeking to throw off imperial rule and the *Tanzimat* was written to save an empire, both groups of reformers were conservative revolutionaries seeking to salvage parts of their historical rights and identity, while at the same time throwing off the yoke of European oppression. It could be said that the representative elements of the *Tanzimat* were far too weak to really represent a liberal mode of governance, but when compared with voting rights in much of Europe in the early and mid-19th century, they look far more robust. The level of toleration and inclusion of minority groups in this imperial system is also distinctive and more liberal than that of the nationalist European states. In trying to strike a balance between pan-Islamic identity, national/linguistic identity, centralization and local autonomy, the Ottoman reform project is truly breathtaking in scope. Though the empire did fall, it would be unfair to say that the reforms failed. Indeed, the seeds they planted in many ways came to fruition with the rise of Ataturk and the secular Islamic republic of Turkey.

It is a similar dynamic of Westernization and retrenchment of Islamic and national identity, as expressed in the much smaller context of 19th Century Tunisia, which this book will now examine, in order to provide the necessary historical context in which to understand the pioneering political theory of Tunisian statesman Khayr al-Din al-Tunisi.

## Chapter 5

# Constitutional Conversations—The Fusing of Political Tradition in Khayr al-Din al-Tunisi's *The Surest Path*

> The Turks of Tunis, confronted with a more stable and more firmly based civilisation, gradually became absorbed into the Tunisian population and founded what can be described as a national dynasty, that of the Husainid beys ... the Turks nevertheless failed to impart any fresh impetus to the age-old Maghrib. In one as in the other, Berber inertia won the day, so that at the beginning of the nineteenth century the entire Maghrib was living, withdrawn into its shell, in accordance with standards that had held for thousands of years, and without having been able to evolve in the direction of statehood in its modern form.[1]

This narrative of Tunisian history aligns nicely with conceptions of North Africa, or the Maghreb, as backward, intransigent, and immune to progress that have been espoused by various thinkers, including Charles Julien, who is quoted above. As seen in the previous chapter however, Tunisia has produced highly original and dynamic thinkers like Ibn Khaldun, so how could it be that thinkers like him could develop in a cultural vacuum of "Berber inertia?" The simple answer is that this view lacks nuance and often says more about the prejudices of the times and places in which it was advanced than it does about North Africa or North Africans. Indeed, the present day is not free from similar conventional wisdom, as the widespread shock at the ardent desire of average citizens in Arab states like Tunisia and Egypt to have democratic government illustrates. This chapter seeks to develop a contextual understanding of the political and social world that Khayr al-Din inhabited when he undertook his only work of actual political theorizing, *The Surest Path to Knowledge Concerning the Condition of Countries*. Written in 1867, it is the product of a very unique set of circumstances and cannot be properly appreciated without a basic acquaintance with what those circumstances were.

In keeping with the constitutional concerns of this book, particular attention will be paid to the Rule of Law in 19th century Tunisia, in addition to its complicated and competing national character(s) and the limits facing various political actors in Tunisia at this time. As these dynamics are highly intertwined, the historical

---

1 Julien, Charles-Andre, C.C. Stewart, Roger Le Tourneau, and John Petrie. *History of North Africa: Tunisia, Algeria, Morocco, from the Arab Conquest to 1830: By Charles-Andre Julien; Translated [from the French] by John Petrie; Edited by C.C. Stewart; Edited and Revised by R. Le Tourneau*. London: Routledge and Kegan Paul, 1970, p. 343.

analysis that follows will proceed largely on chronological, rather than thematic, lines. Following this discussion, a brief biographical sketch of Khayr al-Din will examine the influences and pressures that factored into his conception and execution of his written work. Finally, a detailed analysis of *The Surest Path* will tease out the distinctive elements of Khayr al-Din's political thought and seek to place them within the larger contexts of both Western and Islamic constitutionalism more generally.

## Divine Law and Secular Lawlessness—19th Century Tunisia and the Challenge of Progress

This historical overview of Khayr al-Din's Tunisia necessarily begins in the reign of Ahmad Bey (king). For starters, it was Ahmad Bey whom Khayr al-Din first served as a young mamluk and under whom he received his military and institutional training, both heavily influenced by the Bey's experimental rule. His reformist measures defined the path Tunisia would take for much of the reigns of his next three successors. From 1837–55 he sought to undertake reforms that would strengthen his actual sovereignty and room for maneuver in his affairs with both the Ottoman Sultan, to whom he was ostensibly subject, and with European powers seeking new avenues of commerce and colonization in the Maghreb. In each of these international relationships he was keenly aware of his relative weakness in relation to both military and trade capability. It is an effort to rectify these imbalances that came to absorb much of his energies over the course of his 18 years on the throne. In an effort to understand the particular types of reforms he undertook, one must first gain an appreciation for the influence of geography and climate upon Tunisia's commerce, agriculture, and settlement.[2]

Although clearly part of North Africa and the Arab/Islamic orbit, Tunisia has from very ancient times been firmly embedded in the Mediterranean world. L. Carl Brown goes so far as to say that "the life and times of Ahmad Bey can only be understood as a blend of medieval and modern, of Islam and the West."[3]Another writer notes that Tunisia has

> "two faces on the Mediterranean, one to the north toward Europe and a second to the east toward the Arabo-Islamic heartlands. These two regions have exerted

2 See Perkins, Kenneth J. *A History of Modern Tunisia*. New York: Cambridge University Press, 2004, pp. 12–13. Here he notes that Tunisia's autonomous status within the Ottoman Empire appeared threatened, while simultaneously, the country was being "flooded" by European people, ideas, and products. He interprets Ahmad's reform efforts as an attempt to "relieve the discomforting sensation of being in a vise between more powerful neighbors."

3 Brown, L. Carl. *The Tunisia of Ahmad Bey, 1837–1855*, Princeton Studies on the near East. Princeton, NJ: Princeton University Press, 1974, p. 3.

> significant influences on Tunisia, often in competition with each other. Tunisia's northeastern extremity, the Cape Bon peninsula, defines the approximate midpoint of the Mediterranean Sea. The narrow strait between the peninsula and the Italian island of Sicily links the eastern and western halves of the sea. Tunisia's proximity to this chokepoint has given it strategic importance…"[4]

These two faces are an important part of Tunisia's identity to this day and represent far more than a simple geographic reality. In addition to representing its dual European and Arab political/cultural orbits, they could also represent its two economies (one legal, one black market), its two ruling classes (elite and usually foreign mamluks ruling the cities and tribal chieftains exercising practical control of rural areas), or its two conceptions of law (divine *sharīʿa* and temporal regulation). As Julia Clancy-Smith points out regarding Tunisia's strategic location and coastal outlook,

> Tunisia's ancient, very intense involvement in the Mediterranean world is dictated by her geography. The coastline stretching from Cap Bon in the north to her southernmost tip invites "unregulated commerce," or, from the state's perspective, contraband.[5]

The issue of smuggling is illustrative of larger problems with the rule of law in Tunisia, particularly in the 19th Century when the sovereignty of the state itself was being contested internally by various tribal groups and externally by a variety of imperial designs. To make matters worse, the reign of Ahmad was a time of a total reevaluation of Tunisia's orientation as a Muslim state, and involved a real struggle to accommodate his affinity for European ideas of enlightened monarchy, military strategy, and relationships between the ruler and ruled. The existence of Tunisia within the confines of the Ottoman Empire that had given formal recognition to the ideal of the universal caliphate headed by the Ottoman sultan, and which had afforded the beys a degree of autonomy, was threatened by the Ottoman Empire's own struggle to survive along with the repeated imperial overtures made by France, Britain, and Italy.[6] Ahmad could also not be expected to ignore the large French army camped just across his Western border in Algeria.[7]

---

4 Perkins, Kenneth J. *Tunisia: Crossroads of the Islamic and European Worlds*, Profiles Nations of the Contemporary Middle East. Boulder, CO and London: Westview Press; C. Helm, 1986, p. 1.

5 Clancy-Smith, Julia A. *Rebel and Saint: Muslim Notables, Populist Protest, Colonial Encounters: Algeria and Tunisia, 1800–1904*. Berkeley, CA and London: University of California Press, 1994, p. 159.

6 See Brown (1974), where he states that "Husaynid Tunisia was a Muslim state," but where he also asserts that "The reign of Ahmad Bey might well be epitomized as the period when Tunisia moved from passive observation of Europe to active emulation." p. 108.

7 Perkins (2004), p. 13.

Clearly, evaluating the rule of law in 19th Century Tunisia requires that one first assess the various types and layers of law that were simultaneously at work in this small kingdom.

*A Brief Glimpse at the Beylik*

The Husaynid dynasty of which Ahmad Bey was a member, was founded in 1705 under the threat of Tunisia being invaded by rival factions within the Ottoman Empire, one group emanating from Algeria, the other from Constantinople. The leader of the resistance to the Algerian forces, Husayn bin Ali, gave his name to this dynasty, which lasted uninterrupted until 1957. He and his descendants were not of native Tunisian stock, nor did they consider themselves to be so. As was common in the Ottoman Empire, they saw the natural order of rule as one which emanated from the imperial capital and seat of the caliphate, rather than from the people over whom they ruled. Ahmad Bey was the tenth ruler from this family and like many of his predecessors was the son of a slave mother and royal father. This practice kept the ruling family set apart from other Tunisian families, preserving the tradition of foreign control.[8]

This practice did not result in much actual Ottoman sovereignty, despite the fact that the Beys were granted only the title of "pasha" or governor by the sultan. The Ottoman suzerainty that began in 1574 extended primarily to the recruitment of Tunisia's bureaucrats from Turkey's pool of mamluks, and to occasional supplies of troops, tribute, and pledges of allegiance to the Sultan. Day to day affairs were left more or less to the beys and their associates as Tunisia was too far and relatively unimportant to much concern Constantinople.[9]

As mentioned earlier, this absence of concrete Ottoman power was a double-edged sword. On the one hand, the bey could more or less do as he wished and had more actual monarchic power than many of his European colleagues did. Conversely, he had little reassurance of consistency or practical help from the Ottomans in fending off unwanted European overtures and resisting French encroachment in Algeria spilling over the border into his domains. Thus the approach adopted by Ahmad Bey in the mid-19th century could best be summed up as "If you can't beat them, join them." He launched far-reaching reforms in the way the military was trained, ensuring that they were educated in European tactics and formations. He purchased expensive new military technology from the Europeans so that his soldiers could more effectively mount a display of force when necessary, and he engaged in massive restructuring of Tunisia's trade relationships, taking in large quantities of imported European goods and ensuring that the agricultural sector was geared to exporting the raw materials demanded by European buyers.[10]

8 See Brown (1974), pp. 26–31.

9 Ibid., pp. 25–6.

10 Perkins (2004), pp. 12–14.

These steps were complemented by further radical changes to this once sleepy backwater of the Ottoman Empire. For the first time, the central government instituted conscription from the peasant classes, departing from the time-honored tradition of drawing solely upon "Turks" for military manpower. The purchase of equipment and ships for all these troops also meant that he had to impose a variety of new duties and taxes on exports and other market activities.[11] This sudden change stirred up substantial opposition to the regime amongst the lower echelons of society who faced ruin as their young men were taken from the fields and placed in the barracks. It also provoked Europeans who resented the reassertion of export controls. Even worse, the factories he created to produce basic items like uniforms were poorly utilized and hemorrhaged money at appalling rates. The financial situation of Tunisia quickly progressed from that of a poor, underdeveloped, but relatively debt-free state, to one of fiscal bankruptcy. Coupled with his expensive final act of sending troops to participate in the Crimean War, the Tunisian ship of state was fast succumbing to a flood of unpaid debts.[12]

Lest one be tempted to think that Ahmad's reign was an unmitigated disaster, both Perkins and Brown point out that some of his reforms had long-lasting effects, particularly those of the military academy, which allowed native Tunisians to have a degree of participation in their government for the first time since the pre-Islamic era and which exposed an entire generation of malleable young cadets to the ideas, technologies, and ideologies of Europe.[13] The whole concept of progress and modernization that he imported into Tunisia inculcated into the entire ruling class the expectation that Tunisia should be able to take its place on the world stage, even if it part was a small one, and that it had an identity and future that were distinct from those of the Ottoman Empire. On a more negative note, his ruinous spending sprees opened the door to the massive European interventions in Tunisian political and economic life that was to persist from his death until roughly a century later.[14] It is to the pre-colonial roles played by the European powers, particularly the British and the French, to which this chapter now turns.

11 Ibid., p. 15.

12 Ibid., pp. 15–16. Also see Carl Brown (1974), pp. 303–10 for an account of Ahmad's Crimean adventure and his death in 1855, which spared him the humiliation of discovering his troops had a negligible impact on the war and that Tunisia's debts had indeed become insurmountable.

13 See Perkins (2004), pp. 16–17 and Brown (1974), pp. 310–12. Chapters 9 and 10 of Brown's book provide an excellent summary verdict of the modernizing aspects of Ahmad Bey's rule along with an assessment of his ultimate legacy.

14 Julia Clancy-Smith (1994), p. 157, delivers the following verdict on Ahmad Bey: "Ahmad Bey's reign represents a sea change in modern Tunisia's history, mainly, but not exclusively, because of the reforms imposed upon his largely unwilling subjects ... Upon taking the throne, the bey inaugurated new fiscal policies, organized a conscript army, and established modern commercial, industrial, and educational facilities, patterned upon Western institutions with assistance from European advisors. It was a delicate, and ultimately, ruinous balancing act. Only internal consolidation of Tunisia's population and

## The British and French Consuls and Early Tunisian Constitutionalism

Ahmad Bey's successor, Muhammad Bey, ascended to the throne in 1855, the same year that Tunis hosted the arrival of British consul Richard Wood and French consul Leon Roches. The intense rivalry of these two men and the governments they represented led to a variety of unanticipated outcomes for Tunisia, including the eventual promulgation of the Islamic/Arabic world's first written constitution in 1861.[15] This was part of a much broader program imposed on the Ottomans by Great Britain and France to leverage their participation in the Crimean War into liberal political reforms.

> Although ostensibly most concerned about the sultan's non-Muslim subjects, the European powers hoped that restraints on the arbitrary powers of the ruler and guarantees of basic rights and freedoms would also facilitate their own subjects' commercial ventures in the empire and the latter's integration into the international economy.[16]

The *Tanzimat* era found its Tunisian origination in an environment of similar European leverage, resulting from Tunis' debts and the death sentence of Batto Sfez, a Tunisian Jew convicted of blasphemy.[17] This harsh measure provided cover for the consuls to insist on major judicial reforms. Roches and Wood requested two particular sets of measures. The first was directly related to the Sfez case, and requested the bey to establish a mixed court system to deal with cases involving Europeans and which would establish clearer rights and duties for the ruler and his subjects. The second request (demand may be more accurate), was that Muhammad deal favorably with Europeans seeking to own property and establish businesses in Tunisia.[18] What resulted was known as the 'Ahd al-Aman, or "Security Covenant,"

---

resources could thwart the political ambitions of European and Ottoman suitors; yet his subjects had to remain reasonably content as well. In some cases, Ahmad Bey's reforms expanded state power at the expense of provincial autonomy. Yet in regions distant enough from the political center ... some of these reforms at first had little impact."

15 See Perkins (2004), p. 17 and pp. 26–7. Carl Brown (1974), pp. 320–4, makes a similar point about Ahmad Bey's desire to emulate Europe leading to his abolishing of the Tunisian slave trade in 1841 and the emancipation of slaves in 1846. Interestingly, he was in some ways ahead of those he sought to imitate as the French did not abolish slavery in Algeria until two years later and the former British colonies of the United States famously did not end the practice until a bloody civil war compelled legal emancipation in 1863 (an effort not fully enacted until 1865 and the spirit of which was left unfinished until at least the 1960s).

16 Perkins (1986), pp. 72–3. These reforms would eventually be embodied in the 1857 decree the Hatti Humayun, which was discussed in Chapter 4.

17 Perkins (1986), p. 73.

18 Ibid, pp. 72–3 and Perkins (2004), pp. 18–19. Interestingly, the earlier account of this incident only mentions Roches involvement, whereas the more recent specifically cites Wood as joining Roches in his demand for reform.

which ironically echoed many of the assertions of the 1826 Ottoman Hatt-i Sherif of Gülhane and 1856 Hatt-i Humayun. Among these were the declaration that all of his subjects were equal on both civil and religious grounds, the establishment of modern formalized criminal and commercial statutes, the previously mentioned mixed courts, and an end of state monopolies.[19]

Muhammad Bey's assent to these changes was reluctant and came about primarily because despite the fact that he "inclined toward retrenchment and conservatism," he recognized that the presence of a large French fleet in his waters left him with virtually no room for negotiation or even delay. "European economic interests made it impossible for Muhammad Bey to survive in the shell into which he wished to retreat."[20] His reluctance proved well-founded on two grounds. Firstly, he understood from the legacy of his predecessor what an increase in European economic activity could lead to in terms of debt and loss of power. Additionally, he was well-aware that orthodox understandings of the status of non-Muslims in an Islamic state did not in any way promote equality before the law. Only monotheists had any status (polytheists were at least theoretically to be targeted for conversion or execution), and even these *dhimmis* faced restrictions on military participation and were expected to pay the *jizya* tax designed to both pay for their military protection and humiliate them as people living outside the Muslim *umma*.[21] Muhammad was also under no illusions that one of the major internal poles of power in Tunisia was the Zaituna mosque and the *'ulama* who acted as community leaders and judges in private and family life. These clerics were incensed at the foreign influence creeping into their country, and particularly at the notion that they were on an equal legal and religious footing as their non-Muslim counterparts.[22]

Adding insult to injury, the European powers determined that the issuance of the 'Ahd should be followed by the establishment of a more formal constitution. As far as the *'ulama* were concerned, there was only one constitution and it was the *Holy Qur'an*. The Europeans were already consistently invoking the 'Ahd to protect the commercial and civil interests of their nationals who had entered Tunisia in the flood of speculative investment ushered in under the 1857 reforms. Disgusted and unable to exert any political influence, the *'ulama* withdrew from

19 Perkins (2004), pp. 18–19.

20 Perkins (1986), p. 73. Here it is also noted that initially Muhammad attempted to only grant the judicial reforms without implementing the trade concessions. This is what prompted the French to order their fleet as a final persuasive measure.

21 Tunisian Muslims faced a real challenge to their legal superiority regardless of this decree. Kenneth Perkins (2004), pp. 23–4, points out that at this stage, several non-Muslim and non-Tunisian groups comprised significant minorities of the population and workforce. These included approximately 18,000 Jews; 7,000 Maltese; and 4,600 Italians amongst others. The Italians and Maltese in particular were in direct competition with native Tunisians for jobs at the lower end of the economic scale.

22 Perkins (2004), pp. 19–20.

the constitutional commissions set up by Muhammad.[23] It is at this stage in Tunisian history that Khayr (alternatively transliterated as Khair) al-Din began to play a central role in the affairs of his state. Before delving into his biography however, it is important to briefly overview the developments surrounding the 1861 Constitution, its operation, and legacy.

To a large degree, the constitution or "organic law" that formally came into force after Napoleon III, as Tunisia's quasi-colonial overseer, formally accepted it in 1861 was a restatement of earlier reforms undertaken in the 'Ahd al-Aman. According to various sources, this document's key functions "defined the succession (and) also clarified the responsibilities of the ruler, who was to swear an oath of allegiance to the Fundamental Law at his accession."[24] It also delineated the respective rights and duties of Tunisians and foreigners; "the latter were granted the privileges of work in trades and commerce."[25] Building upon earlier reforms establishment of a governing council for Tunis,

> the fundamental law established a constitutional monarchy whose ministers answered to a sixty-member Grand Council appointed by the ruler. Many of those named to the council were proponents of reform, the most prominent of whom was its president, a mamluk named Khair al-Din al-Tunisi.[26]

Ideally, the existence of the constitution would have established a clear condition of sovereignty for the Tunisian state and its equality provisions would have actually served as a bulwark of protection against European judicial and commercial concessions that were driving Tunisia yet closer to the brink. Although far from being a democratic or representative form of government, the system established by this constitution was revolutionary for an Islamic state in the respect that its inspiration was firmly based in nationalized and secular concerns and principles and disregarded centuries of previous Islamic government practice. As mentioned previously, this innovative quality made the document suspect to both the clerics and the devout, which was only exacerbated by the way in which the constitution was (ab)used by the European powers who compelled its creation. To begin with, there was no lessening of European power as Muhammad al-Sadiq had hoped to achieve as a proper "enlightened monarch." The even more unrealistic nature of the goal of achieving parity with Europe that Ahmad had also cherished was derisively plain. Further incensing native and religious Tunisians was the fact that,

> Despite the powers' advocacy of the constitution, members of the Maltese, Italian, and other European communities disliked its declaration of equality for all residents of Tunisia in so far as that concept resulted in the loss of certain of

23 Perkins (2004), pp. 24–5.

24 Ziadeh (1969), p. 14.

25 Ibid., p. 15.

26 Perkins (2004), p. 27.

> their privileges. Rather than submit to the jurisdiction of Tunisian tribunals, for example, they wanted to retain consular courts, as well as to continue to enjoy exemptions from certain forms of taxation. Nevertheless, they asserted their entitlement to the protections guaranteed by the constitution.[27]

Undoubtedly, the colonizing instinct of the European powers was either blinding them to, or causing them to disregard, the blatant double standard being perpetuated under this arrangement. Between the reckless disregard for the rule of law displayed by the Europeans and the equally corrupt efforts of native power brokers like former Prime Minister Mustafa Khaznadar, the long-term survival of this potentially revolutionary document was doomed from the start. There were too many middlemen who benefitted from corruption, and foreigners who benefitted from a dualistic and inherently unfair judicial arrangement for the reforms to even begin taking effect as intended by the reformers.[28] Ira Lapidus makes the further point that these reforms "could not be fully institutionalized, for there were never sufficiently numerous well-trained troops or administrators."[29]

The doom of the reform effort also spelled doom for Tunisia's attempt to preserve its sphere of autonomy from both Ottoman and European encroachments. The unpopular reforms were paired with failed harvests, business failures, widespread corruption, cleric-led protests over the rapid inflation of basic commodities as a result of the export market, and continual propagation of new and treasury-plundering capital and infrastructure projects.[30] The Zaituna *'ulama* protest of rising wheat and olive oil prices is particularly instructive in assessing the extent to which the reforms were unpopular and relatively ineffective outside of the Bey's inner circle and the interests of foreign business concerns. Following a demonstration in Tunis' souk in 1861 and a march on Bardo Palace, the government quickly neutralized this perceived threat by arresting those demonstrators who were not from the class of *'ulama* and by purchasing the acquiescence of the clerics through "cooption of a few moderate *'ulama* into official positions ... it was well known, both in the royal court and the foreign consulates, that the protestors regarded their economic woes as a consequence of ... rampant foreign influence, which the constitution now symbolized."[31]

The 1861 protest was only a shadow of further developments, in which native Tunisians and European powers eventually came to agree that the constitution

---

27 Perkins (2004), p. 28.

28 Ibid., pp. 24–5. In Perkins (1986), pp. 74–5, he notes that Khaznadar's power had grown under the reforms because of the enormous influx of foreign investors, most of whom were eager to establish contacts with those close to the bey, who could provide information and contacts that would determine the success of their commercial ventures.

29 Lapidus (1988), p. 697.

30 For examples of these events see Ziadeh (1969), pp. 14–16; Perkins (1986), pp. 74–5; and Perkins (2004), pp. 26–8.

31 Perkins (2004), p. 27.

had to be dismantled, albeit for very different reasons. In 1863, Great Britain negotiated and agreed to the Anglo-Tunisian Convention, which

> placed British subjects in Tunisia on the same footing as Tunisians regarding taxation and legal matters, while according them the right to own property and conduct business without restrictions. The Tunisian government accepted this accord because it viewed British interests, unlike those of France, as essentially nonpolitical.[32]

Crucially, this treaty covered both British and Maltese residents, which affirmed full legal jurisdiction for substantial numbers of foreigners and the additional benefit of counterbalancing the influence of the French government.[33] However, this simple arrangement only served to further anger Tunisians already chafing under foreign domination and they staged "a full-scale revolt" in 1864, led by a holy man called Ali ibn Ghdahem. Although the rebellion was quashed through bribery and military reinforcements paid for by Constantinople, it nonetheless was quickly followed by the achievement of one of its key aims of bringing about the repeal of the hated constitution.[34] Angered by the British maneuvers, the French reasoned that the Anglo-Tunisian Convention was binding for only as long as the constitution under which it operated remained in force. Once again, the threat of imminent military invasion proved too persuasive to ignore and Tunisia's constitutional experiment was over before it could really begin. "In short order, the status quo ante, with its virulent competition among Europeans and the absence of restraint on Tunisian officials had returned."[35] It is only with an understanding of the significance of this turbulent era of pre-colonial pressures, technological and industrial revolution, political reform, and burgeoning Tunisian identity that one can make sense of the biography and political theory of Khayr al-Din al-Tunisi, whose work comprises the fulcrum upon which the argument of this book rests.

## Khayr al-Din al-Tunisi—A Man of Multiple Identities and Singular Achievement

Like the country which he would adopt as his homeland, Khayr al-Din al-Tunisi was a man who existed in multiple orbits of culture, power and experience, all of which shaped his outlook on life generally, and the challenges facing Muslim states more specifically. Born in the Ottoman provinces of the Caucasus in approximately 1820–25, as a young man Khayr al-Din was taken as a mamluk slave to Constantinople. "He lived long enough in Constantinople to learn Turkish

32 Perkins (1986), p. 77.
33 Perkins (2004), pp. 28–9.
34 Ibid., pp. 29–30.
35 Ibid., p. 30.

but probably received little, if any, formal education."[36] From there, at roughly 16 years of age, he was sold into the service of Ahmad Bey of Tunisia in 1839. There he was trained in the administrative arts for which the Ottomans and their predecessors were so famed that we still refer to unwieldy bureaucracies as byzantine.[37] Khaldun al-Husry writes this about his early professional training:

> Khayr al-Din arrived in Tunis which was to give him his surname. In the Bay's palace and in the Bardo Military School, newly opened in 1840, Khayr al-Din studied Arabic, and Islamic *'ulum* (sciences, or knowledge in its broadest sense), and the modern military sciences of his day. He had learned French in Turkey. For a time he was trained by the French military mission in Tunis, under Commandant Campenon, who later became Gambetta's minister of war. Khayr al-Din rose quickly to the highest rank in the Tunisian army, becoming a *fariq* (*general de division*) in 1844. He soon abandoned his military career for one in the civil service.[38]

This brief passage makes clear that Khayr al-Din must have been exceptionally capable to have undertaken the range of studies that he did and to rise so quickly (only four years) to a position of military leadership at the age of only 21. G.S. van Krieken also adds to the list of his achievements that his knowledge of the Islamic texts was such that he was familiar with *hadith*, scriptural interpretation, and had memorized the *Qur'an* by heart.[39]

It is hard to imagine what it must have actually been like for him to be taken from his family and raised in this institutional fashion, but there is no sign of self-pity in his own accounts of his life, no hint of wishing for the life he could have had. Rather, in his autobiography he says simply:

> Bien que je sache pertinemment que je suis Circassien, je n'ai conservé aucun souvenir précis de mon pays et de mes parents … Les recherches que j'ai faites … sont toujours restés infructueuses.[40]

36 Brown, L. Carl, "Tunisia in the Time of Khayr al-Din," in Tunisi, Khayr al-D. in, and L. Carl Brown. *The Surest Path: The Political Treatise of a Nineteenth-Century Muslim Statesman*, Harvard Middle Eastern Monographs, 16. Cambridge, 1967, pp. 29–30.

37 Black, Antony. *The History of Islamic Political Thought: From the Prophet to the Present*. Edinburgh: Edinburgh University Press, 2001, p. 296.

38 Husry, Khaldun Sati. *Three Reformers: A Study in Modern Arab Political Thought*. 1st ed. Beirut: Khayats, 1966, pp. 33–4.

39 Van Krieken, G.S., *Khayr al-Dîn et la Tunisie, 1850–1881*, éd. Brill, Leyde, 1976, p. 9

40 Ibid., p. 9. "Although I know full well that I am Circassian, I have kept no precise memory of my country and my parents … The research I've done has always been unsuccessful."

Here one gets the impression that he was naturally curious about his origins but by no means obsessed. It is also important to note that his slave status would not be a cause for humiliation in the world of the 19th century Ottoman Empire. Although he seems to have had no choice in being sent to Tunis, once mamluks like him were purchased and put in post they had an enormous degree of mobility afforded to them and were as free as virtually anyone else in society, perhaps much more free than those in the peasant class who did not share the fortune of their education, access to power, and comfortable lifestyle.[41] In other words, he was little more slave than most professionals who are compelled to work at set times, sometimes for long hours, but who are nonetheless paid well for their work and who have to opportunity for promotion and acknowledgment of success.

The degree to which his success as a military officer placed him on his rapid social and political assent becomes obvious in light of the fact that he actually was placed in charge of the Bardo Military School for a period of time, and "in 1852 was sent by the Bey to Paris to deal with a difficult problem, that of certain claims made by a former minister against the government. He remained in Paris for four years, and for him … they were a formative period. He observed the life of a great political community and applied what he learnt to his own world."[42] It is interesting to note that the "difficult problem" he was sent to deal with related to a colleague of Mustafa Khaznadar named Bin 'Ayad, who absconded from Tunisia with enormous sums of money stolen from the treasury and then took on French citizenship in an effort to avoid the potential consequences of his actions. In a way, this problem would manifest itself in various forms like a virulent hydra throughout his career as he was forced to confront one debt crisis after another, many of them relating to Tunisian corruption and waste and French abuses of power.[43]

In recognition of his lengthy efforts in Paris, Khayr al-Din was made minister of marine in 1857, the same year which marked the beginning of a constitutional approach to Tunisian monarchy under the previously discussed 'Ahd al-Aman.[44] This period of reform, liberalization, and struggle to define the role and identity of Tunisia in a rapidly changing international context was one which saw Khayr al-Din's experience and natural talents put to considerable use. Al-Husry comments

---

41 See Cleveland, William L. "The Municipal Council of Tunis, 1858–1870: A Study in Urban Institutional Change." *International Journal of Middle East Studies*, 9:1 (1978): 36. Here he describes the mamluk class of Tunisia as follows: "Originally white slaves, mainly from the Caucasus region or the Greek islands, the mamluks by the middle of the nineteenth century constituted a relatively solid, if waning class, which dominated the ruling institutions of Husaynid Tunisia—the army and the administration. Protected by the Bey, and sometimes dominating him, they controlled the coercive institutions of society which reached down into the city in the form of a state police, the *hambas*."

42 Hourani, Albert. *Arabic Thought in the Liberal Age, 1798–1939*. Cambridge and New York: Cambridge University Press, 1983, p. 84.

43 Ibid., p. 30.

44 Brown (1967), p. 30.

that some scholars directly attribute Khayr al-Din's influence in the types of reforms undertaken by Ahmad Bey, Muhammad Bey, and Muhammad Sadiq Bey.[45]

His influence with the ruling beys was not based on his philosophical prowess, but on his ability to deliver positive results in their dealings with ever more bold and audacious European powers. Following his successful mission to Paris, he was also asked to undertake yet another foreign mission, but this time it was not to a European state, but to the political heart of Islam in Constantinople. Muhammad Sadiq asked him to complete the customary task of announcing the new ruler's succession and asking for the sultan to issue a formal document of investiture. This in itself was nothing out of the ordinary. However, this routine diplomatic formality was also a cover for a more covert attempt to counterbalance ever stronger French intrusions by persuading the sultan to formally grant Tunis the autonomy it had practiced in a *de facto* sense for hundreds of years. Furthermore, he also requested that the Empire recognize the hereditary nature of the Beylik, in exchange for which, the Bey would pay tribute and also acknowledge the overarching sovereignty of the Ottoman Empire. This was a win-win face-saving measure, but it did stretch both sides' willingness to swallow some pride. It also was clear to the sultan that it was a move certain to anger the French, and this mission failed. It is ironic in some senses that he would be less successful in Constantinople than in Europe, but it possibly had very little to do with Khayr al-Din and very much to do with the Empire's weakness and inability to risk offending the Europeans.[46]

In the run up to the implementation of the constitution of 1861, the Bey first established a municipal council for running Tunis in 1858. The capital being by far the most important urban center and home to a substantial portion of the population, this was an ideal laboratory in which to conduct these new experiments in modernization and consultative government.[47] Importantly, it was at this time that Tunis was also coming under extreme pressure from the potential for conflict between its various ethnic groups and foreigners. Though it was "controlled by Muslims," the rapid changes in Tunis meant that the "segmentation (of social groups) which had obviated the need for a uniform system of regulations and which had kept the urban groupings apart, thus permitting them to co-exist, was difficult to maintain with ... so many Europeans and with increasing state involvement in introducing change."[48]

A passage from British consul Richard Wood meant to justify his suggestion for the creation of the Municipal Council illustrates the graphic nature of the cultural problems confronting Tunis at this time:

45 Al-Husry (1966), p. 34.
46 Hourani (1983), pp. 84–5.
47 Cleveland (1978), p. 33.
48 Ibid., p. 37.

> ... in the present instance, the heterogeneous elements which form the bulk of the ... Christian population of Tunis, their utter disregard of the commonest forms of decency and decorum, their recklessness and usurpation of the principal thoroughfares, which have become impassable and insecure from their having been turned into stables and workshops, and their impatience of control, render indispensable, for the public good, health, and security that some Municipal Regulations should be framed and enforced. In one street alone, besides other animals, there are several hundred pigs which wallow in the public drains and impede progress of passengers. This circumstance in itself is sufficient to produce much irritation and annoyance in a Mussulman city.[49]

In order to rectify the problems of this evolving city, the Council focused on providing what today would be considered very basic social services. These consisted of tasks like policing, controlling the price and quality of goods in the food market, and handling the horrendous overflow of waste and sewage.[50] Khayr al-Din's role on the Municipal Council was indirect but substantial. Amongst its officers were General Abu 'Abdullah Husayn, Muhammad al-'Arbi Zarruq, and Salim Bu Hajib. General Husayn, who was President of the Council for seven years, was also a Circassian mamluk who served with Khayr al-Din on his mission to Paris. His friend would undoubtedly have approved wholeheartedly of this reminder of his to the Bey:

> Those most beloved of God are those who dedicate themselves to the interest of the people. He who spends one hour working toward improving the conditions of the country and the people is more worthy of praise than he who spends his day praying and handling his beads. God Almighty urges action and is pleased by effort.[51]

Likewise, Muhammad al-'Arbi Zarruq and Salim Bu Hajib were intimately involved in the reform efforts being overseen by Khayr al-Din. Zarruq even became "the first director of the Sadiqi College in 1875." Bu Hajib was actually a native Tunisian officer (something that would have been impossible before the reign of Ahmad Bey) who went on to work at the Zaytuna mosque and was a well-known proponent of Khayr al-Din's reforms. His upward mobility from the tribal

49 F.O. 102/55, Wood to Malmesbury, 3 September 1858, no. 25. Quoted in Cleveland (1978), p. 38.

50 Cleveland (1978), pp. 46–54.

51 Ibid., pp. 39–41. The quote from Husayn is yet another instance of a political actor echoing "The Dream of Scipio" in Cicero's *Republic*, although there is no evidence that he was familiar with it. Perhaps this gives yet more credibility to the contention that some political values are both universal and timeless.

Sahel to a position of power was itself a direct testament to the impact that even limited liberalizing reforms could have.[52]

The larger constitutional effort that resulted from the 1861 Constitution was much more directly led by Khayr al-Din, who was named to the presidency of the Grand Council. Prior to its actual enactment, he served the equally, perhaps even more, vital role of serving on the commission that drafted the constitution.[53] Writers have generously called this constitution a "liberal constitution," but it would not be seen as terribly liberal by present-day standards.[54] The Grand Council it created to advise the Bey and to restrict his ability to act autonomously was not democratically elected nor representative, not even in the very limited understanding these ideas would have had in much of 19th century Europe. Rather, its 60 members were appointed by the ruler himself. Crucially, they were tasked with keeping the ministers of the Bey accountable and even more importantly, the Bey himself appointed several pro-reform members to fill its chamber.[55] This move may seem surprising in terms of an authoritarian monarch voluntary limiting his power and placing people willing to speak their minds in an advise and consent capacity. When considered as an act of Tunisian nationalism and attempt to establish international sovereignty and credibility on something approaching the Westphalian model however, it can be seen as an entirely logical attempt for the Bey to promote his government into a league of civilized modern states, while at the same time demonstrating that his legitimacy did not lie in the whims of Constantinople, but on a fundamental social contract with his own subjects. This view is well outside the traditional Islamic mainstream of political philosophy, but well within the currents of European thought that seemed destined to sweep over his nation whether he willed it or not.[56]

This desire to gain more autonomy from the Ottomans while simultaneously fending off European advances by joining the ranks of constitutional states explains the logic in Muhammad Sadiq's choice of Khayr al-Din to lead his new Council. Although the constitution placed real limits on his power locally, as discussed previously the ability of the Bey to project his power outside of Tunis and the major cities had always been limited. Thus, it is mainly for its potential to enlarge his prestige and power abroad and to preserve his domestic standing, that the constitutional path was so attractive, at least on paper, to Muhammad Sadiq. This harmony of interests between the Bey and Khayr al-Din was short-lived however, as Khayr al-Din fully intended to advise the Bey according to what he felt were the best interests of the state, even when these were at odds with the personal interests of its ruler. This led to his angry resignation in 1862 when he argued that

52 Cleveland (1978), pp. 41–2.

53 Hourani (1983), p. 84.

54 See for example, Lapidus (1988), p. 697.

55 Perkins (2004), p. 29.

56 For a similar analysis, see Perkins (1986), p. 74.

ministers were responsible to the Grand Council and not the Bey.[57] Carl Brown highlights his disagreement over Mustafa Khaznadar's plan to obtain a foreign loan to handle Tunisia's mounting debts as the primary reason for his departure.[58] Whether the cause was his argument with the Bey or with his father-in-law (he had married Khaznadar's daughter in what must have been somewhat of a political power marriage), his disgust was strong enough to cause him to resign not only from the Grand Council, but also from his post as minister of marine.[59]

This was a fortuitous misfortune, for it was during this period of self-imposed political exile that Khayr al-Din left Tunisia to travel extensively throughout Europe and when he wrote his book *The Surest Path*, a comparative government text that covered over 20 European state systems, and the introductory section of which summarizes his political thought and approach to reform from within the traditions of Islam. As a detailed analysis of this text comprises the next section of this chapter, it suffices to say that without this time away from the daily political grind to observe and reflect on his adopted homeland and its future *vis a vis* Europe, it may have been impossible for this work to have ever been written in the systematic manner in which it was ultimately produced.[60]

Shortly after the 1867 publication of this work, Khayr al-Din returned to active political life. "In 1869 the worsening situation of Tunisian finances," thanks largely to the loan Khaznadar had advocated, "led to the creation of an International Commission to administer the revenues (of the state), and Khayr al-Din became president of its executive section."[61] In a bizarre twist of fate, it was then Prime Minister Khaznadar himself who asked Khayr al-Din to take on this role because "his advocacy of judicious and responsible government was well known."[62] This reconciliation was very short-lived. It turns out that Khaznadar had not anticipated the enormous scope that the British, French, and Italian-backed debt commission would have in setting policy in all matters relating to Tunisia's fiscal house. Corrupt politicians had far less room to skim profits from activities that could generously be called consultancy, but which were really tantamount to bribery. There was simply little left of the Tunisian treasury to plunder for private gain. Thus, "entirely consonant with his past behavior," Khaznadar tried to "sabotage (the commission) altogether or, failing that, to stonewall directives imperiling his lucrative business arrangements or easy access to state funds."[63]

For Khayr al-Din's part, this task was one that he also found extremely distasteful, albeit for entirely different reasons. He was no fan of putting his beloved and beleaguered Tunisia under foreign domination. However, he also saw

57 Hourani (1983), p. 85.
58 Brown (1967), p. 31.
59 Ibid., pp. 30–1.
60 Ibid., p. 31.
61 Hourani (1983), p. 85.
62 Perkins (2004), p. 31.
63 Ibid, p. 32.

no means of freedom from foreign control in the absence of first attaining freedom from foreign debt.[64] This stand on fiscal responsibility did him no favors in earning the good graces of the Bey, but nonetheless, it demonstrated in a powerful way to the French and Italian members of the commission that he "meant business" and was trustworthy, which ultimately led them to pressuring a very reluctant Muhammad Sadiq to naming him prime minister in 1873.[65] In turn, Khayr al-Din understood the highly competitive and vainglorious nature of the European colonial mindset well enough that he was able to create a degree of autonomy for his own political maneuvering by playing the various powers off one another while they competed to obtain his favor.[66]

Here it is useful to consider the actions he took as prime minister, in order to better appreciate the practical and active follow-up to the political theorizing in *The Surest Path* shortly to be discussed. Here, his achievements in political, social, and cultural spheres amount to something both profound and lasting. Various scholars emphasize different aspects of his activities, but Khayr al-Din himself provides an excellent holistic account in his memoirs, which incorporates most if not all of what his later admirers and scholarly examiners mention on this topic.

> The specific measures which Khayr al-Din listed among his accomplishments included: (1) canceling back taxes; (2) granting a twenty-year tax relief for new plantations of olive and date trees; (3) controlling the exact amount of personal (capitation) tax in order to end the prevarications of the *qa'id*-s;[67] (4) partially canceling the system whereby *spahis* were paid according to the fines collected;[68] (5) reorganizing the customs with a 5 per cent increase on import duties and a reduction of export duties; (6) establishing a regular system to control the *habous* (Muslim endowment) funds; (7) reorganizing studies at Zitouna University;[69] (8) reorganizing the library; (9) paving the streets of Tunis; (10) creating Sadiqi

64 This point is made forcefully and in a very prescient manner throughout *The Surest Path*.

65 Perkins (2004), p. 32.

66 Ibid., pp. 32–3.

67 These are provincial elders and judges who traditionally ruled on a variety of local matters.

68 These are a group of native cavalry units.

69 The mosque was the heart of Islamic learning in Tunisia, and unusually became a place where reform-minded clerics were welcomed and allowed to promote their ideas openly. His reforms meant that clerics would be trained in secular subjects along with their religious studies in order to broaden their worldview and give them a better appreciation of the challenges modernity posed to Islam.

> College "on the model of European lycees"[70]; and (11) stopping the costly system of collecting taxes from the nomads by means of military expeditions.[71]

This laundry list of reforms is important because, as the reader will see, they are close reflections of his earlier ruminations on the role and function of an Islamic government. From this list, it is possible not only to gain an appreciation for the broad scope of his interests and achievements, but also to draw out certain themes about what a state must, should, and can do. Take for instance, the achievements that he mentions toward the end of this list in restructuring the Zaituna curriculum, establishing Sadiqi College, and reorganizing the library. All of these reveal an obvious and passionate conviction that education and knowledge were very much part of "the surest path" to maintaining autonomy and dignity for his people. By introducing secular subjects for the first time to the Zaituna, he both reaffirmed the essential societal role of the *'ulama* while challenging them to expand their understandings of this role in light of a very rapidly changing world which had to contend with far more foreign pressure and influence than at any time since the advent of Islam in the Maghreb. Likewise, the Sadiqi College he founded continues to exist and play an important role in Tunisia to this very day. "The school combined a course of traditional studies, taught in Arabic, with a French-inspired curriculum emphasizing modern languages, mathematics and science."[72] Eventually, Sadiqi graduates began to fill the ranks of the state bureaucracy "forming a tightly knit cadre that preserved and, when possible, acted on Khair al-Din's philosophy well beyond the end of their mentor's ministry."[73]

Azzam Tamimi demonstrates the centrality of the founding of this university by quoting its founding statement as written by Khayr al-Din:

> To teach the Qur'an, writing and useful knowledge, i.e. juridical sciences, foreign languages, and the rational sciences that might be of use to Muslims being at the same time not contrary to the faith. The professors must inculcate in the students love of the faith by showing them its beauties and excellence, in telling them the deeds of the Prophet, the miracles accomplished by him, the virtues of the holy men ... Khairuddin At-Tunisi believed that ' ... kindling the Ummah's potential liberty through the adoption of sound administrative procedures and enabling it to have a say in political affairs, would put it on a faster track toward

70 He was the key figure in the founding of this University which was the first institution in Tunisia to focus on educating its students in modern secular subjects and which became a crucial breeding ground for many subsequent generations of reformers and intellectuals.

71 Brown (1967), p. 33.

72 Perkins (2004), p. 34.

73 Ibid.

> civilization, would limit the rule of despotism, and would stop the influx of European civilization that is sweeping everything along its path.[74]

What is clear is that he views education as a means of reconciling the apparent conflicts between the preservation of Muslim identity and the adoption of "Western" tools for achieving not just this preservation but also the promotion of the state as a Muslim state. Combining a love of faith with a rational training program of science and language, he believes, not only limits abuse of power and makes its use more efficacious, but most importantly holds European encroachment at bay.

Another branch of Khayr al-Din's governing philosophy can be seen in his various uses and reforms of taxation. In canceling back taxes for instance, he was reestablishing trust and assent between the governing class and the governed. He reasoned that people would be less hesitant to come forward to pay their taxes if they knew that in so doing they could avoid potentially ruinous back taxes and regain their legal footing. This same idea animated his determination to stop pursuing funds from the Bedouin by military raid because aside from the farce of raising funds by spending more than they would possibly collect, it seemed to him that "if the state provided security and a regular tax system, then the Bedouin would cease their raids, and trouble-makers would find no refuge from the civil government among the tribes."[75] His other actions in standardizing the means and amounts of tax collection all reveal an attempt to establish legitimacy based on an idea of fairness and justice; fairness in that the state would only collect what was due and without causing harm to its subjects; justice in that the state would communicate with its subjects exactly what was expected of them.

Still another passion of his premiership is his concern for developing domestic production capacity and limiting the taking on of debt via the import of foreign finished goods. This explains his increase of import and decrease of export duties, along with his plantation tax relief. Taken as a group, they clearly represent an investment in Tunisia's future economic well-being. This too is behind his ensuring that Tunis, the state's capital and largest city, was paved. What could be more basic to an economy than the ability to transport goods efficiently? The Romans found roads vital for commercial and military ventures and this lesson remained true for all subsequent empires. Indeed, some would trace part of the economic predominance of the United States to the building of its interstate highway system. Efficiency also factored into his appointment of the highly respected cleric Muhammad Bairam a *habus* to head the *Habus* Council, which was charged with responsibly administering, for the good of the people, the 25 percent of Tunisian land that had been designated as a pious trust.[76]

---

74 Khairuddin At-Tunisi, Aqwam Al-Masalik Fi Taqwim Al-Mamalik (Tunis, 1972), p. 185. As quoted in Tamimi, Azzam. "Islam and Democracy from Tahtawi to Ghannouchi." *Theory, Culture & Society,* 24:2 (2007): 39–58.

75 Brown (1967), p. 33.

76 Perkins (2004), p. 34.

Uniting each of these strands of his efforts as prime minister is an over-arching and very traditional Islamic view that government is primarily about stewardship. Carl Brown claims this is consistent with even medieval Islamic thought and defines it as "a rigid separation between the rulers and the ruled, whose mutual relations were guided by the parallel of the shepherd and his flock."[77] As will be seen later in his text, Khayr al-Din remained deeply committed to an Islamic vision of the state, even as he was committed to reforming the way an Islamic state functioned in a world that had moved well beyond the confines of the Medieval and Renaissance periods.

Despite, or perhaps because of, his many successes as prime minister, Khayr al-Din's time in power was over by 1877 after only four years. The same foreign powers that conspired to have him appointed prime minister, and who curried his favor, ultimately decided that his time was up. The French in particular were upset by his affinity for the Ottomans and his business deals with the British. Once British resources and attention were diverted to more pressing and long-standing concerns in their more traditional Egyptian sphere of influence, there was nothing stopping the French from ensuring he was removed from office.[78]

Even this unfortunate turn of events did not spell the end of his political career. Towards the end of 1878, he was asked by Sultan 'Abd al-Hamid, "who had read *The Surest Path*," to be Grand Vizier of the Ottoman Empire. Although this stint at the pinnacle of the traditional seat of Muslim power was extremely short-lived and was the final act of his political life, he remained in Constantinople until his death in 1889.[79] Before turning to the analysis of *The Surest Path*, it is helpful to consider how its translator, Khayr al-Din scholar Carl Brown sums up the legacy of its author.

> At first sight Khayr al-Din's efforts seem to have been as short-lived as those of Ahmad Bey. Nothing approaching accountability was established in Tunisian administration ... Even Sadiqi College, established in 1875 to train the needed new cadres for sound administration, by 1881 was on the verge of closing as a result of neglect and mismanagement. One could go on tolling a like fate for the other specific measures of Khayr al-Din. Yet an approach that overlooks the slow, stumbling manner in which societies change and that ignores the importance of ideas, even when they survive for a time only in the heads of a small number of insignificant people, would completely miss the essence of Tunisian reformism... Khayr al-Din's efforts appear to have been completely frustrated, but something remained—a few persons, a few ideas, a small body of experience. Without this saving remnant, the Young Tunisian movement ... might not have existed at all. It is from this movement (including its many mistakes) that one can trace the beginning of Tunisian nationalism. Bechir Safr,

77 Brown (1967), p. 32.
78 Perkins (2004), p. 36.
79 Brown (1967), p. 35.

> a leader of the Young Tunisians, had been a protégé of Khayr al-Din. He was called affectionately the "Second Father of the Reawakening." The first, of course, was Khayr al-Din.[80]

Thankfully, the ideas of Khayr al-Din were not simply in the heads of some insignificant people for a brief time, but were carefully enumerated and persuasively argued in his 1867 text, *Aqwam al-masalik fi ma'rifat ahwal al-mamalik*, or *The Surest Path to Knowledge Concerning the Condition of Countries*. It is to an understanding and analysis of this text that this discussion now turns.[81]

## *The Surest Path*—Khayr al-Din's Islamic Solution to the Challenge of the West

During his time in exile, Khayr al-Din remained preoccupied with affairs of state. His time away from active office seems to have provided him with the needed leisure to systematize his thoughts into a coherent idea of how a Muslim state should be properly constituted and run, how this might be achieved, and why it was both necessary and in accordance with the principles of the *sharīʿa*. This last consideration gives his work a decidedly defensive tone, but considering the persistence of doubts to this day from both Muslim and Western thinkers about the compatibility of orthodox Islam with constitutional government and reform this is manifestly understandable. In his *A History of Modern Tunisia*, Kenneth Perkins describes *The Surest Path* as drawing upon "the three most important components of Khair al-Din's intellectual heritage: Muslim piety, the traditional statecraft incorporated into his training as a mamluk, and the modern culture of the West first encountered in Ahmad Bey's service but comprehended more fully as a result of his residence in France."[82] Rather than proceed through the text in a linear fashion, this analysis will seek to draw out the three constitutional themes that comprise the focus of this work. As a writer who is both a devout Muslim and an experienced high-ranking official who has had extensive exposure to European ideas and politics, Khayr al-Din's work is distinctly heterodox. It is as eloquently forceful in its discussion of European virtues and advantages as it is in defending the timelessness of Islam and its *sharīʿa*. As such, the way he deals with a concept like the rule of law is concerned with aspects of this question that would resonate with Muslim and European audiences. His views on the restriction of governmental power derive mainly from the same concerns at preventing tyranny and corruption that animate the writers of *The Federalist Papers*, yet do so by

80 Brown (1967), pp. 35–6.

81 A more detailed, excellent and accessible biographical account of Khayr al-Din al-Tunisi is available in Wasti, Syed Tanvir. "A Note on Tunuslu Hayreddin Paşa." *Middle Eastern Studies*, 36:1 (2000): 1–20.

82 Perkins (2004), p. 33.

appealing to various *hadith* and *sunna* that had widespread legitimacy amongst Tunisia's elite, in particular the influential *'ulama* to whom he addresses many of his appeals and criticisms. Likewise, his analysis of the qualities of various nationalities and how they are fitted for their governments uses the traditional language of the *umma*. Even the publication of *The Surest Path* in both Arabic and French authorized versions shows the dual audiences and traditions that Khayr al-Din had in mind as he wrote.

After assessing each of the various constitutional concepts in *The Surest Path*, a final look at the idea of progress is essential. As a true believer in the modernist vision, Khayr al-Din's work is aimed squarely at economic, technological, and military advancement, all of which are presented as the ends which can be gained through the means of good government and political reform. In this sense, he is more in the philosophical company of someone like Hayek or other political economists than he is with either Western or Islamic political philosophers from earlier times. Once his constitutional concepts and his goal of progress are analyzed, it will then be possible to assess the extent to which his work successfully fuses the two constitutional traditions, to what degree it is indeed concerned with constitutionalism, and what its implications were and are.

### The Surest Path to the Rule of Law—The De-Personalization of Power

Khayr al-Din's writings have not received the same level of scrutiny as those of Sayyid Qutb, al-Afghani, or even Tahtawi. However, his name does crop up in various scholarly considerations of Islamic reform, constitutionalism, and/or modernism. This passage from Gudrun Kramer is illustrative of the general consensus of his view of the rule of law and his place in the Islamic canon of political theory, if such a thing exists.

> What emerges as a core concern for modern Muslims is to check and limit arbitrary personal rule and to replace it with the rule of law. That had already been the preoccupation of the 19th century Arab and Ottoman constitutionalists, ranging from 'Abd al-Rahman al-Kawakibi and Khair al-Din al-Tunisi to Namik Kemal.[83]

This very brief statement shows that Khayr al-Din is considered to be a constitutionalist and that this has something to do with de-personalizing power and replacing it with the rule of law. Although his concerns do very much involve tyranny, the context in which he was writing was very different from that of modern European authors. As such, he is far less concerned about the tyranny of the majority than he is with the tyranny of one despot and the ruinous effects it can have on a

83 Kramer, Gudrun. "Islamist Notions of Democracy." *Middle East Report*, 183 (1993): 6.

state. His perspective is of one who lives in a state that is being overwhelmed by foreign influences, money, and residents. Even worse, as discussed earlier, these foreigners did not submit to Tunisian authority and maintained their own courts and rules and relied upon the military and economic pressure of their home states to extract ever more egregious legal exceptions that made their participation in Tunisia's economy more advantaged than that of its own citizens. If anything then, it is the tyranny of the minority, the miniscule minority of an autocrat and his sycophants, and the larger foreign minority interests which concern him most. For this reason, and because of the distinctive Islamic views on the unity of sovereignty, it is necessary to analyze Khayr al-Din's view on the rule of law alongside and in combination with his views on the restriction of governmental power. The endemic corruption of the Tunis regime is also an important factor in the amount of attention he pays to courting an audience of the *'ulama*. His vision of the rule of law and the role of government as being analogous to that of shepherd and flock neatly coincided with the role played by the *'ulama* as local leaders and spiritual shepherds. In view of the political realities he acknowledged that "any mandate for change had necessarily to come from above, but it also had to fall within the parameters of Islamic values, and confirmed by its endorsement of the *'ulama*, the guardians of those values."[84] These two concepts are inextricably linked in the historical, political, cultural context in which he is writing.

It is telling that in *The Surest Path* his discussion of the rule of law begins in the context of discussing Europe's historical experience with this constitutional ideal. He makes the pointed observation that

> The present situation in the kingdoms of Europe has not long been established. After the attacks of the northern barbarians and the fall of the Roman Empire in 476, Europe fell into a shocking state of savagery, lawlessness and oppression, beginning in a movement of decline—which is naturally quicker than that of advance.[85]

The words "savagery, lawlessness and oppression," are all familiar terms in 19th century political discussion, but primarily in European discussions of other civilizations, including "Oriental" groups into which they often classified Muslim societies. Here they have been turned on their head to remind his fellow Muslims that European claims to superiority in these matters are recent developments in the grand scale of history. He goes on to reject claims that this progress is based upon the Christian religion of most of Europe, because even though "it does urge the enforcement of justice and equality before the law, Christianity does not interfere in political behavior."[86] As further proof that Christianity does not ensure the rule of law in its domains, he gives the example of the "imperfection"

84 Perkins (2004), p. 33.

85 Tunisi, Khayr al-Din (1967), p. 80.

86 Ibid.

of the Papal States.[87] Contrary to the common Western belief that Islam is inferior in its ability to provide sound principles for governance, Khayr al-Din says first that Europe has become prosperous and powerful simply because of "*tanzimat* based on political justice."[88] Secondly, he contrasts the Christian passivity toward politics with the active engagement in politics required by Islam, particularly in predominantly Muslim societies. The idea that good governance and fairness, along with the application of knowledge leads to prosperity is "well known from our Holy Law," as attested to in Muhammad's statement that "Justice brings glory to religion, probity to constituted authority and strength to all orders of the people, high and low. Justice guarantees the security and well-being of all subjects."[89]

After an extensive discussion on the nature of kingship and the need for its restraint, Khayr al-Din begins making his case for accountable ministerial government's effectiveness at establishing and maintaining the rule of law. He even cites Mill's observation that "The English nation reached its highest peak during the reign of George III who was mad," noting that this happy result was no accident, but rather was possible "only through the participation of those qualified to loosen and bind, to whom the ministers were responsible."[90] Translator L. Carl Brown's footnote on "those qualified to loosen or bind" (*Ahl al-hall wa al-'aqd*) reveals that this phrase has an original legal usage meaning:

> those qualified to act for the *umma* in appointing and deposing the caliph or any ruler. In fact, the term came to mean a more loosely-defined group of those actually possessing political power plus the eminent religious scholars, leading merchants, and other notables whom the political leadership were likely to consult (or *ought* to consult, according to whether the term was being used in a descriptive or normative sense).[91]

Here then, is an interesting juxtaposition of European historical precedent with Islamic political terminology. The phrase he chose is not only powerful in that it hearkens to the election of the caliph, who was the leader of all Muslims, but it also can be traced back to the very first instance in which the Islamic *umma* had to appoint a political successor to Muhammad. It thus became a tradition that any new caliph, including the Ottoman sultans, had to have their role assented to by "those qualified to loosen and bind," although in practice this became a

---

87 This is a rather understated criticism of the disarray found in 19th century Italy.

88 *Tanzimat* is not capitalized in most instances in Khayr al-Din's work as it is the general project of constitutional reform and not merely the specific Ottoman reforms earlier discussed as *Tanzimat* to which he is referring.

89 Tunisi (1967), p. 81. It is notable that this quote mentions the security and well-being of subjects, which are two aims typically seen as essential in establishing the legitimacy of the state.

90 Tunisi (1967), p. 86.

91 Ibid., p. 85.

mere formality. Later Muslim thinkers use this historical precedent from the earliest days of Islam, in much the way that Christians might cite the apostles, to emphasize the legitimacy and even requirement that Muslim rulers allow and are responsive to *shura*, or consultation.[92] This term which initially evoked tribal elders conferring their blessing on their leaders' decisions has come to be used in a variety of ways, including advocating limited constitutional government and even full liberal representative democracy.

Khayr al-Din never advocates the creation of a representative republic outright. It could be that he felt that Tunisia was not yet ready for this degree of self-rule, or that he simply did not foresee that this would come to be seen by many as the only legitimate type of government. Regardless, his continuation of the topic reveals a strong democratic strain in his thought. Keeping his clerical audience in mind, he reminds them that promoting the rule of law through institutionalizing government and making rulers and ministers accountable is not in contradiction to the *sharīʿa* principle that the ruler is appointed by God and has jurisdiction and power over his entire flock. Rather than a derogation of authority, it is a delegation of authority in much the same way that Moses asked God to designate his brother Aaron as his *wazir* or helper, pleading that He "'Increase my strength with him and cause him to share my task.'... Therefore, if the imam's sharing his power with the delegated vizierate ... is permissible and is not deemed a diminution of his executive authority, then his sharing of power within a group-those qualified to loosen and bind—in all aspects of policy is even more permissible."[93] This provides a key link between the idea that the task of governing should be shared and that the rule of law requires that those who share in governing must be chosen. The example of Moses and Aaron could lead one to accept, as was Ottoman practice, that the obligation of *shura* could be met by the appointment, by the king, of a minister who would advise him and act alongside him to enforce the law. Khayr al-Din supports his more radical view by alluding to the requirement of Umar ibn al-Khattab that succession to the caliphate required consultation of six people in which at least four of them agreed on a candidate. The will of the four was always meant to be followed over that of the other two, regardless of who those two people were.[94]

Having established that a constitutional view of the rule of law is compliant with the *sharīʿa*, Khayr al-Din next discusses the secular laws meant to address the contingencies a state may face that are not directly addressed in traditional

92 Modernist Muslims like Rida argue this group endowed with authority to advise the ruler in a binding manner includes everyone in "whom the *umma* has faith: they would include scholars, the leaders of the army, and the leaders of various sectors of society who promote the general interests of the people." See Khan, M.A. Muqtedar (2006), *Islamic Democratic Discourse: Theory, Debates, and Philosophical Perspectives.* Lexington Books: Oxford, p. 43 for further discussion.

93 Tunisi (1967), pp. 88–9.

94 Ibid., pp. 89–90.

Islamic jurisprudence.[95] He specifically mentions that after the Muslims lost Spain it was the Ottomans who saved the *dar al-Islam* from total chaos, "when Sultan Suleyman Selim at the beginning of the tenth century [1495–1591 A.D.] established his beneficial *qānūn* in order to extirpate the means by which defects befall kingdoms. In doing this he sought the help of the active *'ulama* and the wisest statesmen."[96] The ordinances, or *qānūns*, he proposed including reorganizing the army, police, property system, etc. and actually led to his gaining the moniker of al-Qanuni.[97] These very practical concerns make up a considerable percentage of the business of a modern state, yet are not typically considered to be decisions with moral implications. Just the same, this famous monarch sought out advice and consultation. Khayr al-Din explains the significance of his method of rule as follows:

> The essential feature of the *qānūn* was to make the *'ulama* and the viziers responsible for the ruler's administration, making it possible for them to investigate princes and sultans should they deviate. This is because Islamic sovereignty is based upon the Holy Law whose principles, already referred to, include the duty of consultation and of resisting actions disapproved by God. The *'ulama* are the most knowledgeable about such matters just as the viziers are most knowledgeable about politics and the requirements of various situations. If the *'ulama* and viziers are apprised of something which violates the *sharī'a* and the *qānūn* which serves it, then they will do what the religion requires. This is, first, to speak out against what is wrong, and if this works then the desired effect is achieved. If not, then they should inform the army leaders that their admonition has been to no avail. In the above-mentioned *qānūn* it is made clear what will happen if the sultan should remain determined to carry out his wish even if it is against the public interest. He would be deposed and another member of the royal family would take his place. In this way certain obligations and commitments would be imposed by the *'ulama* and the statesmen, and the situation would continue in this manner.
>
> Thus according to the provisions of the *qānūn* the position of the *'ulama* and the viziers with authority to hold the sultans accountable for their actions is like that of representatives in Europe ... Or, more precisely, the authority of the former is greater since the secular restrainer of accountability is supported among us by a religious restrainer.[98]

---

95 For instance, Muhammad never proposed traffic regulations for automobiles because they did not yet exist.

96 Tunisi (1967), p. 112.

97 For further information on Suleiman's reign and impact, including his legacy as a lawgiver, see J.M. Rogers and R.M. Ward's (1998) *Suleyman the Magnificent*.

98 Tunisi (1967), pp. 112–13.

From this passage, a rough outline of Khayr al-Din's solution to arbitrary rule can be sketched. The "essential feature" of this good example of Islamic governance from the glory days of the Ottoman Empire is not found in any elaborate institutional arrangements or popular sovereignty, but simply in accountability. This is because in order for the clerics and political elites to discharge their duty and responsibility for the "ruler's administration," it was critical that they also gain the corresponding power to investigate their rulers. Although Khayr al-Din does not lay out a specific procedure for how this investigative power may be used, he mentions that it would have to be a matter of violating the law, whether the sacred *sharīʿa* or the secular *'qānūn*. This is an important development because there were plenty of historical examples of Islamic rulers being overthrown for religious violations, but it was unheard of that he should also be removed from office for violating the ordinances which he himself promulgated and over which he was theoretically sovereign. This is, in European terms, a development that would make an Islamic monarch less like the classic French rulers who reigned on the theory of "L'État, c'est moi," and more like a British ruler, with all the attendant expectations that he would be bound to the laws of God, nature, and of his own state and accountable to a group representing the interests of the whole state.

Furthermore, the first action required of the state's ruling class is that they verbally inform and warn the king of the error which he has committed or is in danger of committing, after which, they have the right to appeal to the military to undertake a limited form of coup d'état in order to depose the unrighteous or lawless monarch.[99] This theory has its venerable roots in both the West, as seen in the frequent overthrow of Roman emperors by rival military leaders, and in Islam, as witnessed in the enormous power wielded by the Ottoman janissaries.[100] Khayr al-Din's conclusion to this passage is instructive, in that it acknowledges the link to the ways of Europe (the model for the successful and prosperous state) by referring to this group of *'ulama* and viziers as acting in the same capacity as "representatives in Europe."[101] The real advantage for the Islamic state in applying this model is that, whereas European states only have their own secular

99 Khayr al-Din augments this argument at the conclusion of *The Surest Path*'s Introduction, pp. 176–8. Here he discusses the ancient practice of appointing a dictator at times of national crisis, enacting a temporary delegation of authority into the hands of one autocrat. Crucially, this ruler is given power for a defined period of time, after which his emergency powers must be renewed by the delegating authority (i.e. the Roman Senate) or automatically be rescinded. Following his time in power, he would also be held accountable by the assembly for the manner in which he ruled and subject to punishment should his actions be found manifestly unjust. In contrast to recent experiences in states like Egypt, with decades of "emergency rule," Khayr al-Din emphatically states that "it is surely obligatory to restore liberty after the disappearance of these special circumstances."

100 In fact, this pattern reasserts itself time and again with Tunisia, Egypt, Turkey, and Pakistan all experiencing military coups in the 19th, 20th, and 21st centuries.

101 Note that this is highly reminiscent of the argument made roughly 150 years later by Noah Feldman (2008) in his *The Fall and Rise of the Islamic State*.

constitutions and laws to appeal to in enforcing accountability and justice, Muslim rulers, viziers, and *'ulama* have the additional authority that comes from having a "religious restrainer."[102]

Slightly later in *The Surest Path*, Khayr al-Din undertakes the thorny issue of pluralism, multi-ethnic states, and democratization. This is important because it shows that a thinker can be extremely constitutionally-minded without necessarily being a dyed in the wool advocate of democracy. Contrary to the expectations generated by his frequent inclusion in the group of "liberal Islamic political thinkers," he actually argues against the demands of groups within the Ottoman Empire for "laws to be established and protected" by a truly representative, popularly-elected assembly.[103] This is troubling to him, not because he is opposed to democracy wholesale, but rather because he has (very well-founded) fears that behind this opposition movement lay several foreign powers vying for the diminution of Ottoman power and sovereignty so that they can promote their own economic and political interests with less hindrance.

Khayr al-Din's assessment of the liberal movements in the Ottoman Empire of his day is that the political agitators showed

> no signs of good faith toward the state. Instead, they often showed a desire to draw closer to those of their own race (*jins*) by complaining about the state's official conduct and by stirring up confusion. This is due to their being constantly subject to corruption by foreigners who plant in their chests the seeds of "protection" for purposes which cannot be hidden. It is possible that the establishment of liberty in the way demanded above, before giving consideration to those obstacles would merely facilitate these ulterior aims. Among the requisites of this liberty is the equality of all subjects in all political rights, and this includes access to the highest state positions. However, among the important preconditions for granting this freedom is the agreement among all of the subjects concerning the interest of the kingdom and the strengthening of the state's authority.[104]

This reveals a common critique of liberal democracy that persists to this day, namely, that by presuming democracy to be the *de facto* best form of government, failure to achieve a certain degree of democratization leads to a state itself being considered less than a full member of the family of civilized nations, when

102 This is yet another example of the sort of two-pronged argument employed by Khayr al-Din throughout his writings. He is forceful in arguing for the benefits of certain European behaviors and institutions, but even more forceful in his belief that the benefits of Islam will make them even more effective in a Muslim polity.

103 Examples and explanations of the view of Khayr al-Din as a liberal Muslim thinker can be found in books ranging from Albert Hourani's (1983) *Arabic Thought in the Liberal Age* to Al-Suwaidi's (1995) *Arab and Western Conceptions of Democracy* to Antony Black's (2001) *The History of Islamic Political Thought.*

104 Tunisi (1967), pp. 116–17.

perhaps there are underlying reasons that democracy has not yet blossomed.[105] In the case mentioned here, the problem would seem to be that modern notions of liberal government conceive of the state as being necessarily a nation-state, acting in the best interests of the overarching nation it represents both internally and internationally, whereas clearly there was no one nation to which all Ottomans allied themselves. Rather, the extreme nature of pluralism in the vast empire, traditionally governed by the autonomous *millet* system which encouraged separation in settlement and private legal matters, meant that the residents of the empire had stronger loyalties to their own clans, which in turn sometimes had significant ties from outside the empire. As opposed to European history, in which national groups tended to coalesce into political units and either absorb or expel foreign peoples into their more or less homogenous societies, Islamic societies were traditionally highly tolerant of other religious and national groups living and conducting commerce within their borders. At the same time, the binding ideal of an Islamic *umma* which existed apart from and above all other peoples, meant that there was little precedent for intermixing between religious groups and even less of a sense of national loyalties as being on a par with, let alone superior to, the religious loyalty due to other believers. This is why Muslim scholars spoke of the House of Islam and the House of War in discussing international matters because it was assumed that there was only one sovereign of the Muslims, God, and only one deputy of God, the caliph. How then, can an Islamic state be a nationalist state? It thus makes sense that Khayr al-Din does not believe a coherent national identity to be a prerequisite of democracy, but rather a coherent and unifying idea of what is in the public interest (*maslaha*) and how the power which promotes that interest can best be strengthened so as to protect it.

Though it does not follow next in Khayr al-Din's work, it would seem logical to briefly examine his conception of liberty, "since what we have been presenting on this subject indicates that liberty is the basis of the great development of knowledge in the European kingdoms."[106] In exploring this concept, he sums it up as follows:

> "Liberty" is used by the Europeans in two senses. One is called "personal liberty." This is the individual's complete freedom of action over himself and his property, and the protection of his person, his honor, and his wealth. He is equal before the law to others so that no individual need fear encroachment upon his person nor any of his other rights. He would not be prosecuted for anything not provided for in the laws of the land duly determined before the courts. In general, the laws bind both the rulers and the subjects … The second sense of liberty is political liberty which is the demand of subjects to participate

105 For an excellent critique of the pitfalls of conflating constitutionalism with democratization, particularly in an Islamic context, see Nathan Brown's (2002) *Constitutions in a Non-Constitutional World.*

106 Tunisi (1967), p. 160.

> in the politics of the kingdom and to discuss the best course of action. This is similar to what the second caliph, 'Umar ibn al-Khattab, may God be pleased with him, referred to in saying, "Whoever among you sees any crookedness then let him set it straight," meaning any deviation in his conduct or governance of the *umma*.[107]

The advantage of presenting liberty in this perfunctory manner, making it a European *fait accompli*, is that he can avoid the philosophical debates as to what liberty should be, who grants it, what its origins are, etc., and can instead focus on the types of liberty that actually already exist in the European states whose prosperity he seeks to achieve on behalf of his own *umma*. Al-Husry argues that for Khayr al-Din, liberty is one of the *usul*, or principles, embodied in the *sharīʿa*.[108] The first type of liberty is an inherently negative set of freedoms which limit the state's interference in its subjects' lives by guaranteeing their rights and the protection of that which they already have through publication and fair adjudication of the laws of the land. This is also a very individualistic type of liberty that will later be used to make a variety of political economy based arguments as to the creative and commercial energies it can unleash.[109] The second type of liberty is more communitarian, and it is not surprising that it is this type that he explicitly links to Islamic tradition, begging the question whether a good example of personal liberty was not readily apparent in his extensive store of knowledge from the *Qurʾan* and *hadith*. The freedom to participate politically and arrive at an agreed course of action for the well-being of the state epitomizes the title of his work in that he sees it as the means by which a ruler or state can avoid "deviation" and remain on "the surest path."

Part of staying on the straight and narrow path, to borrow from Christian terminology, relies upon an expansion of what political freedom means in practice beyond the simple mechanics of creating representative institutions and electing their members. Particularly important in this effort, is "something else which is called freedom of the press." Oddly, this term which is now largely taken for granted is carefully defined to mean that "no one can be prevented from writing that which it seems to him to be in the public interest in books or newspapers

107 Tunisi (1967), pp. 160–1.

108 Al-Husry (1966), pp. 41–3. Here Al-Husry also points out that the Arabic word Khayr al-Din uses for the word "liberty" is *hurriyya*, which is "an abstract noun formed from *hurr*, free." Traditionally, it is a legal term meaning the opposite of slavery and only appears as a political term from the 19th century onwards. Other writers of this era, like Tahtawi, felt compelled to explain its meaning as equating to the Islamic ideas of equity and justice. The first instance of its political use is actually found in Napoleon's first proclamation to Egypt. Al-Husry ultimately concludes that Khayr al-Din's non-traditional use of *hurriyya* is not in fact in accordance with the *sharīʿa* or traditional Islamic theory.

109 This particular form of liberty has resonances with thought stretching back at least to Cicero's argument that the state should not be in the business of confiscating wealth but protecting it, and extends forward to the political economic thought of leaders like Ronald Reagan and Margaret Thatcher.

which can be read by the public."[110] This would seem to be a fairly expansive view of this freedom because the body that determines the public interest value of the writings is not the *'ulama*, a board of censors, or the state, but rather "what seems to him," the writer, to be "in the public interest." As the state cannot claim to read the minds of the writers in its domains to know with certainty if they intend to write on behalf of the public interest, this would seem to be a fairly good guarantee of journalistic freedom. Likewise, he specifies that not only can anyone write what he wishes, but he can also publish it so that "it can be read by the public." This means that opposition to government policy or even to the regime does not need to be privately registered in order to be legal, but is legitimate in the public sphere.[111]

The freedom of the press and political liberty are circumscribed to an extent in his following discussion of how some European states have granted both personal and political liberty, whereas others have only granted personal liberty along with varying degrees of political liberty "because the conditions of kingdoms vary according to the aims of their subjects."[112] This would seem to be an implicit statement of his view that not all Muslim states would be immediately ready for what he terms "absolute liberty," but would need to first achieve an internal consolidation of the public will so that the essential political questions would enjoy enough broad consensus to confer legitimacy on the decisions made on the day to day affairs of the state by its various organs.

In speaking about the variety of European states' readiness for absolute liberty, he could easily be speaking about any number of Islamic states. Those which are ready have subjects who "resist their kings only in order to have a right of opposing the state if it turns aside from the straight path, and to draw it toward a policy of benefit for the kingdom."[113] In other states, there is not even agreement about which form the government should ultimately take, let alone what its aims should be, allowing various parties to harbor potentially detrimental "ulterior motives." "As a result of this belief some kings deem it permissible to abstain from granting complete liberty."[114] This would seem to advocate for what would now be considered commonplace, or "universal," rights like free expression and freedom of the press, but his willingness to grant the ruler discretion in how much freedom to allow his subjects could also advocate for a variety of political measures that could be seen as repressive. One might ask Khayr al-Din how a consensus about the form and aims of the state can be achieved and legitimized absent an

110 Tunisi (1967), p. 162.

111 It is important to remember that Khayr al-Din himself is credited with creating the first consistently running printing press and newspaper in Tunisia, along with significantly expanding its library holdings during his own premiership. Clearly he intended to practice what he preached.

112 Tunisi (1967), p. 162.

113 Ibid., p. 162.

114 Ibid., pp. 162–3.

open public debate on the matter, which would necessarily require freedom of expression, assembly, the press and some type of popular vote.[115]

Khayr al-Din's solution to the problem of how to advance the goal of a free and prosperous society in a measured way in the presence of a king who can unilaterally grant or deny freedoms as he deems appropriate is to ensure that the king himself is properly educated and trained in an argument that hearkens back to the neo-Platonism so popular with earlier Muslim thinkers like al-Farabi. He thinks that Muslim rulers should imitate their European counterparts in the education of future rulers by choosing "proficient masters who will teach him science and knowledge appropriate to his standing, the aim being whatever trains his character and broadens his knowledge." They should also travel to foreign countries to gain a wider view of the world and to ascertain their "progress in development," taking advantage of the beneficial customs and practices to be found in various places, and avoiding "things which would hold back his own country." Following this training via tourism, the future king is groomed for power through gradual initiation and elevation in political life by attending, then speaking, and then presiding over the assembly.[116]

It becomes clear in the follow up to this summary, that in the guise of discussing European royal customs, Khayr al-Din is actually advocating that Muslim states do the same. He says:

> What is required of kings is not simply settling private disputes—as seen in some Islamic countries. Nor is it getting involved in details of administration which can be carried out by other functionaries. Rather, what is required of rulers is over-all supervision—knowing the men appropriate for public office, testing them, investigating them closely in order to guide them in their ignorance and restrain their feigned ignorance, inspecting the conditions of the subjects, assisting with increase of industries and sciences leading to the training of character and growth of wealth, showing a concern for the organization of the army and navy, fortifying the frontiers with material for resistance and defensive forces in order to protect the religion and the homeland, regulating the political and commercial relations with foreign states in a way which will cause the honor and wealth of the kingdom to grow, and other such general things.
>
> The worldly happiness and misery of kingdoms depend on the success or failure of its kings in these matters and upon the possession of political *tanzimat* based on justice which is recognized and respected by those in charge.[117]

115 For an example of the legacy of Khayr al-Din's writings on consensus and voting, see Ahmad, Aziz. "Sayyid Aḥmad Khān, Jamāl Al-Dīn Al-Afghānī and Muslim India." *Studia Islamica*, 13 (1960): 74.

116 Tunisi (1967), p. 158.

117 Ibid., pp. 158–9.

What is less than clear is why he does not at least more fully discuss the possibility of these same duties being discharged by a representative group or assembly. His own Ottoman and Tunisian context of being steeped in monarchy was surely a significant factor in Khayr al-Din's seeming obsession with discussing political merit and reforms in the context of kingship, but one would think his years in France would have graphically illustrated that a state with "absolute freedom" is very likely mature enough to dispense with the need for a single wise ruler to guide its affairs. Perhaps it is simply that his work is aimed largely at the Tunisian elites in the *'ulama* and political classes who derive many tangible benefits from the presence of a monarch.

In response to the European cynics and Muslim critics of the *tanzimat* reforms that he feels will promote a broader vision of a shared public interest for Muslim states (not least of which because the previously discussed Ottoman reforms granted full legal equality to all subjects and placed them under the same jurisdictions, taxation laws, and military obligations), Khayr al-Din says that it is ridiculous to claim that "rulers of Muslim states" are universally and forever incapable of reforming to an extent that they can be trusted to be fair with Europeans living and doing business in their domains. Some of these very European powers, he points out, also struggled for generations to implement political reform, suffering setbacks and reversals until "they finally succeeded (in consolidating political reforms in accordance with justice) with the support of their inhabitants in carrying out its provisions without hardship."[118] Indeed, the very writing of *The Surest Path* would seem to be meant to generate the legitimacy for reform within his own society because without "this support of the population, one cannot hope to attain any results."[119]

In the long-term it would seem that Khayr al-Din believes that Muslim states are capable of lasting and significant reform and progress in establishing equality and the rule of law, although the manipulation of European powers makes the task extraordinarily difficult. He laments that in some countries a given European power may advocate reform, whereas in another it may say "'These *tanzimat* are not appropriate for your situation and it is preferable for you to return to your previous condition,' although such advice is in conflict with the political principles of their own countries."[120] Fed up with the contradiction of European policy toward Muslim states, he nonetheless is aware of their power and proposes a temporary compromise meant to assuage European

118 Tunisi (1967), p. 119.

119 Ibid., pp. 119–20. See also Perkins (2004), p. 33. Unlike many other scholars, Perkins offers a slightly more nuanced view of Tunisi's liberalism, emphasizing that Khayr al-Din "understood that Western institutions had undergone a centuries-long process of maturation within a specific cultural context and that their successful transplantation in societies not embedded in Western culture hinged on laying the groundwork in a similar, albeit telescoped, process."

120 Tunisi (1967), p. 122.

fears of injustice should all people, including foreign residents, of an Islamic state be treated as fully equal before the law and subject to the same courts.[121] For a time, there could be a special group of courts that would be under the state's jurisdiction but in operation especially for foreigners and with a few basic guarantees. Following the establishment of trust that running these courts successfully would engender, it might then be possible to convince fair-minded Europeans that "finally they could be placed under our jurisdiction."[122] This would be key to the larger move that he feels is "incumbent upon the Islamic states," to "remove these disadvantages (of the capitulation treaties) by granting these guarantees and making them known abroad."[123] This effort is very similar to a newly reconstituted state or regime proving its good faith to the international community by signing on to certain humanitarian treaties and conventions that bind them to certain internationally agreed standards of conduct in their dealings with their own citizens and with foreigners, which is then reciprocated by a fuller granting and respect for that state's sovereignty.

Once an Islamic state successfully throws off the restraints of the capitulation treaties and establishes universal jurisdiction over all people living in its lands, the question remains what type of laws it should enact in order to achieve the level of development that Khayr al-Din seeks. Here again, as with his discussion of the training of future monarchs, he uses European practice as both a model and a foil for advocating similar, but Islamicized measures in Tunisia and the broader Ottoman Empire.[124] Intriguingly, he begins his discussion of the types of European law, how they are made, and how they are enforced by reminding his readers that Europeans have found after much long suffering experience that "the granting of unlimited freedom of action to kings and statesmen leads to oppression resulting in the kingdom's ruin." This is why they "have decided on the necessity of having those qualified to loosen and bind participate (as will be shown) in all aspects of politics while placing responsibility for administering the kingdom upon the executive ministers."[125] By using this terminology he is giving yet another overt indication that this is a pattern which he would gladly see emulated in the lands of Islam, although without necessarily subscribing to the social contract or representation theories that the European models of government by "those qualified to loosen and bind" would normally employ.

He then breaks down European law into two categories: laws "observed between the state and the subject," and laws "drawn up to decide legal actions between individuals, adjust the taxes and grants among the population according

121 See Hourani (1983), p. 91.

122 Tunisi (1967), p. 122.

123 Ibid., p. 123.

124 For an interesting discussion of Khayr al-Din's success, or lack thereof in using Islamic ideas for his proposed reforms, see al-Husry (1966), pp. 51–3.

125 Tunisi (1967), p. 170.

to the profits and merits of each, and other such domestic matters."[126] These two categories just happen to dovetail nicely with the Islamic categories of *sharīʿa* and *qānūn*, a point which he does not need to make explicitly to any *'ulama* reading his work. The first set of laws between the ruler/state and subjects/citizens is roughly equivalent to the types of law considered to be simple ordinances or codes in Islamic jurisprudence. They are not terribly concerned with forbidding immorality or promoting morality in any direct fashion, but rather they

> cover the sovereign's rights and duties ... Many things are included in this category such as liberty for the masses secured by the guarantee of their rights, determination of the type of regime whether republic or hereditary monarchy, execution of the laws, the conduct of domestic and foreign policy, which includes making war and negotiating terms of peace and of commerce, designation of official duties, appointment of ministers and other officers ... expenditures of tax revenues for their designated purposes, and other such matters relating to the administration of the kingdom provided they do not go beyond the purpose of it laws.[127]

These *qānūn* comprise much of the day to day business of any state and Khayr al-Din seems to advocate an executive and bureaucratic approach to the conduct of this branch of law by saying that "these things are among the prerogatives of the ruler with the aid of his ministers."[128] In an answer to the earlier question as to why he seems so obsessed with presenting rule in a monarchic context, it is clear from his presentation of the French system that in theoretical terms the word "ruler" could be applied to any executive authority, even one that is elected or is somehow embodied in an institution of multiple individuals. It must be then, that the particular context of kingly rule is used to make his argument more Islamic, Ottoman, and Tunisian. In fact, the first group of executive laws is created in the way that they would be in an ideal version of the Tunisian monarchy. In France, they are "established by the agreement of those adults who are in full possession of their civil and political rights. Other states have additional conditions such as an educational qualification, ownership of property ... or belonging to the class of distinguished persons called by them the *noblesse*."[129] These are the same types of people already given precedence in Tunisia, but the important distinction is that the Bey was under no obligation to follow the advice of his nobility. The European rulers, on the other hand, are legally obliged to acquiesce to the authority of this upper parliament by taking actions such as allowing ministers to be questioned

126 Ibid., p. 171.

127 Tunisi (1967), pp. 170–1.

128 Ibid., p. 171. Albert Hourani (1983), p. 93, provides proof of the centrality of a coherent and just legal order in Khayr al-Din's actual political life, stating that for a time he "seriously considered" creating a "modern and uniform system of Islamic law."

129 Tunisi (1967), p. 171.

by the upper legal chamber and compelled to answer their questions, and in the case of disapproval of the ministers or the executive's policy, the ministers must be dismissed, or parliament dissolved, and a new set of representatives given the chance to resolve the dispute. They either agree with the king or continue to oppose him, but in either case the rule of the people wins out. Khayr al-Din couldn't have summed it up better when he says that

> The benefit to the country comes in firmly establishing the rectitude of those in charge of the country's interests. Thus, it is easy for the country to appropriate her wealth and the blood of her sons since it is for her own benefit. In this way the situation of both the state and the country is properly secured even if the king be a prisoner of his own appetites or endowed with poor judgment.[130]

The system he proposes then, is one in which the responsibility for both making and executing the law is shared between the king and a group of wise advisors. Beyond this, the actual form of government and the corresponding institutions, rights, and duties remain a question that is open to the contingent circumstances of any give state. This is less assertive in its promotion of freedom than might be hoped for by those labeling Khayr al-Din as a liberal thinker, but if his view that political development must be natively and gradually driven is taken into account, it still leaves plenty of room for the true self-determination of a populace that liberalism's institutions aim to achieve.[131] At the end of the day, the rule of law must reign supreme for Khayr al-Din's vision of a prosperous Islamic state to be achieved. It is this achievement that would satisfy the requirements of the wise ancient Greek refugee quoted near the end of his text, who in answer to the question of were he and his fellow Greeks should settle answered simply, "In any land where the law is stronger than the ruler."[132]

## *The Surest Form* of Legitimacy—The Role of the Islamic umma in History and Political Reform

Having examined Khayr al-Din's views on the need for the rule of law and its interrelationship with the depersonalization of political power, this chapter will now turn to the question of the role national character plays in his constitutional thought. In sharp contrast to most European writing on this idea, his notion of

130 Tunisi (1967), p. 173. The previous summary of how executive law is made can be found on pp. 170–3.

131 Black (2004), p. 298, characterizes Khayr al-Din's support for the democratizing efforts of groups like the Young Ottomans as "cautious support."

132 Tunisi (1967), p. 175.

nationality will be shown to be intimately related to a pan-Islamic identity.[133] Just as his ultimate views on the form and size of government are highly flexible, so too are the ways in which he would define the nature and scope of those being ruled by an Islamic regime. In order to convince his readers of not only the compliance of political reform with the principals of *sharīʿa* but also its feasibility in an Islamic context, he seeks to simultaneously demystify Europe's success and the decline of Islamic states, saying

> One could cite other nations that had attained the ultimate in stability only by respecting their legal system which was based on just government. In the same way disregard for these rules was the cause of their decline.
>
> It should not be imagined that this was due to a divine grace in the holy laws of the nations mentioned. Actually, these were laws derives from human reason based on due consideration to worldly authority. If laws should also be endowed with divine grace and sanctity, as is the case with our immaculate *sharīʿa*, then their being violated would be even more likely to cause decline in this world, not to mention the punishment which would ensue in the next. Whoever follows the history of the nations referred to and of the Islamic *umma* will see this clearly.[134]

Thus it is seen that it is not any special innate quality of European states that has led to their relative success, but primarily that their legal systems are "based on just government." The laws which they have instituted, he argues, are not inexplicable and should be easily seen by Muslims to be in accordance with reason. If Europeans can derive a just legal order from reason, how much more then should Muslim states be able to create a just state given the "divine grace and sanctity" underlying obligatory *sharīʿa* that would surely inform the decrees of the state? If reason and order explain European success, Islamic decline is presented as a matter of punishment for failing to live up to the principles dictated by the *sharīʿa*. It is not the case then that the reforms of the Ottoman Empire and or various Islamic kingdoms contradict God's law that is the problem, but rather that corruption and a lack of respect for the law have violated the spirit of the spiritual law.

Having debunked the idea that Islam and Islamic civilization are somehow inherently contradictory or inferior to European norms, Khayr al-Din turns to his Muslim critics and their claims that "the *tanzimat* are not suitable for the condition of the Islamic *umma*." This belief, he says, is based on four "objections", which are as follows:

---

133 See for example the analysis of Khayr al-Din's writings and political life in Hourani (1983), pp. 93–6, where he never refers to questions of restoring Tunisian power or protecting Tunisian identity, but always couches his reform ideas in terms of their benefit to the Muslim *umma* writ large.

134 Tunisi (1967), pp. 175–6.

1. The *tanzimat* are contrary to the *sharī'a*.

2. They are inappropriate since there is no disposition on the part of the *umma* to accept the civilization on which they are based.

3. They will almost certainly lead to the loss of rights given the long time needed to settle lawsuits, and identical delays will be seen throughout the administrative system.

4. The increased government employment required for the various administrations will require an increase in taxation.[135]

He answers the first and second objections in a strident affirmation of the ability of Muslim people to apply European-style reforms to their own countries in a successful manner by claiming that "impartial observers" will attest to the "superior native intelligence" of the Muslim masses and that the historical experience and venerable civilization of the Islamic *umma* "still bearing the influence of the pious predecessors should be able to acquire what will set right its present situation and expand the scope of its civilization."[136] This, for his *'ulama* audience, would be tantamount to an intellectual and political call to arms, a type of liberal progressive *jihad*. By embracing reform they can tap into the superior nature of Islamic society and not only fend off European advances but perhaps even expand the influence of Islam. The technocratic element of his call can be seen in his assertion that "the *umma's* latent freedom can be kindled by precise *tanzimat* which will facilitate its integration into political affairs." If only the people were ruled justly and properly, then the society could mature politically until it was ready to use its "latent freedom" productively.

Khayr al-Din's next point is one that would resonate with many Muslim thinkers today. He remarks upon the fact that some of the European states that have successfully introduced reforms were more or less culturally, politically, and economically backward before undertaking them. "Moreover, we still see today disparities among these states in the refinement of their *tanzimat* and the knowledge and virtue of their judges, but these disparities have not prevented the most advanced subjects upon entering these countries from being under the jurisdiction of the most backward."[137]

---

135 Tunisi (1967), p. 129. Perhaps it was this belief, if he did in fact believe the Muslim masses to have superior intelligence, which led him to so thoroughly transform Tunisia's intellectual landscape with the founding of the Sadiqi College, reforming the Zaituna Mosque curriculum, establishing libraries, and ensuring the first regular operation of a printing press, as related in Perkins (2004), pp. 32–5.

136 Tunisi (1967), p. 130.

137 This recalls a quote in an article from the 31 January, 2011 issue of *Slate* magazine, entitled "The Shame Factor: When will dictators learn not to treat their people like fools?"

In order to further drive home his contention that the various Islamic peoples are indeed well-suited to the reforms he is advocating, Khayr al-Din turns from the case of European success to recounting the well-known and unprecedented successes of the early Islamic empires. The case he makes, is one that

> reveals the expansive development, extent of wealth and military strength growing out of justice, consensus, fraternal relations among the provinces and political unity professed by the Islamic *umma*, not to mention the concern for the sciences, industries and other such recognized achievements which have appeared in Islam. The Europeans followed in the footsteps of the Islamic *umma*, and those among them who are impartial concede this priority to the Islamic *umma*.[138]

The concept of nationhood presented in this short passage is of a dual nature. The pressing concerns of his time to resist European pressure commended to Khayr al-Din the strategic advantage, and perhaps even necessity, of the Islamic states being able to present a united front to the Europeans. This is why his era of prosperity is portrayed as one of consensus, "fraternal relations," and "political unity." In truth, these conditions rarely prevailed after the earliest days of the House of Islam, but the idea that they should remains powerful to the present day. It is important to note that he does give tacit recognition to political disunity, or at least autonomy, when he mentions relations between "provinces." Whereas European provinces tended to have a very circumscribed set of local powers, those in the Ottoman Empire enjoyed almost complete de facto autonomy, even if de jure they were under the suzerainty of the sultan.

In support of his arguments, he then quotes extensively from the French historian Duruy, who lends additional credibility to the former glory and present potential Khayr al-Din sees within the *umma* because he is a non-Muslim European, and therefore ostensibly impartial in his account. The descriptive language he borrows is very inspiring and poetic, as when he cites Duruy's line: "While the people of Europe were lost in the deepest darkness of ignorance seeing only the slightest light as if through the eye of a needle, there radiated from the Islamic *umma* a powerful light of literature, philosophy, the arts, industries, etc."[139] In addition to their past achievements the binding power of the Arabic language is also cited as one which " has a depth and wide scope which cannot be hidden to those who know it." It is commonly accepted that

---

In it, the late Christopher Hitchens recounts a recent conversation a close friend of his had with the heir of an unnamed Arab Muslim dictator, in which the young aristocrat asked "is it true that there are now free elections in Albania?" Upon receiving a reply in the affirmative, he lamented, "In that case, what does that make us? Are we peasants? Children?" Accessed 08 February, 2011 at http://www.slate.com/id/2283168/.

138 Tunisi, Khayr al-Din (1967), p. 99.

139 Tunisi (1967), p. 99.

language is an important part of national identity, and this may very well be one reason why Khayr al-Din's nationalist appeals, if they can be called that, are largely pan-Islamic.[140] Duruy takes this argument further in regards to Arabic, arguing that its high number of synonyms, especially for those words rooted in the historical desert origins of the Arabs and Arabic, such as the "80 words for honey, 200 for the snake, 500 for the lion, 1,000 for the camel, a like number for the sword and more than 4,000 for misfortune," are demonstrative of the need of Arabic speakers to have "a powerful memory," and as they managed to successfully comprehend their language and use it to develop the poetic arts, for instance, then it becomes clear for Duruy that "the Arab undoubtedly has a powerful memory and a keen intellect."[141] Khayr al-Din's agreement that this is indeed the case means that surely, the Arabic-speaking peoples are capable of developing and using a lexicon for modern statecraft that draws upon their deep well of vocabulary and accumulated historical experience.

The rest of Khayr al-Din's excerpt from Duruy's work traces the development of these early linguistic advantages (which must also translate into advantages for the *Qur'an* which was revealed and transmitted in its pure Arabic form) into the advantages born of successful conquest. The sweep of Muslim armies throughout the Middle East, Eastern Europe, and North Africa, put them into contact with a dizzying array of cultures and customs. Much as Khayr al-Din advocates copying useful European practices in his own time, these early Muslims "mingled with nations who had preceded them in civilization," coming across the writings of Aristotle (albeit indirectly) and saving them for posterity. They also took advantage of the knowledge of men brought from Constantinople by Caliph al-Ma'mun to make significant strides in mathematical knowledge and improved upon ancient Mediterranean discoveries in geography, physics, astronomy, and medicine.[142]

In terms of economic development, Medieval Muslims "learned all of the industries when they conquered the great Roman cities, and they eventually became the most proficient masters in all of these fields." This is yet another example of Muslims borrowing knowledge that was good and bringing their own creativity to it to create far greater levels of expertise. The examples given here are more of a manufacturing and economic nature than the discoveries mentioned earlier, which were largely in the arts and theoretical aspects of science. Arab excellence in crafting products is given "sufficient witness" in "the swords of Toledo … the silks of Granada, the blue and green broadcloth of the city of Cuenca, the saddles, harnesses and leathers of Cordova." In other words, there is absolutely no excuse for the utter lack of industrial development and prowess in the assorted Muslim

140 Antony Black's (2004), p. 296, analysis of Khayr al-Din's work is that it was a call to restore "the independence and strength of the Islamic world community."

141 Tunisi (1967), p. 100.

142 See pp. 100–4 for the full account Khayr al-Din gives of Islamic advances and innovations.

domains. After all, "Europeans used to buy these commodities at high prices and vie with each other for them ... In sum, Spain achieved such a fame for its development from the time of the caliphs in the early centuries that is was even more of an attraction than the East'."[143]

Of course, this spectacular Islamic rise was followed by a humiliating series of defeats and decay, but the latent power of the idea of the Islamic nation, the *umma*, meant that the "disruption of the Islamic states did not stop the Arabs' work in the sciences and literature ... The Christians who drove the Muslims out of Spain obtained through contacts with them in wars their knowledge, industries, and discoveries. The Mongols and the Turks who successively dominated Asia became in the sciences the servants of those they had conquered."[144] In other words, even in defeat, the Islamic ethos and civilization maintained, and Khayr al-Din would probably argue could regain, a victorious stature in the fields of knowledge, practical science, and culture.[145] Indeed, in recalling his comparison between Islamic and European histories in discussing the Islamic *umma*, he says that the purpose of using Europe as a comparative case in successful development is "that we may choose what is suitable to our own circumstance which at the same time supports and is in accordance with our *sharīʿa*. Then, we may be able to restore what was taken from our hands and by use of it overcome the present predicament of negligence existing among us."[146]

Having laid out the dual historical developments in the Islamic and European civilizations and made a strong case for the compatibility and readiness of Islamic civilization and modern reforms, Khayr al-Din also sought to lay out a vision of progress and prosperity that was in keeping with Islamic mores suspicious of foreign innovations and yet proud of their own illustrious past.[147] By packaging this effort as a recapturing of knowledge and skills once already in Muslim hands, he attempts to circumvent the objections based on innovation's corrosive effects and to re-brand it as a mere continuation of the legacy of Islam. Thus in the next section of this chapter, Khayr al-Din's advocacy of progress and Western-style liberalization (even though he would not have employed that term) will be assessed in order to understand how he perceived it to be the solution to "the present predicament of negligence" he identified above.

143 Tunisi (1967), p. 105.

144 Ibid., pp. 107–8.

145 Hourani (1983), p. 89, says that Khayr al-Din's use of Duruy and Sedillot in the manner discussed above is "characteristic of later writers," and is meant to prove the greatness of Islamic civilization by virtue of its recognition as quoted in these modern European writers.

146 Tunisi (1967), p. 73.

147 Al-Husry (1966), p. 38.

### The Surest Path to Progress—Innovation through Reclamation

In many ways, Khayr al-Din's account of the meaning and importance of progress is a restatement of his arguments on the rule of law and nationhood. It uses the same types of arguments from Muslim scripture, history, and references to European experiences. The reason for examining it in its own right, however, is that Khayr al-Din himself says near the beginning of *The Surest Path* that in order to achieve the goal of independence and prosperity

> The first task is to spur on those statesmen and savants having zeal and resolution to seek all possible ways of improving the condition of the Islamic *umma* and of promoting the means of its development by such things as expanding the scope of the sciences and knowledge, smoothing the paths to wealth in agriculture and commerce, promoting all the industries and eliminating the causes of idleness. The basic requirement is good government...[148]

This identifies one primary audience that Khayr al-Din addresses throughout his work, although rarely in the same direct fashion he uses with the *'ulama*. These are the people who would have worked alongside him in government, who control the various levers of power and influence in the state. This is a prodding reminder that their aim should not be self-improvement but "improving the condition of the Islamic *umma*." It is a well accepted principle that one of the primary reasons certain states do not perform well economically is that they are too plagued by corrupt and/or inept government. An additional reason for looking at Khayr al-Din's use of the concept of progress in his work is that he states that *The Surest Path's* "second task" is

> to warn the heedless among the Muslim masses against their persistent opposition to the behavior of others that is praiseworthy and in conformity with our Holy Law simply because they are possessed by the idea that all behavior and organizations of non-Muslims must be renounced, their books must be cast out and not mentioned, and anyone praising such things must be disavowed. This attitude is a mistake under any circumstances.[149]

Although it would appear that his other audience is the Muslim population at large, as seen in the rest of his book, it appears more likely that he is addressing their most influential local leaders and their spokesmen in the *'ulama* class. That is why he bluntly criticizes blind rejection of outsiders' ideas even when they are morally good or neutral and would prove beneficial to society. He hammers this home with a well-chosen paraphrase of al-Ghazali's maxim, stating that "It is not according to man that truth is known. Rather, it is by truth that man is known.

148 Tunisi (1967), p. 74.

149 Ibid., p. 74.

Wisdom is the goal of the believer. He is to take it wherever he finds it."[150] He goes on to cite the ultimate source of authority, the Prophet Muhammad, who, in the Battle of the Trench, took the advice of Salman the Persian in digging a trench around Medina in order to better defend it. It was this willingness to consult and learn from others that establishes the Islamic bona fides of both the principle of consultation and of using what is beneficial from others for the good of the *umma*. "If it was permissible for the virtuous ancestors to take such things as logic from outside their own religious community and to translate it from Greek … then what objection can there be today to our adopting certain skills that we greatly need in order to resist intrigues and attract benefits?"[151] This shows that it is ultimately Khayr al-Din's preoccupation with avoiding occupation by Europeans that motivates his push for progress as much as it is the result of his desire to restore pride to the *umma*.

In a development which he found particularly pernicious and perverse, Khayr al-Din later mocks those who reflexively reject European ideas that could gain their society more independence, development, and wealth, while at the same time "vying with each other in clothing, home furnishings and such everyday needs just as in weapons and all military requirements. The truth is that these are things are European products."[152] The evil is not in the purchase of these products but that in perpetuating a cycle of indebtedness whereby Tunisia (or other Muslim states presumably) produces primary agricultural and raw materials, which are exported to Europe at low cost, where they are turned into manufactured goods and resold to Tunisians at a much higher price in reflection of the value added in manufacture. He ominously and accurately predicts that "if the value of imports exceeds the exports, ruin will unavoidably take place."[153] His economic analysis continues throughout the text, making reference to the advantage of regulating taxes, promoting inventions through state competitions and recognition, educating youths, and the development of a robust financial industry.[154]

Each of these economic strands is intimately tied up with the two types of freedom alluded to earlier. Khayr al-Din paints a vivid picture of the type of future freedom could afford the *umma* in his reference to the gains already realized in Europe.

150 Ibid., p. 75.

151 Ibid., pp. 75–6.

152 Ibid., p. 77.

153 See ibid., pp. 77–8. This fear was realized immediately following Khayr al-Din's term as prime minister with the creation of the European debt commission that came to take over the functions and sovereignty of the state in all but name, in order to insure that European creditors were paid back. Also see Perkins (2004), pp. 33–5 for an account on Khayr al-Din's time in office and his experiences with European debt commissioners.

154 See ibid., p. 81, 133, 135, 155, 157, 163 and 167.

> Among the most important things the Europeans have gathered from the lofty tree of liberty are the improvements in communications by means of railroads, support for commercial societies, and the attention given to technical training. By means of the railroads products can be imported from distant lands quickly enough to be useful, whereas there their importation was formerly impossible ... With these societies the circulation of capital is expanded, profits increase accordingly, and wealth is put into the hands of the most proficient who can cause it to increase.[155]

The picture that emerges from this view of progress is that Khayr al-Din has an impressive grasp of capitalist economics and the centrality of infrastructure given the lack of familiarity he would have gained with well-managed development in Tunisia. He could potentially even be seen as a proto-Keynesian who advocates significant state involvement in paying for various social and capital investments meant to generate the capacity for industry and wealth to be created and to eventually pay the state back with a solid return on this investment in the form of increased productivity, decreased need to provide social welfare, and increased tax revenues. He also reveals free market stripes in his belief that capital markets that are well-run result in wealth being "put into the hands of the most proficient who can cause it to increase." This is, from a holistic perspective, a very balanced approach to economics and progress, much as his approaches to the use of European principles in the rule of law applied on behalf of the Islamic *umma* is also one which strikes a careful balance.[156]

## *A Sure Success?*—Assessing the Practical and Theoretical Legacy of Khayr al-Din

In reflecting upon the narrative woven by Khayr al-Din in making his case for *tanzimat*, it is clear that each of the constitutional themes discussed above cannot be applied to his theory in a piecemeal fashion. Each of these pillars is part of a mutually reinforcing structure. Although some of his contemporaries and some present-day contemporary scholars display disappointment that this work and his later work do not explicitly advocate that Tunisia return to constitutional rule, it is important to bear in mind the historical context that made the constitution engender such native hostility that the idea of its restoration was perhaps even

155 Ibid., pp. 163–4.

156 For a fascinating example of Khayr al-Din's economic philosophy in practice, see Byron, D. Cannon. "Administrative and Economic Regionalism in Tunisian Oleiculture: The Idarat Al Ghabah Experiment, 1870–1914." *The International Journal of African Historical Studies*, 11:4 (1978): 584–628.

more unpopular with the Tunisians than it was with the French business and political interests who found its provisions inconvenient.[157]

Various students of Khayr al-Din have come to a number of conclusions about how successfully he fused European and Islamic political ideas, and how successfully he put his ideas into practice when he later regained political power. In terms of his effort to fuse two traditions with their own sets of questions, problems, and answers, Khayr al-Din's results would seem to be mixed. His rule of law is situated firmly in both the Western and Islamic orbits. It advocates limited, accountable government, recourse to the courts, and uses the language of rights and duties found throughout Western constitutional discourse. This does not detract from its simultaneous anchoring in Islamic values as enshrined in the *sharīʿa*, which provide authentic and ardent motivation for Muslims to this day.[158] His views on nationhood, on the other hand, are decidedly and emphatically Muslim. There may have been a time when the idea of Christendom had a certain resonance, but it is doubtful that it has ever matched the imaginative and political power represented by the Dar al-Islam, with its united *umma*, and sovereign caliph. This is because Christendom never fully embodied itself as a political reality and instead remained a unity of faith and ideas, whereas the historical Muslim experience found success in the marriage of this same type of faith with political power. It is a restoration of this power that Khayr al-Din most desires, and to his mind, progress in the guise of economic and political development is the "surest path" to achieving this goal.

In terms of constitutionalism, Khayr al-Din is not the most original, the most devout, or the most liberal thinker. In a sense, this is his genius. His constitutionalism is one which reflects his Tunisian context. It is not merely Muslim, it is Mediterranean, aware of the world, and keenly, painfully aware of the real humiliation caused by imperialism and an inability to compete

157 See Hourani (1983), p. 94. Here he recounts how in response to critics who questioned his lack of advocacy for the reestablishment of constitutionalism in Tunisia, he replied that two conditions were necessary in order for this type of governance to succeed. The ruler had to be "willing to promulgate them," and the subjects have to be able to understand them and "be willing to accept them." The fact he had to be so cautious on his return to power would seem to indicate that *The Surest Path* was not immediately successful in its aim to convince the Tunisian ruling class of the virtues of reform.

158 Al-Husry (1966) is one of the more critical commentators on Khayr al-Din's Islamicizing of Western political ideas. He summarily renders his verdict as follows: "Khayr al-Din's main preoccupation was to find in traditional political theory and practice precedents for those Western political institutions and practices that he admired and hoped his coreligionists would adopt. He himself admits, unwittingly but clearly, the final failure of his attempt, when at the very end of his book he apologizes to the reader for using foreign terms for which he can find no equivalent in Arabic. Among the terms are: 'constitution', 'dictator', 'jury', and 'camera (in a parliament)'." Of course, one could argue his use of these terms is no different than a Western writer using words like *umma*, *jihad*, or *asabiyya* in describing concepts which have venerable and particular meanings in the Islamic tradition without exact correlations in the West.

economically and politically with European states. His appeals to a glorious Muslim past, a constitutionalism based on longstanding and well-known principles of consultation, and his goal of Tunisian autonomy speak to many constituencies; clerics, historians, nationalists, and the working classes would all find something appealing in his argument. In this sense we find surprising echoes of Thomas Hobbes' strident appeals to reason to nearly every possible English constituency (secularists, clerics, scientists, mathematicians, and devout citizens) that the avoidance of foreign domination and civil war required a fundamentally new understanding of the social contract.

Likewise, Khayr al-Din is well aware that power in Tunisia is diffuse. Ostensibly under Ottoman control, it is actually governed by the administration of the Bey, tribal elders, and at the level of civil society, by the ulama. Each of these groups must have a stake in the game if they are to support the new constitutional path. This bears striking and vitally important foreshadowing of the way in which Tunisia, uniquely amongst all Arab Spring states, functioned in the aftermath of the downfall of its dictator. Important social and political groups, along with religious factions, were all brought together to create a process for drafting a new constitution. This in turn was put to referendum and structured so that the parties mutually agreed to respect the results of the election and to continue operating inclusively even should their own side be victorious. Khayr al-Din's *Surest Path* and his work on the first Tunisian constitution are well-known within Tunisia and they form part of a shared cultural legacy of respect for political diversity, inclusiveness, and genuine constitutionalism that have persisted despite the painful and problematic legacies of colonial domination and strongman rule.

Indeed, one of the more promising and exciting avenues for applying the work of Khayr al-Din to present discourses lies in the idea of reclamation and reinvention. It is not enough for Muslim-majority states to simply claim adherence to religious law or to hearken back to a supposed golden age. No amount of mental gymnastics or political manipulation can recreate the conditions of the early days of Islam. The world is fundamentally changed. Recognizing this contingency is one of Khayr al-Din's real strengths. By citing Western virtues that have clearly led to prosperous and stable states he risks alienating his audience. However, by claiming they first existed within Islam and were appropriated by Europeans, he turns the traditional European account of being the birthplace of civilization on its head and makes the urgency of reclaiming the Muslim world's legacy of tolerance, trade, and transnational power all the more potent. It also disarms one of the most powerful arguments of Islamist movements, in that it clearly rejects the Western/Islamic dichotomy and makes the question not whether values like democracy are foreign or un-Islamic, but rather emphasizes the venerability of concepts like *shura* and demonstrates how their application to modern politics is not only recommended, but actually required. Ultimately, according to Khayr al-Din, lawful and righteous government, government according to the spirit and letter of the *sharīʿa,* is government which is accountable to the people, equitable in its treatment of them, and responsible for promoting the good of society at large; in other words, *sharīʿa*-based government is constitutional in every sense and leaves institutional arrangements up to the will of the people they are to govern.

To conclude these reflections on the introduction of *The Surest Path*, it is sufficient to consider these words from Khayr al-Din: "We have seen that the countries which have progressed to the highest ranks of prosperity are those having established the roots of liberty and the constitution, synonymous with political *tanzimat*."[159] Thus, the practical implications of this comparative examination of constitutional thought in the West and Islam, and the legacy of the work of Khayr al-Din and others, as seen in the Arab Spring and its aftermath, will be examined in the concluding chapter.

159 Tunisi (1967), p. 164.

# Chapter 6

# The Arab Spring—Constitutional Thought in Contested Political Space, Questions and Conclusions

> Yes, there will be perils that accompany this moment of promise. But after decades of accepting the world as it is in the region, we have a chance to pursue the world as it should be.
>
> Of course, as we do, we must proceed with a sense of humility. It's not America that put people into the streets of Tunis or Cairo: It was the people themselves who launched these movements, and it's the people themselves that must ultimately determine their outcome.
>
> Barack Obama, 19 May 2011

In the speech quoted above, given in the immediate aftermath of the Arab Spring uprisings, President Obama identifies both the promise and the perils that the Arab Spring has come to symbolize: the promise that people in these states might have governments that protect their rights and respect their aspirations, and the peril that these revolutions may ultimately be in vain and simply lead to new forms of political oppression or token political concessions. The movement is one which has echoes in earlier revolutions, such as those seen during the fall of communism in Eastern Europe, but which also has a number of unique factors. A variety of analyses have already been published, generally regarding the causes of the Arab Spring and its prospects for engendering long-lasting political change. Factors ranging from the historical to the economical, to the rise of social media are often cited in these studies. All of these are useful ways of trying to make sense of this series of events that so greatly shook the political landscape of the Middle East and North Africa. However, this chapter will utilize the constitutional norms developed in this book, to articulate a number of questions regarding the prospects for constitutional reform in the post-Arab Spring era. It will then use each of these questions as an analytical framework for looking at three different Arab Spring states, each of which experienced a rapid overthrow of the *ancient regime*, yet which conversely experienced very divergent political and constitutional paths subsequent to the initial uprisings. Egypt will be assessed for prospects of a coherent rule of law, the difficulties in reconciling this notion with a religious/sectarian understanding of the state, and the risk of backlash when such efforts fail to produce the promised results. This section seeks to answer questions such as how majority-Muslim states can resolve the tension between representing majorities that often call for more religious involvement in the state and the need to protect minorities who differ in their religious practice or belief? What basis exists for the rule of law in states which privilege a particular sect over others, particularly when it leads to unequal treatment of citizens in terms of qualification for political office or other interactions with the state?

Following this study, the chapter will turn to Libya, which emerged from the despotism of Qaddafi only to erode into a failed state of warring fiefdoms and factions. Orientalist writers have often referred to Islamic government as prone to charismatic leaders (implying this legacy began with Muhammad himself), and have argued that the location of power within a person (caliph, sultan, etc.) rather than in a constitution or institutions, has left many states open to extreme despotism. In this argument, there is an historical case that can be made which gives legitimacy to these claims. However, the diagnosis of the cause of this despotism, a supposed Muslim or Oriental affinity for authoritarian, arbitrary rule, seems both ignorant and misplaced. As the case study of Libya will show, the problem was not an over-reliance on Muslim identity or principles, but rather an open hostility to the creation of any political identity that was not completely wrapped up in loyalty to the person of Qaddafi. This is the utter and profound antithesis of representation, which is the second constitutional principle detailed in this book. In Qaddafi's Libya, much as in Louis XIV's France, the ruler and the state were conflated to the point of becoming indistinguishable. Thus, the resulting chaos in the aftermath of his death makes a compelling argument for the inclusion of genuine representation as a central constitutional value. Furthermore, it directly invokes the tribalism and social dynamics discussed in Ibn Khaldun, allowing it to demonstrate a direct link between the proto-nationalism of Montesquieu and the "group feeling" of Khaldun. This section aims to answer questions such as, what identity or identities Arab Spring states can mobilize to legitimize their regimes? How will they use them to justify any institutional changes, or lack thereof, meant to address protestors' demands? Will these be inclusive enough to truly ensure representation for all?

Finally, in keeping with the principle of limiting and separating government powers, the chapter will examine why Tunisia, uniquely, has experienced a relatively untroubled transition to constitutional governance and why it also seems to be the sole Arab Spring state which has fundamentally changed in a long-lasting constitutional direction. The crucial recognition of Tunisians that their social allegiances are multiple and plural, and thus that they will sometimes be in the majority and sometimes in the minority on given political questions, neatly echoes that of *The Federalist* writers, who contended that the real protection of minorities within democracies existed in the division of power into such a diversity of groups and institutions, that no one group could possibly dominate all aspects of society. This would ensure that every political actor and stakeholder continued to have a legitimate interest in the game of politics and its outcomes. The Tunisian genesis and consolidation of the Arab Spring allow us to ask in light of the fact most of the Arab Spring movements were launched in response to repression and/or authoritarianism, what new political and institutional arrangements are being tried to avoid a return to the past? How do any limits they place on specific personal or institutional powers influence the power of individual citizens to interact with and influence their governments? Does the creation of multiple layers of government allow more groups to experience political victory (and defeat) and thus ensure that elections remain more than foregone conclusions and motivate political actors to produce results because they are more fully convinced the electorate will hold them accountable?

## Egypt and the Struggle for Definition of the Rule of Law

One of the most contentious issues facing nearly all the states involved in the Arab Spring uprisings is dealing with the contradictory demands that they represent their majority populations, many of whom have been ruled by minority sects or clans with little regard for their aspirations, and that they likewise protect minority groups and allow them various individual freedoms in regards to religion, gender, and political opinions. As the Arab-speaking world's most populous state, Egypt has been a particularly vivid example of the perils entailed in this quest. The promise of Tahrir Square of 2011, when people Egyptians proclaimed "The people and the military are one hand," has been sorely tested and indeed betrayed, first by the lack of inclusiveness by the Morsi regime and subsequently by the remilitarization of the state and coronation of General Sisi as new de facto ruler.

Even prior to the military ouster of President Morsi, there were clear signs that all was not well in the state of Egypt. As Stepan and Linz point out, it was only by entering into a number of secret understandings with the military that the Muslim Brotherhood was able to consolidate power ahead of elections and to ensure powerful officers would not actively oppose its plans to reform the state to make it more Islamic. They claim that "more than is commonly understood, the cost of the Brotherhood's gains (which included the presidency of Egypt) included a special position for the military in the new constitutional order, the economy, and the regional government." Supporting this claim they cite various provisions which require that the Minister of Defense must be a serving military officer, the giving of various regional governorships to powerful members of the military, and the establishment of the military's right to hold military trials for civilians accused of crimes that "harm the armed forces."[1] When it turned out that this very same Minister of Defense, a heretofore unknown officer called Abdul Fatah al-Sisi, responded to anti-Morsi riots in June 2013 by siding with the protestors, rather than with the regime, the split between the political and military wings of the state was laid bare. There are a number of factors which contributed to this unrest, economics, perceptions of favoritism, resistance to the Brotherhood's

1 Alfred Stepan and Juan J Linz, "Democratization Theory and the 'Arab Spring'," *Journal of Democracy*, 24:2 (2013): 22.

form of Islamicization of the state, but the fact that the military was allowed to maintain an overt role as ultimate arbiter of political disputes seems to be the most important factor in the way in which President Morsi and much of the post-revolutionary government were deposed by the armed forces.

Rather than speculating on Egypt's future, an examination of the rhetoric from this time of existential crisis for the Morsi regime allows for the constitutional dilemmas surrounding the rule of law in post-revolutionary (or still revolutionary?) Egypt to be brought forward. Looking at the ultimatum delivered to President Morsi by the military, followed by a selection from his response in a 45-minute speech to the nation will reveal not only the deep divisions between these actors, but also the centrality of the rule of law means for Egypt and its people, and the way in which differing perceptions of it lead to radically different visions for the role and responsibilities of the entire state.

On 1 July, 2013, the Egyptian military released the following public pronouncement:

> Egypt and the whole world witnessed yesterday demonstrations by the great people of Egypt expressing their opinion in an unprecedented, peaceful and civilized way.
>
> Everyone saw the movement of the Egyptian people and heard their voices with the greatest respect and concern. It is necessary that the people receive a reply to their movement and the call from every party with any responsibility in the dangerous circumstances surrounding the nation.
>
> As a main party in the considerations of the future and based on their patriotic and historic responsibilities to protect security and stability, the Armed Forces state the following:
>
> - The Armed Forces will not be a party in the circles of politics or governance and are not willing to step out of the role defined for them by the basic ideals of democracy based on the will of the people.
>
> - The national security of the state is exposed to extreme danger by the developments the nation is witnessing, and this places a responsibility on us, each according to his position, to act as is proper to avert these dangers. The armed forces sensed early on the dangers of the current situation and the demands the great people have at this time. Therefore, it previously set a deadline of a week for all political forces in the country to come to a consensus and get out of this crisis. However, the week has passed without any sign of an initiative. This is what led to the people coming out with determination and resolve, in their full freedom, in this glorious way, which inspired surprise, respect and attention at the domestic, regional and international levels.

- Wasting more time will only bring more division and conflict, which we have warned about and continue to warn about. The noble people have suffered and have found no one to treat them with kindness or sympathize with them. That puts a moral and psychological burden on the armed forces, which find it obligatory that everyone drop everything and embrace these proud people, which have shown they are ready to do the impossible if only they feels (sic) there is loyalty and dedication to them.

- The Armed Forces repeat their call for the people's demands to be met and give everyone 48 hours as a last chance to shoulder the burden of the historic moment that is happening in the nation, which will not forgive or tolerate any party that is lax in shouldering its responsibility.

- The Armed Forces put everyone on notice that if the demands of the people are not realized in the given time period, it will be obliged by its patriotic and historic responsibilities and by its respect for the demands of the great Egyptian people to announce a road map for the future and the steps for overseeing its implementation, with participation of all patriotic and sincere parties and movements—including the youth, who set off the glorious revolution and continue to do so—without excluding anyone.

A salute of appreciation and pride to the sincere and loyal men of the Armed Forces, who have always borne and will continue to bear their patriotic responsibilities toward the great people of Egypt with determination, decisiveness and pride.

God save Egypt and its proud, great people.[2]

Ironically, this statement goes to great lengths to put the people of Egypt forward as the ultimate decision-makers in how the state should be run. Their protests are given priority in justifying the military's response to mass unrest and rioting. Just as the people declared that they and the military were one following the downfall of Mubarak, the military was now embracing this same statement in setting up the downfall of Morsi and the Brotherhood. The primary words in this text are not ideological or religious, they are nationalistic. Egypt, Egyptians, and the people are the phrases which figure most potently throughout this brief statement. In other words this is a populist appeal to a popular uprising. Even the youth, who comprise the bulk of the disaffected, are specifically mentioned in an effort to placate them and reassure them that the armed forces are one their side.

That said, it does not require terribly deep thought to see that the military "doth protest too much." In particular, the phrase which precedes the actual demands of the text is especially revealing: "As a main party in the considerations of the future

2 As translated by the Associated Press and published on http://www.huffingtonpost.com/2013/07/01/egyptian-military-ultimatum-text_n_3529987.html.

and based on their patriotic and historic responsibilities to protect security and stability, the Armed Forces state the following…"

In a true democratic regime the military would not see itself as "a main party in the considerations of the future." Rather, they would be a main party in enforcing the wishes and policies, usually foreign policies, of the political rulers of the state, who in turn would be representing the collective will of the citizens. This is far more than an issue of semantics. It is a rare instance of truth-telling by a united group of power brokers who have a large stake, perhaps the largest stake, in the ultimate economic and political direction of Egypt. The military's entanglement in every layer of society which might offer power and/or wealth had never been a secret in Egypt, but it was supposed to become a relic of the past in the post-Mubarak era. Indeed, not only were the rest of the words of the document proven utterly hollow when the military failed to endorse the civilian solutions to this crisis and installed its own leader as top executive prior to organizing an election/coronation to legitimize it, even its justification of providing security is highly questionable.[3]

An interesting contrast to this military message is immediately apparent in Muhammad Morsi's response, delivered on July 2, 2013 and addressed to the entire nation:

> It is normal after revolution for there to be opposition and support. We wrote a constitution and it was (passed) via referendum. We had legitimacy afterwards, and this legitimacy is what guarantees for us that there be no infighting between us and no bloodshed if we respect it … My message to you all, to the opposition, is that I will stand by this legitimacy. And to the supporters who respect democracy and love legitimacy, safeguard Egypt and the revolution. Don't let the revolution be stolen from you, opponents and supporters … I will safeguard legitimacy with my life … I want to say some clear points … There is no alternative for legitimacy, constitutional legitimacy, legal legitimacy, the legitimacy of elections held before … I decided there is no alternative for legitimacy and keeping an open channel for dialogue … Legitimacy is the only guarantee against violence. The old regime won't return … If this initiative isn't accepted, the country will go down a dark road and we'll be back to square one … We have to prove to the world that we are capable of democracy … peacefully we protect the legitimacy … legitimacy is our only guard from future faults … I do not accept anyone saying anything or taking steps against legitimacy; this is completely rejected … To save the nation we need to sacrifice, but not against each other … when we announce jihad that must be against foreign enemies and not against each other. We sacrifice for our country and I am the first to sacrifice. If the cost for legitimacy is my blood I will give it easily … Legitimacy and legitimacy

---

3 For example, see Mohammad Ayatollahi Tabaar, "Assessing (in) Security after the Arab Spring: The Case of Egypt," *PS: Political Science & Politics*, 46:4 (2013). He offers an excellent analysis of how shifting political and military alliances have drastically shifted power to the military and simultaneously undermined socio-political stability.

> alone, the constitution and constitution alone, and the elections and the elections alone … My iron will is with my people and is unshaken.[4]

Where the military statement was nationalistic and appealed to the unity of Egypt, Morsi's speech is undeniably ideological, emotional, and obsessed with one key concept—Legitimacy. Indeed, in a word cloud created by an analysis of the speech (see below), it is the significant word used by far the most in the speech, coming to a total of 57 uses, or more than one per minute.

**Figure 6.1 Word Cloud of President Morsi's July 1, 2013 Speech to the Nation of Egypt**

*Source:* Available at: http://www.bbc.co.uk/news/world-middle-east-23161987.

After this concept, "people," "Egypt," and "God" round out the top keywords. As a speech meant to address massive dissatisfaction with his government and to heal divisions that were literally tearing his country apart, this seems uniquely disconnected from the actual concerns of his opposition. There was little dispute in the country that Egypt had formed a new democratically-elected government and that Morsi was the legitimate head of that government. On the other hand, there was no end of disputes as to the legitimacy of his actions in that role, the legitimacy of excluding non-Islamists from key positions of power, or the legitimacy of Morsi's office interfering with Egypt's supposedly autonomous judiciary branch.

It would seem that by Morsi's definition, legitimacy is simply a product of elections. Thus, in explaining why he would continue to remain in power, he is compelled only to recite the mantra: "Legitimacy, and legitimacy alone. The constitution, and the constitution alone. And the elections, and the elections alone." Certainly elections can endow a regime with a layer of legitimacy and thus empower it to transform the promises made during the campaign into actual policies. However, legitimacy is much more than a popular mandate to rule. It is an ongoing negotiation between a state, its present government, and its people

---

4 As reported in *Al Ahram*, 2 July, 2013: Available at: http://english.ahram.org.eg/NewsContent/1/0/75511/Egypt/Live-updates-Millions-on-streets-in-Egypt-as-defia.aspx.

as to how all the citizens of the state can be fairly treated, how their lives and livelihoods may be improved, and how they as a united people can create a meaningful and lasting identity that contributes to social cohesion and which alleviates the worst potential effects of political disagreements. In other words, it is the product of a state committed to transparency, accountability, responsiveness, and most importantly the rule of law.

Alluding back to the analysis of Cicero and al-Farabi in this text, one could argue that what Egypt has lacked in practice following the Arab Spring is a unifying vision of the state and its distant future, one which can transcend partisan and religious divides, and one which can form a vision of the state as an entity composed of its citizens, yet larger than them in the sense that it should outlive them. Instead, this vision has been substituted by a policy of responding to individual shareholders in the state, lurching from crisis to crisis and uprising to uprising. Ruling in a state of emergency was one of the primary flaws of the Mubarak regime and it seems that Egypt's rulers intend to repeat this mistake for the sake of exigency, when what is called for is a thoroughly debated, well thought out reconsideration of what Egypt is, who its people are, and what they represent as part of the larger world. Given its mythical and powerful past, the need to create and sustain this vision should be only too clear. Only when Egypt (and most of the other Arab Spring states) has formed a government which meets the above conditions, only once it has carefully defined the basis of its law, the mechanisms for enforcing and changing that law, and the means by which society can engage with it, only then will it truly be ruled by law, and only then will it have the legitimacy so earnestly and errantly claimed by President Morsi.

## Libya, Yes, but are there Libyans?

The new Libya which emerged from Qaddafi's 1969 coup lacked the sociopolitical bases of highly institutionalized states; power rested on neither the balance of classes and groups typical of Western pluralism nor the massive political and bureaucratic organizations of communist societies. Rather, the core of the new regime was the relation between the charismatic leader and his (often armed) followers; political power grew out of personal leadership, ideological proselytization, and the barrels of the Free Officers' guns. The leader assumed enormous personal power to govern in the interest of substantive justice or the common good as he saw it, unconstrained by traditional or legal limits. Indeed, he adopted the role of prophetic "law-giver," reshaping and recasting according to an ideology of transformation—virtually a "political religion"—Libya's fluid social and political structures with a freedom unknown in more structured societies.[5]

5 Raymond A. Hinnebusch, "Charisma, Revolution, and State Formation: Qaddafi and Libya," *Third World Quarterly*, 6:1 (1984): 59.

Of all the states involved in the Arab Spring uprisings, Libya is perhaps the most extreme example of the spectacular fall of a dictator and the equally spectacular dissolution of society in the subsequent void. The above quote, written in 1984, points out a number of reasons why this is the case, and highlights an important commonality in all of the Arab Spring states, namely that these are countries which have emerged from colonial pasts during earlier revolutions. Seen in this light, the Arab Spring uprisings are the continuation of the post-colonial desire to establish self-rule and self-respect, both domestically and internationally. Thus, the centrality of finding an identity that is distinct from that imposed during the colonial era, which respects the pasts of these states, and which somehow represents all of the people, many of whom come from religious or tribal minorities, is clear. In Libya's case, the post-colonial era was initially one in which Western rule was cast off in favor of a non-institutionalized, personified politics, embraced and embodied in the person and personality of Muammar al-Qaddafi. Much like Mao Tse Tung, Qaddafi was a revolutionary warrior leader who was driven by a sense of his own destiny and its being fundamentally intertwined with that of his state. Also like Mao, he wrote a political treatise laying out various maxims for achieving the ideal government, *The Green Book.*

On the question of representation, *The Green Book* is explicitly hostile. Here Qaddafi writes: "There can be no representation in lieu of the people and representation is fraud … THE GREEN BOOK presents the ultimate solution to the problem of the instrument of government, and indicates for the masses the path upon which they can advance from the age of dictatorship to that of genuine democracy."[6]

The discussion continues to describe how the state will set up various councils in which all citizens will participate and thus create the first true direct democracy.

Unfortunately, this idealized state was never realized and representation was scorned in favor of personification and total identification of Libya with Qaddafi. Being bereft of institutions which could provide any type of expertise or continuity in governing, Libyans were faced with a unique set of circumstances following Qaddafi's capture and execution. On the one hand, there were very few political actors who could pose any sort of ongoing threat to a new state. There would be no need to reprogram the state or the people against Qaddafi because his downfall was the ultimate renunciation of his regime and his ideology. Alternatively, Libya had no political or social society to speak of at a national level. Tribalism, sectarianism, and militia groups dominated and continue to dominate the country, with little prospect of agreeing on a unified vision for the state, let alone the institutional organs that could best achieve such a vision.

Fundamentally, Libya is the best argument in favor of Ibn Khaldun and Montesquieu's argument that the state needs to be more than a positivist constitution or a set of laws, but must instead embody the spirit of its people and

6 Muammar Al Qaddafi, *The Green Book* (Public Establishment for Publishing, Advertising and Distribution, 1980), 6.

create a sense of national self. For Montesquieu, the case of Libya could represent an instance in which different tribes may be accommodated with representation in the government and input into the fundamental law in accordance with their primary occupations and cultural preoccupations. Likewise, Ibn Khaldun would easily recognize the centrality of the tribe and tribal *asabiyya* in Libya, and one could apply this theory to argue that what Libya most earnestly requires is a stronger national identity that transcends the tribe and which could draw upon the shared historical experiences of first overcoming colonial domination, and then uniting to overthrow totalitarian political and social domination in the tyrranicide of Qaddafi.

The descent into tribalism had led, amongst other things, to the violation of ancient rules of conduct in regards to embassies and the killing of the US Ambassador to Libya, the withdrawal of most major foreign residents and ambassadorial staff, economic stagnation and the continued imprisonment and abuse of people seen to have been on the wrong side of the revolution.[7] Despite all of this, in keeping with the argument of this text that Monstesquieu and Khaldun are descriptive rather than determinist thinkers, there are scholars who argue that the fatalism and determinism which predominate discussions of Libya's future are premature and obscure the uniquely positive aspects of its lack of pre-existing institutions and the positive elements of its post-Arab spring history as a state.

In a piece that forms one part of an article entitled "Arab Winter," which has ominous undertones of cold, unforgiving death, Ryan Calder claims that there are many reasons to be optimistic about Libya's long-term prospects. Among these are the conduct of elections in 2012 that were seen both domestically and internationally as free and fair, the general agreement amongst social actors that Islam should form the fundamental basis for state law (and more importantly wide consensus on the type of Islam best suited to Libya), and the fact that "Libyans have not given up on the 2011 revolution and still appreciate their hard-won freedoms—a fact lost in news reports of domestic chaos. In the words of Libyan-American poet Khaled Mattawa: 'Somewhere, an earthly sun is shining on us, with us, again. There is air in the air again'."[8]

A shining sun and air to breathe are not guarantees of future life, but they are indicators that Libya does have a national life at the present. Furthermore, this brief look at Libya in the post-Arab Spring suggests that if foreign powers wish to see improvement from its very fragile state to one of robust health, then they would be unwise to pull the plug on the various types of economic, political, and social assistance they have been offering and instead may wish to consider pulling out all the stops to establish a physical and political space in which the various tribal and militia actors could convene, act as representatives of their various

7 See Seth G. Jones, "Mirage of the Arab Spring: Deal with the Region You Have, Not the Region You Want" *Foreign Affairs*, 92(2013): 58.

8 Calder, Ryan, "Libya's cautious optimism," in Charles Kurzman et al., "Arab Winter," *Contexts*, 12:2 (2013): 19–20.

parties, and agree upon new institutional means for Libyans to represented in a larger national context.

## Tunisia, Continuing on the Surest Path?

> Freedom is a great, great adventure, but it is not without risks … . There are many unknowns.
>
> Fathi Ben Haj Yathia (Tunisian author and former political prisoner), *New York Times*, 21.2.2011[9]

Beginning her article "The Arab Spring: Religion, revolution, and the public sphere," written in the relatively early days of the Arab Spring, Seyla Benhabib cites the above quote to contradict critics of the revolutions and their assertions that revolutionaries were insufficiently aware of the challenges and dangers that lay ahead of them. For Benhabib, the early and eager dismissal on the part of some commentators of the Arab Spring as a movement doomed to ultimate failure smacks of Orientalism and Islamophobia. As she puts it, these thinkers traditionally argue there are only three possibilities for Islamic government: 1) Corrupt Autocracies ( such as Saudi Arabia, and Egypt), 2) Islamic Fundamentalisms (a catchall term including theocracies as varied as Iran and some aspects of its nemesis Saudi Arabia), or 3) Terrorisms (another catchall term for groups that often have a basis in very particular places and contexts).[10] The subsequent dispersion of political power in Libya and rise of fundamentalist militias, the quelling of unrest in Bahrain, and the re-entrenchment of military rule in Egypt provide some vindication for these critics and raise serious challenges to those who argue, as this author does, that what it means for a state to be Islamic is contingent upon how the Muslims in that state define it, and that furthermore it does not necessarily preclude a politics and political system that are pluralist, respectful of individual freedoms, and which are stable and prosperous.

The birthplace of Muslim constitutionalism in the modern era, and the birthplace of the Arab Spring, Tunisia, is perhaps the last and best argument in a practical sense for the rejection of such determinism and the continuation of constitutional discourse between the traditionally Christian Western states and majority Muslim states in the Middle East, North Africa, and Far East. In recognition of its efforts to negotiate a mutually acceptable constitution between liberals and Islamists, urbanites and rural dwellers, Freedom House awarded Tunisia a ranking of 3 on

9 Quoted in Seyla Benhabib, "The Arab Spring: Religion, Revolution and the Public Sphere," *Eurozine* (10 May 2011). Available at: http://www.eurozine.com/articles/2011-05-10-benhabib-en.html (2011): 1.

10 "The Arab Spring: Religion, Revolution and the Public Sphere," *Eurozine* (10 May 2011). Available at: http://www.eurozine.com/articles/2011-05-10-benhabib-en.html (2011): 2.

its 7-point scale of political rights, the highest rating in over 30 years of any Arab country.[11] This achievement has come with great effort and at great cost. Tunisia, like most post-revolutionary states, faces the very real danger that those who speak freely will be silenced or killed by more popular voices, and the equally daunting task of bringing groups with opposing ideologies together into a coherent government. Despite these challenges, it has avoided the tribalism of Libya and the militarism of Egypt. Why has Tunisia succeeded thus far where these other states have failed?

To begin with, Tunisia is a state with an inherently constitutional identity. Whether populist dictatorships or opportunistic autocrats, nearly all of its post-colonial leaders have felt compelled to at least pay lip service to the idea that they and their regimes are constitutional (evidenced by the *Dastour* and *neo-Dastour* parties). Perhaps because of this, the various leaders of the factions that overthrew Ben Ali worked together to formulate a vision for how Tunisia would function after his downfall and how they would negotiate various election scenarios to ensure that all Tunisians felt represented by the new state, even if their particular party did not win a majority in the elections.[12]

Following a multi-year effort, Tunisia adopted a new constitution, and did so in a thoroughly constitutional fashion. A freely-elected constituent assembly drafted a text in consultation with all major political parties, debated its provisions and made alterations where necessary, and finally agreed upon a text which could be presented to the country as a whole. Although an exhaustive analysis of this new constitution is clearly warranted, a more limited examination of some key provisions will allow the basic constitutional and ideological underpinnings of the text to be revealed, along with a general understanding of how these are being incorporated into political institutions that are truly representative of Tunisia's people and which are designed to safeguard their hard-won human rights.[13]

> We, the representatives of the Tunisian people, members of the National Constituent Assembly,
>
> Taking pride in the struggle of our people to gain independence and to build the State, to eliminate autocracy and achieve its free will, as a realisation of the objectives of the revolution of freedom and dignity, the revolution of 17 December 2010–14 January 2011, out of loyalty to the blood of our blessed martyrs and the sacrifices of Tunisian men and women over generations, and to break with oppression, injustice and corruption;

11 Stepan and Linz, "Democratization Theory and the 'Arab Spring', p. 18.

12 For a more complete discussion of these distinctly Tunisian approaches to post-revolutionary governance, see "Democratization Theory and the 'Arab Spring'," pp. 23–4.

13 English translations of various constitutional articles all come from The Jasmine Foundation's unofficial translation of the final text. Available at: http://www.jasmine-foundation.org/doc/unofficial_english_translation_of_tunisian_constitution_final_ed.pdf.

> Expressing our people's commitment to the teachings of Islam and its open and moderate objectives, to sublime human values and the principles of universal human rights, inspired by our civilisational heritage accumulated over successive epochs of our history, and from our enlightened reformist movements that are based on the foundations of our Islamic-Arab identity and to human civilisation'sachievements, and adhering to the national gains achieved by our people;
>
> With a view to building a participatory, democratic, republican regime, under the framework of a civil State where sovereignty belongs to the people through peaceful rotation of power through free elections, and on the principle of the separation of powers and balance between them; in which the right to association based on pluralism, neutrality of administration and good governance constitute the basis of political competition; and where the State guarantees supremacy of the law, respect for freedoms and human rights, independence of the judiciary, equality of rights and duties between all male and female citizens and fairness between all regions;
>
> Based on the dignified status of humankind; enhancing our cultural and civilisational affiliation to the Arab Islamic nation, on the basis of national unity that is based on citizenship, brotherhood, solidarity, and social justice; with a view to supporting Maghreb unity as a step towards achieving Arab unity,integrating with the Muslim and African nations, and cooperating with the peoples of the world; supporting the oppressed everywhere, and the people's right to self-determination, and for just liberation movements at the forefront of which is the Palestinian liberation movement; and standing against all forms of occupation and racism;
>
> Being aware of the necessity of contributing to a secure climate and the protection of the environment to ensure the sustainability of our natural resources and the sustainability of a safe life for coming generations; and achieving the will of the people to be the makers of their own history, while believing in knowledge, work, and creativity as sublime human values, seeking to become pioneers, and aspiring to contribute to civilisation, on the basis of the independence of national decision-making, world peace, and human solidarity;
>
> We, in the name of the people, draft this Constitution with God's blessings.

The preamble of the constitution begins in typical fashion with "We." In this case, "We, the representatives of the Tunisian people," is a refreshingly honest admission that this text is created on behalf of all the people, but that not all the people have contributed to it or even necessarily support it. This is an example of a conscientious humility found throughout the text. Despite winning the largest share of votes in the elections to draft the constitution, the Islamist Ennahda party demonstrates a keen awareness that it represents only one significant portion of Tunisian society and not all Tunisians. This is in stark contrast to the fatal mistake made by Morsi in his assertion that simply winning an election gave him and the Muslim Brotherhood legitimacy to rule according to their political program without the need to consult other major political and social groups.

The text continues to affirm Islam as the official religion of the state, but again offers the clarification that for the writers of this text it has "open and moderate objectives." It furthermore makes a direct reference to its inspiration in "our civilizational heritage accumulated over successive epochs in our history, and from our enlightened reformist movements."

The preamble also shows that Tunisia's constitution drafters are aware of its place in a larger North African, Arab, Islamic, and global context and that a key aspect of its identity in all of these contexts is as an example of a successful "liberation movement."

Having established a basis for its rule of law in Islam and its history, and its identity as a state with a positive role to play in the world as an example of political liberation, the text goes on to specify the various rights enjoyed by Tunisia's citizens along with the roles and responsibilities of different government organs. Notably, there is one significant concession to the Islamists in the requirement that the President of the Republic, who acts as Head of State, must be a Muslim (Article 74). However, this person can be male or female and can even hold dual nationality so long as this is revoked prior to taking office. The explicit inclusion of women here is complemented by Article 21, which clearly states total political equality between men and women and, which perhaps as or more importantly, prohibits "any discrimination" in the eyes of the law. Another liberal facet of the text includes the lack of any religious qualification whatsoever for election to the Chamber of Deputies, and consequently to Prime Minister, which is the most politically powerful role in the entire system (Article 53).

Aside from treading a careful path of accommodation to its various social factions, the constitution lays out a somewhat unique institutional arrangement which is generally parliamentary, with a popularly elected legislative parliament, parliamentary-approved Prime Minister and government ministers, an independent judiciary, an armed forces that is subject to the laws of the land and obedient to the will of the government, and a President with executive powers similar to those of the US President. Thus far, this would seem to largely emulate existing constitutional arrangements along American and French lines. However, the constitution also gives the President a role in the religious identity and policy of the state as he or she appoints the General Mufti of Tunisia, who speaks as the religious voice of the state (Article 78).

The overall result of the Tunisian constitution is a testament to the ability of political actors who are committed to a broad set of ideals to overcome and accommodate their respective differences. Much like the American founding fathers, who felt compelled to write works like *The Federalist Papers* to justify their institutional arrangements as necessary to the public good and protected from arbitrary abuse in a post-revolutionary setting, the Tunisian founders demonstrate throughout their text an absolute commitment to compromise in the name of national unity and personal political freedom. Although he is long dead, they are true heirs of the legacy of Khayr al-Din and the wider Tunisian constitutional movement.[14]

## Civilizations in Concert

This text argues that constitutionalism is a mode of governance which is applicable to diverse societies and contexts, and which is dependent upon states' adherence to a basic level of the rule of law, representation of their citizens' cultures and identities, and clearly defined roles for various power holders and institutions. The detailed examination of a very limited sample of canonical works from the Western and Muslim traditions of political thought offered here reveals that there are a number of shared values, goals, and constitutional concepts which could form the basis of better understanding between states which are often posed as polar opposites. Indeed, far from being anti-constitutional, innately authoritarian, incapable of reform, or dismissive of personal freedom, these thinkers and many others demonstrate a shared commitment to a very basic set of ideas that people have organized themselves into states, that these states are tasked with creating and enforcing a set of laws with equal application to all citizens, that all citizens must likewise be represented by the state, and finally that the institutions of the state should be arranged so as to clearly define and restrict their powers so that both personal and social freedoms can flourish.

Furthermore, there is genuine value in placing thinkers from differing traditions in a sort of imagined conversation with one another.[15] In a globalized, pluralist, media-saturated world it is deeply unsatisfactory to consider constitutional government as purely in the province of Western political thought, or as a universal given about which there is little debate as to the values and contours that comprise it. Rather, the very contingency of these ideas, their derivation from particular people, times, and places cries out for a re-examination of their meaning, both within and beyond their immediate contexts, and for a complete reconsideration of the impact earlier waves of global interaction (such as the Crusades) had on the cross-fertilization of political and social ideas. The dichotomy of Islam and the West is useful as a device for creating artificial divisions that highlight the divergent paths Christian (or historically Christian) states and Muslim states have

14 Indeed, even a quick reading of the constitution reveals that it closely mirrors virtually all of the social concerns of Khayr al-Din's *Surest Path* and his reforms of the municipal government of Tunis. The role of reform (*Tanzimat*), the centrality of young people and education, the identification with Islam and the wider Muslim world (much like the Ottoman Empire), and the balancing of secular rights with institutional restrictions are all traceable to his on-going influence.

15 I do not subscribe to the Straussian notion of a conversation of the greats, but I do accept that scholars often place them in conversation with one another in the context of their own new work.

taken in the last few hundred years. Indeed, this tool is an excellent alternative explanation that masks the more concrete legacies of colonialism and exploitation and the despotism and unconstitutional nature these types of rule imposed on most of the Muslim world. Perhaps it is these European legacies which shaped the largely authoritarian nature of 20th and early 21st century political regimes in Muslim states.

Ultimately, placing blame for despotism is a pointless exercise. The fact that millions of people felt abused by law, ignored by their supposed government representatives, and unable to access or participate in their own states, indeed unable to even have the assurance of the necessities of life, is what led to the Arab Spring. This uprising was clearly economic in origin, but political and constitutional in aspiration and direction. Yes people demanded food and jobs, but they also wanted fair, representative, accountable government. Although the prospects for success in achieving these goals seem dim, this book nonetheless demonstrates that constitutionalism is at the very heart of political life, that although its concerns vary in each state they nonetheless seem to always include certain basic elements, and that by comparing disparate constitutional canons it is possible to generate novel and native solutions to the problems of governance plaguing much of the world today.

To conclude, it is worth repeating the words of Khayr al-Din's friend and colleague General Abu 'Abdullah Husayn, who perhaps unconsciously echoes the religious devotion to the state of his fellow Mediterranean statesman Cicero:

> Those most beloved of God are those who dedicate themselves to the interest of the people. He who spends one hour working toward improving the conditions of the country and the people is more worthy of praise than he who spends his day praying and handling his beads. God Almighty urges action and is pleased by effort.[16]

16 William L. Cleveland, "The Municipal Council of Tunis, 1858–1870: A Study in Urban Institutional Change," *International Journal of Middle East Studies*, 9:1 (1978): 39–41.

# Bibliography

Abou El Fadl, Khaled. *Islamic Law and Muslim Minorities: The Juristic Discourse on Muslim Minorities from 8th to 17th Century Ce/2nd to 11th Hijrah*. Muis Occasional Papers Series. Singapore: Islamic Religious Council of Singapore, 2006.

———. *Reasoning with God: Rationality and Thought in Islam*. Oxford: Oneworld, 2002.

Abou El Fadl, Khaled, Joshua Cohen, and Deborah Chasman. *Islam and the Challenge of Democracy*. Princeton, NJ: Princeton University Press, 2004.

Abou El Fadl, Khaled, Joshua Cohen, and Ian Lague. *The Place of Tolerance in Islam*. Boston: Beacon Press, 2002.

Abu-Rabi, Ibrahim M. *The Blackwell Companion to Contemporary Islamic Thought*. Blackwell Companions to Religion. Malden, MA: Blackwell, 2006.

Ahmad, Aziz. "Sayyid Aḥmad Khān, Jamāl Al-Dīn Al-Afghānī and Muslim India." *Studia Islamica*, 13 (1960): 55–78.

al-Farabi, Abu Nasr, and Richard Walzer. *Al-Farabi on the Perfect State: Abu Nasr Al-Farabi's Mabadi Ara Ahl Al-Madina Al-Fadila: A Revised Text with Introduction, Translation, and Commentary*. Oxford: Oxford University Press, 1985.

Al Qaddafi, Muammar. *The Green Book*. Public Establishment for Publishing, Advertising and Distribution, 1980.

Allan, T.R.S. *Constitutional Justice: A Liberal Theory of the Rule of Law*. Oxford and New York: Oxford University Press, 2001.

Aristotle, and Jonathan Barnes. *The Complete Works of Aristotle: The Revised Oxford Translation*. Bollingen Series 71:2. Princeton, NJ: Princeton University Press, 1984.

Arjomand, Said Amir. *Constitutional Politics in the Middle East: With Special Reference to Turkey, Iraq, Iran, and Afghanistan*. Oñati International Series in Law and Society. Oxford and Portland, OR: Hart Publishing, 2008.

———. *Constitutionalism and Political Reconstruction*. International Comparative Social Studies. Leiden and Boston: Brill, 2007.

———. *The Political Dimensions of Religion*. Suny Series in near Eastern Studies. Albany, NY: State University of New York Press, 1993.

Arjomand, Said Amir, and Nathan J. Brown. *The Rule of Law, Islam, and Constitutional Politics in Egypt and Iran*. Suny Series. Pangaea Ii: Global/ Local Studies. Albany, NY: State University of New York Press, 2013.

Arjomand, Said Amir, and Edward A. Tiryakian. *Rethinking Civilizational Analysis*. Sage Studies in International Sociology 52. London and Thousand Oaks, CA: SAGE Publications, 2004.

Arnason, Johann P. and Georg Stauth. "Civilization and State Formation in the Islamic Context: Re-Reading Ibn Khaldūn." *Thesis Eleven*, 76:1 (February 1, 2004): 29–48.

Asconius Pedianus, Quintus, R.G. Lewis, Jill Harries, and Albert Curtis Clark. *Commentaries on Speeches of Cicero* [in Latin text with English translation and commentary.]. Clarendon Ancient History Series. Oxford and New York: Oxford University Press, 2006.

Backer, Larry Cata. "From Constitution to Constitutionalism: A Framework for Analysis of Nationalist and Transnational Constitutionalism." (2008). Available at: http://works.bepress.com/larry_backer/1.

Bailyn, Bernard. *The Debate on the Constitution: Federalist and Antifederalist Speeches, Articles, and Letters During the Struggle over Ratification*. The Library of America 62–3. New York: Library of America: Distributed to the trade in the U.S. and Canada by Viking Press, 1993.

Beeman, Richard R., Stephen Botein, Edward Carlos Carter, and Institute of Early American History and Culture (Williamsburg, VA). *Beyond Confederation: Origins of the Constitution and American National Identity*. Chapel Hill: Published for the Institute of Early American History and Culture, Williamsburg, Virginia, by the University of North Carolina Press, 1987.

Bellamy, Richard. *Political Constitutionalism: A Republican Defence of the Constitutionality of Democracy*. Cambridge: Cambridge University Press, 2007.

Benhabib, Seyla. "The Arab Spring: Religion, Revolution and the Public Sphere." *Eurozine* (10 May 2011), Available at: http://www.eurozine.com/articles/2011-05-10-benhabib-en. html (2011).

Berkes, Niyazi. *The Development of Secularism in Turkey*. New York: Routledge, 1998.

Berkey, Jonathan Porter. *The Formation of Islam: Religion and Society in the Near East, 600–1800*. Themes in Islamic History V. 2. New York: Cambridge University Press, 2003.

Bingham, T.H. *The Rule of Law*. London and New York: Allen Lane, 2010.

Black, Antony. *The History of Islamic Political Thought: From the Prophet to the Present*. Edinburgh: Edinburgh University Press, 2001.

———. "Religion and Politics in Western and Islamic Political Thought: A Clash of Epistemologies?". *The Political Quarterly*, 81:1 (2010): 116–22.

———. *The West and Islam: Religion and Political Thought in World History*. New York: Oxford University Press, 2008.

Bobbio, Norberto, and Maurizio Viroli. *The Idea of the Republic*. Cambridge: Polity Press, 2003.

Boucher, David. *The Limits of Ethics in International Relations: Natural Law, Natural Rights, and Human Rights in Transition*. Oxford: Oxford University Press, 2009.

———. *Political Theories of International Relations: From Thucydides to the Present*. Oxford and New York: Oxford University Press, 1998.

Boucher, David, James Connelly, and Tariq Modood. *Philosophy, History and Civilization: Interdisciplinary Perspectives on R.G. Collingwood*. Cardiff: University of Wales Press, 1995.

Boucher, David and P.J. Kelly. *Political Thinkers: From Socrates to the Present*. 2nd ed. Oxford and New York: Oxford University Press, 2009.

———. *The Social Contract from Hobbes to Rawls*. London and New York: Routledge, 1994.

———. *Social Justice: From Hume to Walzer*. London and New York: Routledge, 1998.

Brett, Michael. "The Way of the Nomad." *Bulletin of the School of Oriental and African Studies*, 58:2 (1995): 251–69.

Briton Cooper, Busch. "Divine Intervention in the "Muqaddimah" of Ibn Khaldūn." *History of Religions*, 7:4 (1968): 317–29.

Browers, Michaelle and Charles Kurzman. *An Islamic Reformation?* Lanham, MD: Lexington Books, 2004.

Brown, Chris, Terry Nardin, and N.J. Rengger. *International Relations in Political Thought: Texts from the Ancient Greeks to the First World War*. Cambridge and New York: Cambridge University Press, 2002.

Brown, L. Carl. *The Tunisia of Ahmad Bey, 1837–1855*. Princeton Studies on the near East. Princeton, NJ: Princeton University Press, 1974.

Brown, Nathan J. *Constitutions in a Nonconstitutional World: Arab Basic Laws and the Prospects for Accountable Government*. Suny Series in Middle Eastern Studies. Albany, NY: State University of New York Press, 2002.

———. *The Rule of Law in the Arab World: Courts in Egypt and the Gulf*. Cambridge Middle East Studies 6. Cambridge and New York: Cambridge University Press, 1997.

Brown, Rebecca L. "Accountability, Liberty, and the Constitution." *Columbia Law Review*, 98:3 (1998): 531–79.

Brudner, Alan. *Constitutional Goods*. Oxford and New York: Oxford University Press, 2004.

Burke, Edmund and David Bromwich. *On Empire, Liberty, and Reform: Speeches and Letters*. The Lewis Walpole Series in Eighteenth-Century Culture and History. New Haven, CT: Yale University Press, 2000.

Burke, Edmund and Brian W. Hill. *Edmund Burke on Government, Politics, and Society*. London: Fontana, 1975.

Burke, Edmund and J.G.A. Pocock. *Reflections on the Revolution in France*. Indianapolis, IN: Hackett Publishing Co., 1987.

Byron, D. Cannon. "Administrative and Economic Regionalism in Tunisian Oleiculture: The Idarat Al Ghabah Experiment, 1870–1914." *The International Journal of African Historical Studies*, 11:4 (1978): 584–628.

Calder, Norman. "Friday Prayer and the Juristic Theory of Government: Sarakhsī, Shīrāzī, Māwardī." *Bulletin of the School of Oriental and African Studies,* 49: 01 (1986): 35–47.

Carey, George W. "Separation of Powers and the Madisonian Model: A Reply to the Critics." *The American Political Science Review*, 72:1 (1978): 151–64.

Carol Riphenburg. "Afghanistan's Constitution: Success or Sham?". *Middle East Policy*, 12:1 (2005): 31–43.

Carothers, Thomas. *Promoting the Rule of Law Abroad: In Search of Knowledge*. Washington, DC: Carnegie Endowment for International Peace, 2006.

Chandler, David. *Constructing Global Civil Society: Morality and Power in International Relations*. Houndmills, Basingstoke and New York: Palgrave Macmillan, 2004.

Chandler, David and Gideon Baker. *Global Civil Society: Contested Futures*. Routledge Advances in International Relations and Global Politics. London and New York: Routledge, 2005.

Choudhry, Sujit. *Constitutional Design for Divided Societies: Integration or Accommodation?* Oxford and New York: Oxford University Press, 2008.

Cicero, Marcus Tullius, Miriam T. Griffin, and E.M. Atkins. *On Duties*. Cambridge Texts in the History of Political Thought. Cambridge and New York: Cambridge University Press, 1991.

Cicero, Marcus Tullius, Niall Rudd, and J.G.F. Powell. *The Republic; and, the Laws*. Oxford World's Classics. Oxford and New York: Oxford University Press, 1998.

Clancy-Smith, Julia A. *Rebel and Saint: Muslim Notables, Populist Protest, Colonial Encounters: Algeria and Tunisia, 1800–1904*. Berkeley, CA: University of California Press, 1994.

Cleveland, William L. "The Municipal Council of Tunis, 1858–1870: A Study in Urban Institutional Change." *International Journal of Middle East Studies*, 9: 1 (1978): 33–61.

Cobban, Alfred. *Edmund Burke and the Revolt against the Eighteenth Century: A Study of the Political and Social Thinking of Burke, Wordsworth, Coleridge, and Southey*. London: G. Allen & Unwin, 1929.

Cohen, Elizabeth F. "Jus Tempus in the Magna Carta: The Sovereignty of Time in Modern Politics and Citizenship." *PS: Political Science & Politics*, 43:3 (2010): 463–66.

Collingwood, R.G. and David Boucher. *Essays in Political Philosophy*. Oxford: Clarendon Press, 1989.

———. *The New Leviathan, or, Man, Society, Civilization, and Barbarism*. Rev. ed. Oxford and New York: Clarendon Press, 1992.

Collingwood, R.G., David Boucher, Wendy James, and Philip Smallwood. *The Philosophy of Enchantment: Studies in Folktale, Cultural Criticism, and Anthropology*. Oxford and New York: Oxford University Press, 2005.

Cornell, Saul and Omohundro Institute of Early American History & Culture. *The Other Founders: Anti-Federalism and the Dissenting Tradition in America, 1788–1828*. Chapel Hill: Published for the Omohundro Institute of Early American History and Culture, Williamsburg, Virginia, by the University of North Carolina Press, 1999.

Cotran, Eugene, Adil Umar Sherif, and University of London. Centre of Islamic and Middle Eastern Law. *Democracy, the Rule of Law and Islam*. Cimel Book Series. London: Kluwer Law International, 1999.

Countryman, Edward. *What Did the Constitution Mean to Early Americans?: Readings*. Historians at Work. Boston: Bedford/St. Martin's, 1999.

Crone, Patricia. *God's Rule: Government and Islam*. New York: Columbia University Press, 2004.

Dale, Stephen Frederic. "Ibn Khaldun: The Last Greek and the First Annaliste Historian." *International Journal of Middle East Studies*, 38:3 (2006): 431–51.

Dallmayr, Fred. "Beyond Monologue: For a Comparative Political Theory." *Perspectives on Politics*, 2:2 (2004): 249–57.

———. "Introduction: Toward a Comparative Political Theory." *The Review of Politics*, 59:3 (1997): 421–28.

Dallmayr, Fred R. *Beyond Orientalism: Essays on Cross-Cultural Encounter*. Albany, NY: State University of New York Press, 1996.

———. *Border Crossings: Toward a Comparative Political Theory*. Global Encounters. Lanham, MD: Lexington Books, 1999.

———. *Integral Pluralism: Beyond Culture Wars*. Lexington, KY: University Press of Kentucky, 2010.

Davison, Roderic H. "Turkish Attitudes Concerning Christian-Muslim Equality in the Nineteenth Century*." *The American Historical Review*, 59:4 (1954): 844–64.

Denny, Frederick M. "Ummah in the Constitution of Medina." *Journal of Near Eastern Studies*, 36:1 (1977): 39–47.

Dhaouadi, Mahmoud. "Ibn Khaldun: The Founding Father of Eastern Sociology." *International Sociology*, 5:3 (September 1, 1990): 319–35.

Donohue, John J. and John L. Esposito. *Islam in Transition: Muslim Perspectives*. New York: Oxford University Press, 1982.

Durkheim, Emile. *Montesquieu and Rousseau: Forerunners of Sociology*. Ann Arbor: University of Michigan Press, 1960.

Dyck, Andrew R. and Marcus Tullius Cicero. *A Commentary on Cicero, De Legibus*. Ann Arbor: University of Michigan Press, 2004.

———. *A Commentary on Cicero, De Officiis*. Ann Arbor: University of Michigan Press, 1996.

Dyer, Justin Buckley. "Slavery and the Magna Carta in the Development of Anglo-American Constitutionalism." *PS: Political Science & Politics*, 43:3 (2010): 479–82.

Edwards, Jason. *The Radical Attitude and Modern Political Theory*. New York: Palgrave Macmillan, 2007.

Elster, Jon, Rune Slagstad, and Maison des sciences de l'homme (Paris France). *Constitutionalism and Democracy*. Studies in Rationality and Social Change. Cambridge and New York: Cambridge University Press, 1988.

Emerson, Steven and Investigative Project on Terrorism (Organization). *Jihad Incorporated: A Guide to Militant Islam in the Us*. Amherst, NY: Prometheus Books, 2006.

Esposito, John L. *Islam: The Straight Path*. 3rd ed. New York and Oxford: Oxford University Press, 1998.

———. *Islam and Politics*. Contemporary Issues in the Middle East. 4th ed. Syracuse, NY: Syracuse University Press, 1998.

Esposito, John L. and John O. Voll. "Islam and the West: Muslim Voices of Dialogue." *Millennium—Journal of International Studies*, 29:3 (December 1, 2000): 613–39.

Euben, Roxanne L. "Comparative Political Theory: An Islamic Fundamentalist Critique of Rationalism." *The Journal of Politics*, 59:1 (1997): 28–55.

———. "Contingent Borders, Syncretic Perspectives: Globalization, Political Theory, and Islamizing Knowledge." *International Studies Review*, 4:1 (2002): 23–48.

Ewin, R.E. *Virtues and Rights: The Moral Philosophy of Thomas Hobbes*. Boulder, CO: Westview Press, 1991.

Feldman, Noah. *After Jihad: America and the Struggle for Islamic Democracy*. 1st paperback ed. New York: Farrar, Straus and Giroux, 2004.

———. *The Fall and Rise of the Islamic State*. Princeton, NJ: Princeton University Press, 2008.

Finn, John E. *Constitutions in Crisis: Political Violence and the Rule of Law*. New York: Oxford University Press, 1991.

Flandreau, Marc and Nathan Sussman. "Old Sins: Exchange Rate Clauses and European Foreign Lending in the 19th Century." *SSRN eLibrary* (2004).

Forsyth, Murray Greensmith, and H.M.A. Keens-Soper. *A Guide to the Political Classics: Plato to Rousseau*. Oxford and New York: Oxford University Press, 1988.

———. *The Political Classics: Green to Dworkin*. Oxford and New York: Oxford University Press, 1996.

Forsyth, Murray Greensmith, H.M.A. Keens-Soper, and John Hoffman. *The Political Classics: Hamilton to Mill*. Oxford and New York: Oxford University Press, 1993.

Franco, Paul. *The Political Philosophy of Michael Oakeshott*. New Haven, CT: Yale University Press, 1990.

Franklin, Daniel P. and Michael J. Baun. *Political Culture and Constitutionalism: A Comparative Approach.* Comparative Politics Series. Armonk, NY: M.E. Sharpe, 1995.

Freeman, Michael. *Edmund Burke and the Critique of Political Radicalism.* Chicago, IL: University of Chicago Press, 1980.

Friedrich, Carl J. *Constitutional Reason of State: The Survival of the Constitutional Order*. The Colver Lectures in Brown University. Providence, RI: Brown University Press, 1957.

Garnham, David and Mark A. Tessler. *Democracy, War, and Peace in the Middle East.* Indiana Series in Arab and Islamic Studies. Bloomington, IN: Indiana University Press, 1995.

Gaudefroy-Demombynes, Maurice. *Muslim Institutions*. Westport, CT: Greenwood Press, 1984.

Gaus, Gerald F. and Chandran Kukathas. *Handbook of Political Theory*. London and Thousand Oaks, CA: SAGE, 2004.

Gearhart, Suzanne. "Reading De L'esprit Des Lois: Montesquieu and the Principles of History." *Yale French Studies*, 59 (1980): 175–200.

Gebhardt, Jürgen. "Political Thought in an Intercivilizational Perspective: A Critical Reflection." *The Review of Politics*, 70:1 (2008): 5–22.

Gelderen, Martin van, and Quentin Skinner. *Republicanism: A Shared European Heritage.* 2 vols. Cambridge and New York: Cambridge University Press, 2002.

Green, Arnold H. "Political Attitudes and Activities of the Ulama in the Liberal Age: Tunisia as an Exceptional Case." *International Journal of Middle East Studies*, 7:2 (1976): 209–41.

Gwyn, William B. "The Indeterminacy of the Separation of Powers and the Federal Courts." *George Washington Law Review*, 57 (1988–1989): 474–506.

Haddad, Yvonne Yazbeck, and John L. Esposito. *Islam, Gender, & Social Change.* New York: Oxford University Press, 1998.

Hamilton, Alexander, James Madison, John Jay, and Ian Shapiro. *The Federalist Papers: Alexander Hamilton, James Madison, John Jay.* Rethinking the Western Tradition. New Haven, CT:: Yale University Press, 2009.

Hamilton, Alexander, James Madison and John Jay. *The Federalist.* edited by Jacob Ernest Cooke. 1st ed. Middletown, CT: Wesleyan University Press, 1961.

Hammond, Robert. *The Philosophy of Al Farabi and Its Influence on Medieval Thought.* New York: Hobson Book Press, 1947.

Hampsher-Monk, Iain. *The Political Philosophy of Edmund Burke.* Documents in Political Ideas. London and New York: Longman, 1987.

Harrison, Ross. *Hobbes, Locke, and Confusion's Masterpiece: An Examination of Seventeenth-Century Political Philosophy.* Cambridge and New York: Cambridge University Press, 2003.

Harvey, W. Burnett. "The Rule of Law in Historical Perspective." *Michigan Law Review*, 59:4 (1961): 487–500.

Haskell, Henry Joseph. *This Was Cicero: Modern Politics in a Roman Toga.* London: Secker & Warburg, 1943.

Hayek, Friedrich A. von. *The Constitution of Liberty*. Chicago, il: Regnery, 1972.
Helmholz, R.H. "Magna Carta and the Ius Commune." *The University of Chicago Law Review*, 66:2 (1999): 297–371.
Hinnebusch, Raymond A. "Charisma, Revolution, and State Formation: Qaddafi and Libya." *Third World Quarterly*, 6:1 (1984/01/01 1984): 59–73.
Hobbes, Thomas, and Richard Tuck. *Leviathan*. Cambridge Texts in the History of Political Thought. Cambridge and New York: Cambridge University Press, 1991.
Hopton, T.C. "Grundnorm and Constitution: The Legitimacy of Politics." *McGill Law Journal*, 24 (1978): 72–91.
Hourani, Albert. *Arabic Thought in the Liberal Age, 1798–1939*. Cambridge and New York: Cambridge University Press, 1983.
Hulsebosch, Daniel Joseph. *Constituting Empire: New York and the Transformation of Constitutionalism in the Atlantic World, 1664–1830*. Studies in Legal History. Chapel Hill: University of North Carolina Press, 2005.
Huntington, Samuel P. *The Clash of Civilizations and the Remaking of World Order*. New York: Simon & Schuster, 1996.
Husry, Khaldun Sati. *Three Reformers: A Study in Modern Arab Political Thought*. 1st ed. Beirut: Khayats, 1966.
Hutchings, Kimberly. "Dialogue between Whom? The Role of the West/Non-West Distinction in Promoting Global Dialogue in Ir." *Millennium—Journal of International Studies*, 39:3 (May 1, 2011): 639–47.
Ibn Hisham, Abd al-Malik, Muhammad Ibn Ishaq, and Alfred Guillaume. *The Life of Muhammad*. London, New York: Oxford University Press, 1955.
Inayat, Ham id. *Modern Islamic Political Thought: The Response of the Shi'i and Sunni Muslims to the Twentieth Century*. London and New York: I.B. Tauris, 2005.
Jackson, Vicki C. *Constitutional Engagement in a Transnational Era*. Oxford and New York: Oxford University Press.
Jones, Seth G. "Mirage of the Arab Spring: Deal with the Region You Have, Not the Region You Want, The." *Foreign Affairs*, 92 (2013): 55.
Julien, Charles Andre, C.C. Stewart, Roger Le Tourneau, and John Petrie. *History of North Africa: Tunisia, Algeria, Morocco, from the Arab Conquest to 1830: By Charles-Andre\0301 Julien; Translated [from the French] by John Petrie;* Edited by C.C. Stewart; Edited and Revised by R. Le Tourneau. London: Routledge & Kegan Paul, 1970.
Kamm, F.M. *Morality, Mortality*. Oxford Ethics Series. New York: Oxford University Press, 1993.
Kammerhofer, Jörg. "Constitutionalism and the Myth of Practical Reason: Kelsenian Responses to Methodological Confusion." *SSRN eLibrary* (
Kedourie, Elie. *Politics in the Middle East*. Oxford and New York: Oxford University Press, 1992.
Keene, Edward. *International Political Thought: A Historical Introduction*. Cambridge and Malden, MA: Polity, 2005.

Keener, Frederick M. *The Chain of Becoming: The Philosophical Tale, the Novel, and a Neglected Realism of the Enlightenment: Swift, Montesquieu, Voltaire, Johnson, and Austen*. New York: Columbia University Press, 1983.

Kelsen, Hans, Anders Wedberg, and Wolfgang Herbert Kraus. *General Theory of Law and State*. 20th Century Legal Philosophy Series: Vol. I. Cambridge, MA: Harvard University Press, 1945.

Khadduri, Majid. *The Islamic Conception of Justice*. Baltimore, MD: Johns Hopkins University Press, 1984.

Khan, M.A. Muqtedar. *Islamic Democratic Discourse: Theory, Debates, and Philosophical Perspectives*. Oxford: Lexington Books, 2006.

Kinzer, Bruce L., Ann P. Robson, and John M. Robson. *A Moralist in and out of Parliament: John Stuart Mill at Westminster, 1865–1868*. Toronto and Buffalo: University of Toronto Press, 1992.

Kirk, Russell. *The Conservative Constitution*. Washington, D.C. Lanham, MD: Regnery Gateway; National Network [distributor], 1990.

Klabbers, Jan, Anne Peters, and Geir Ulfstein. *The Constitutionalization of International Law*. Oxford and New York: Oxford University Press, 2009.

Kramer, Gudrun. "Islamist Notions of Democracy." *Middle East Report*, 183 (1993): 2–8.

Kriesel, Karl Marcus. "Montesquieu: Possibilistic Political Geographer." *Annals of the Association of American Geographers*, 58:3 (1968): 557–74.

Kurzman, Charles. *Modernist Islam, 1840–1940: A Sourcebook*. Oxford and New York: Oxford University Press, 2002.

Kurzman, Charles, Dalia F Fahmy, Justin Gengler, Ryan Calder, and Sarah Leah Whitson. "Arab Winter." *Contexts*, 12:2 (2013): 12–21.

Ladavac, Nicoletta Bersier. "Hans Kelsen (1881–1973) Biographical Note and Bibliography." *Eur J Int Law*, 9:2 (January 1, 1998): 391–400.

Laks, André, and Malcolm Schofield. *Justice and Generosity: Studies in Hellenistic Social and Political Philosophy: Proceedings of the Sixth Symposium Hellenisticum*. Cambridge and New York: Cambridge University Press, 1995.

Lapidus, Ira M. *A History of Islamic Societies*. Cambridge: Cambridge University Press, 1988.

Lerner, Ralph. "Review: Beating the Neoplatonic Bushes." *The Journal of Religion*, 67:4 (1987): 510–17.

Levi, Edward H. "Some Aspects of Separation of Powers." *Columbia Law Review*, 76:3 (1976): 371–91.

Locke, John, and Mark Goldie. *Locke: Political Essays*. Cambridge Texts in the History of Political Thought. Cambridge and New York: Cambridge University Press, 1997.

Locke, John, and Peter Laslett. *Two Treatises of Government*. Cambridge Texts in the History of Political Thought. Student ed. Cambridge and New York: Cambridge University Press, 1988.

Loughlin, Martin, and Neil Walker. *The Paradox of Constitutionalism: Constituent Power and Constitutional Form*. Oxford and New York: Oxford University Press, 2007.

Lutz, Donald S. *Principles of Constitutional Design*. Cambridge and New York: Cambridge University Press, 2006.

———. "Thinking About Constitutionalism at the Start of the Twenty-First Century." *Publius*, 30:4 (2000): 115–35.

Lyons, David. *Rights, Welfare, and Mill's Moral Theory*. New York: Oxford University Press, 1994.

Macfarlane, Alan. *The Riddle of the Modern World: Of Liberty, Wealth and Equality*. Houndmills, Basingstoke and New York: Macmillan Press, 2000.

MacKendrick, Paul Lachlan, and Karen Lee Singh. *The Philosophical Books of Cicero*. New York: St. Martin's Press, 1989.

Macpherson, C.B. *The Political Theory of Possessive Individualism: Hobbes to Locke*. Oxford: Clarendon Press, 1962.

Maddox, Graham. "A Note on the Meaning of 'Constitution'." *The American Political Science Review*, 76:4 (1982): 805–9.

Madison, James, Alexander Hamilton, and John Jay. *The Federalist Papers*. Classics of Conservatism. New Rochelle, NY: Arlington House, 1966.

Mandler, Peter. *The English National Character: The History of an Idea from Edmund Burke to Tony Blair*. New Haven, CT and London: Yale University Press, 2006.

March, Andrew F. "Islamic Foundations for a Social Contract in Non-Muslim Liberal Democracies." *American Political Science Review*, 101:2 (2007): 235–52.

Marquez, Xavier. "Cicero and the Stability of States." *SSRN eLibrary* (1905).

Mason, Sheila Mary. *Montesquieu's Idea of Justice*. International Archives of the History of Ideas 79. The Hague: Martinus Nijhoff, 1975.

McIlwain, C.H. "The English Common Law, Barrier against Absolutism." *The American Historical Review*, 49:1 (1943): 23–31.

———. "A Fragment on Sovereignty." *Political Science Quarterly*, 48:1 (1933): 94–106.

———. "The Historian's Part in a Changing World." *The American Historical Review*, 42:2 (1937): 207–24.

———. "Mediaeval Institutions in the Modern World." *Speculum*, 16:3 (1941): 275–83.

———. "Sovereignty Again." *Economica*, 18 (1926): 253–68.

McIlwain, Charles Howard. *The American Revolution: A Constitutional Interpretation*. Clark, NJ: Lawbook Exchange, 2005.

———. *Constitutionalism & the Changing World: Collected Papers*. Cambridge University Press. Library Editions. Cambridge: Cambridge University Press, 1939.

———. *Constitutionalism: Ancient and Modern*. Rev. ed. Indianapolis, IN: Amagi/Liberty Fund, 2007.

———. *The Growth of Political Thought in the West, from the Greeks to the End of the Middle Ages*. New York: The Macmillan company, 1932.

McLaren, Lauren M. "Explaining Opposition to Turkish Membership of the Eu." *European Union Politics*, 8:2 (June 1, 2007): 251–78.

Mill, John Stuart, Harriet Hardy Taylor Mill, and John M. Robson. "Essays on Equality, Law, and Education." *Collected Works of John Stuart Mill*. Toronto: University of Toronto Press, 1984.

Mill, John Stuart, and John M. Robson. *An Examination of Sir William Hamilton's Philosophy and of the Principal Philosophical Questions Discussed in His Writings*. Collected Works of John Stuart Mill. Toronto and Buffalo: University of Toronto Press, 1979.

———. *John Stuart Mill: A Selection of His Works*. College Classics in English. Toronto and New York: Macmillan of Canada; St. Martin's Press, 1966.

Mill, John Stuart, and G.W. Smith. *John Stuart Mill's Social and Political Thought: Critical Assessments*. Critical Assessments of Leading Political Philosophers. 4 vols. London and New York: Routledge, 1998.

Montesquieu, Charles de Secondat, Anne M. Cohler, Basia Carolyn Miller, and Harold Samuel Stone. *The Spirit of the Laws*. Cambridge Texts in the History of Political Thought. Cambridge and New York: Cambridge University Press, 1989.

Montesquieu, Charles de Secondat, and David Lowenthal. *Considerations on the Causes of the Greatness of the Romans and Their Decline*. Agora Editions. New York: Free Press, 1965.

Moore, Clement H. "Review: [Untitled]." *Middle Eastern Studies*, 6:2 (1970): 234–36.

Müftüler-Bac, Meltem, and Yannis A. Stivachtis. *Turkey-European Union Relations: Dilemmas, Opportunities, and Constraints*. Lanham, MD: Lexington Books, 2008.

Mufti, Malik. "Jihad as Statecraft:Ibn Khaldun on the Conduct of War and Empire." *History of Political Thought*, 30 (2009): 385–410.

Muller, Jerry Z. *Conservatism: An Anthology of Social and Political Thought from David Hume to the Present*. Princeton, NJ: Princeton University Press, 1997.

Murden, Simon. *Islam, the Middle East, and the New Global Hegemony*. The Middle East in the International System. Boulder, CO: Lynne Rienner Publishers, 2002.

Murphy, Walter F. *Constitutional Democracy: Creating and Maintaining a Just Political Order*. The Johns Hopkins Series in Constitutional Thought. Baltimore, MD: Johns Hopkins University Press, 2007.

Na'im, Abdullahi Ahmad. *African Constitutionalism and the Role of Islam*. Philadelphia, PA: University of Pennsylvania Press, 2006.

Nederman, Cary J. "The Liberty of the Church and the Road to Runnymede: John of Salisbury and the Intellectual Foundations of the Magna Carta." *PS: Political Science & Politics*, 43:3 (2010): 457–61.

Nourse, Victoria. "Toward a "Due Foundation" for the Separation of Powers: *The Federalist Papers* as Political Narrative." *Texas Law Review*, 74:3 (February 1996): 447–522.

O'Brien, Bruce R. "Forgers of Law and Their Readers: The Crafting of English Political Identities between the Norman Conquest and the Magna Carta." *PS: Political Science & Politics*, 43:3 (2010): 467–73.

O'Gorman, Frank. *Edmund Burke: His Political Philosophy*. Political Thinkers, 2. London: Allen and Unwin, 1973.

O'Rourke, K.C. *John Stuart Mill and Freedom of Expression: The Genesis of a Theory*. London New York: Routledge, 2001.

Oakeshott, Michael. *Rationalism in Politics, and Other Essays*. New York: Basic Books Publishing Co., 1962.

Osborn, Annie Marion. *Rousseau and Burke: A Study of the Idea of Liberty in Eighteenth-Century Political Thought*. London, New York [etc.]: Oxford University Press, 1940.

Paine, Thomas. *Rights of Man*. The Penguin American Library. Harmondsworth, and New York: Penguin Books, 1984.

Pallitto, Robert. "The Legacy of the Magna Carta in Recent Supreme Court Decisions on Detainees' Rights." *PS: Political Science & Politics*, 43:3 (2010): 483–86.

Parkin, Charles W. *The Moral Basis of Burke's Political Thought, an Essay*. Cambridge: Cambridge University Press, 1956.

Perkins, Kenneth J. *A History of Modern Tunisia*. New York: Cambridge University Press, 2004.

———. *Tunisia: Crossroads of the Islamic and European Worlds*. Profiles Nations of the Contemporary Middle East. Boulder, CO and London: Westview Press, 1986.

Piscatori, James P. and Royal Institute of International Affairs. *Islam in the Political Process*. [London]; Cambridge and New York: Royal Institute of International Affairs; Cambridge University Press, 1983.

Plato, G.R.F. Ferrari, and Tom Griffith. *The Republic*. Cambridge Texts in the History of Political Thought. Cambridge and New York: Cambridge University Press, 2000.

Polin, Raymond. *Plato and Aristotle on Constitutionalism: An Exposition and Reference Source*. Avebury Series in Philosophy. Aldershot and Brookfield, VT: Ashgate, 1998.

Pound, Roscoe, Charles Howard McIlwain, and Roy F. Nichols. *Federalism as a Democratic Process: Essays*. Washington: Zenger Publishing, 1978.

Powell, J.G.F. *Cicero the Philosopher: Twelve Papers*. Oxford and New York: Clarendon Press, 1995.

Rabkin, Jeremy A. *Law without Nations?: Why Constitutional Government Requires Sovereign States*. Princeton, NJ: Princeton University Press, 2005.

Reeves, Richard. *John Stuart Mill: Victorian Firebrand*. London: Atlantic Books, 2007.

Reid, John Phillip. *Constitutional History of the American Revolution*. 4 vols Madison, WI: University of Wisconsin Press, 1986.

Resnick, Philip. "Montesquieu Revisited, or the Mixed Constitution and the Separation of Powers in Canada." *Canadian Journal of Political Science/ Revue canadienne de science politique*, 20:1 (1987): 97–115.

Richter, Melvin. "Comparative Political Analysis in Montesquieu and Tocqueville." *Comparative Politics*, 1:2 (1969): 129–60.

———. "An Introduction to Montesquieu's 'an Essay on the Causes That May Affect Men's Minds and Characters'." *Political Theory*, 4:2 (1976): 132–8.

———. "Montesquieu and the Concept of Civil Society." *The European Legacy: Toward New Paradigms*, 3:6 (1998): 33–41.

Robson, John M. *The Improvement of Mankind: The Social and Political Thought of John Stuart Mill*. University of Toronto. Dept. Of English. Studies and Texts, 15. Toronto and London: University of Toronto Press: Routledge and K. Paul, 1968.

Robson, John M. and Michael Laine. *A Cultivated Mind: Essays on J.S. Mill Presented to John M. Robson*. Toronto and Buffalo: University of Toronto Press, 1991.

Robson, John M., Michael Laine, and University of Toronto. *James and John Stuart Mill: Papers of the Centenary Conference*. Toronto and Buffalo: University of Toronto Press, 1976.

Rousseau, Jean-Jacques, and Victor Gourevitch. *The Social Contract and Other Later Political Writings*. Cambridge Texts in the History of Political Thought. Cambridge and New York, NY, USA: Cambridge University Press, 1997.

Rubin, Uri. "The "Constitution of Medina" Some Notes." *Studia Islamica*, 62 (1985): 5–23.

Ruedy, John, and Georgetown University. Center for Contemporary Arab Studies. *Islamism and Secularism in North Africa*. New York and Washington, DC: St. Martin's Press; Center for Contemporary Arab Studies, Georgetown University, 1994.

Salvadori, Massimo. *European Liberalism*. Major Issues in History. New York: Wiley-Interscience, 1972.

Sánchez Valencia, Víctor. *The General Philosophy of John Stuart Mill*. International Library of Critical Essays in the History of Philosophy. Aldershot and Burlington, VT: Ashgate, 2002.

Sartori, Giovanni. "Constitutionalism: A Preliminary Discussion." *The American Political Science Review*, 56:4 (1962): 853–64.

Sayeed, Khalid B. *Western Dominance and Political Islam: Challenge and Response*. Albany, NY: State University of New York Press, 1995.

Scheuerman, William E. "Carl Schmitt's Critique of Liberal Constitutionalism." *The Review of Politics*, 58:2 (1996): 299–322.

Sharp, Malcolm P. "The Classical American Doctrine of 'the Separation of Powers'." *The University of Chicago Law Review*, 2:3 (1935): 385–436.

Shaw, Stanford J. "The Nineteenth-Century Ottoman Tax Reforms and Revenue System." *International Journal of Middle East Studies*, 6:304 (1975): 421–59.

Shklar, Judith N. *Montesquieu*. Past Masters. Oxford and New York: Oxford University Press, 1987.

Skinner, Quentin. *The Foundations of Modern Political Thought*. 2 vols. Cambridge and New York: Cambridge University Press, 1978.

Soares, Benjamin F. and René Otayek. *Islam and Muslim Politics in Africa*. 1st ed. New York: Palgrave Macmillan, 2007.

Starr, June. *Law as Metaphor: From Islamic Courts to the Palace of Justice*. Albany, NY: State University of New York Press, 1992.

Steinberger, Peter J. "Ruling: Guardians and Philosopher-Kings." *The American Political Science Review*, 83:4 (1989): 1207–25.

Steinmetz, George. *State/Culture: State-Formation after the Cultural Turn*. The Wilder House Series in Politics, History, and Culture. Ithaca, NY: Cornell University Press, 1999.

Stepan, Alfred, and Juan J. Linz. "Democratization Theory and the 'Arab Spring'." *Journal of Democracy*, 24:2 (2013): 15–30.

Strauss, Leo. *The Political Philosophy of Hobbes, Its Basis and Its Genesis*. Oxford: The Clarendon Press, 1936.

Sturm, Douglas. "Constitutionalism: A Critical Appreciation and an Extension of the Political Theory of C.H. Mcilwain." *Minnesota Law Review*, 54 (1969): 215–44.

Syse, Henrik. *Natural Law, Religion, and Rights: An Exploration of the Relationship between Natural Law and Natural Rights, with Special Emphasis on the Teachings of Thomas Hobbes and John Locke*. South Bend, IN: St. Augustine's Press, 2007.

Tabaar, Mohammad Ayatollahi. "Assessing (in) Security after the Arab Spring: The Case of Egypt." *PS: Political Science & Politics*, 46:4 (2013): 727–35.

Tamimi, Azzam. "Islam and Democracy from Tahtawi to Ghannouchi." *Theory, Culture & Society*, 24:2 (March 1, 2007): 39–58.

Taylor, Quentin P., Alexander Hamilton, James Madison, and John Jay. *The Essential Federalist: A New Reading of the Federalist Papers*. Constitutional Heritage Series, 1st ed. Madison, WI: Madison House, 1998.

Tessler, Mark. "Islam and Democracy in the Middle East: The Impact of Religious Orientations on Attitudes toward Democracy in Four Arab Countries." *Comparative Politics*, 34:3 (2002): 337–54.

Treister, Dana S. "Standing to Sue the Government: Are Separation of Powers Principles Really Being Served?". *California Law Review*, 67 (1993–1994): 689–726.

Tunisi, Khayr al-Din, and L. Carl Brown. *The Surest Path: The Political Treatise of a Nineteenth-Century Muslim Statesman*. Harvard Middle Eastern Monographs, 16. Cambridge: Distributed for the Center for Middle Eastern Studies of Harvard University by Harvard University Press, 1967.

Vatikiotis, P.J. *Islam and the State*. London and New York: Croom Helm, 1987.

Vile, M.J.C. *Constitutionalism and the Separation of Powers*. Oxford: Clarendon P., 1967.

Waddicor, Mark H. *Montesquieu and the Philosophy of Natural Law*. International Archives of the History of Ideas, V. 37. The Hague: Nijhoff, 1970.

Waldron, Jeremy. *'Nonsense Upon Stilts': Bentham, Burke, and Marx on the Rights of Man*. London and New York: Methuen, 1987.

Walzer, Richard. "Aspects of Islamic Political Thought: Al-Farabi and Ibn Khaldun." *Oriens*, 16 (1963): 40–60.

Warrender, Howard. *The Political Philosophy of Hobbes, His Theory of Obligation*. Oxford: Clarendon Press, 1957.

Watt, W. Montgomery. *Muhammad at Mecca*. Oxford: Clarendon Press, 1953.

———. *Muhammad at Medina*. Karachi and New York: Oxford University Press, 1981.

Weiker, Walter F. "The Ottoman Bureaucracy: Modernization and Reform." *Administrative Science Quarterly*, 13:3 (1968): 451–70.

Weingast, Barry R. "The Political Foundations of Democracy and the Rule of Law." *The American Political Science Review*, 91:2 (1997): 245–63.

Welsh, Jennifer M. *Edmund Burke and International Relations: The Commonwealth of Europe and the Crusade against the French Revolution*. St. Antony's/ Macmillan Series. Houndmills, Basingstoke; New York: Macmillan Press, in association with St. Antony's College, Oxford, 1995.

Wert, Justin J. "With a Little Help from a Friend: Habeas Corpus and the Magna Carta after Runnymede." *PS: Political Science & Politics*, 43:3 (2010): 475–78.

White, Hayden V. "Ibn Khaldûn in World Philosophy of History." *Comparative Studies in Society and History*, 2:1 (1959): 110–25.

Wittke, Carl Frederick. *Essays in History and Political Theory in Honor of Charles Howard Mcilwain*. Cambridge, MA: Harvard University Press, 1936.

Worcester, Kent. "The Meaning and Legacy of the Magna Carta." *PS: Political Science & Politics*, 43:3 (2010): 451–56.

Ziadeh, Nicola A. *Origins of Nationalism in Tunisia*. Beirut: Librarie du Liban, 1969.

# Index

Printed in Great Britain
by Amazon